LIBERALIZING LYNCHING

Liberalizing Lynching

BUILDING A NEW RACIALIZED STATE

Daniel Kato

OXFORD
UNIVERSITY PRESS

OXFORD
UNIVERSITY PRESS

Oxford University Press is a department of the University of Oxford.
It furthers the University's objective of excellence in research, scholarship,
and education by publishing worldwide. Oxford is a registered trade mark
of Oxford University Press in the UK and in certain other countries

Published in the United States of America by
Oxford University Press
198 Madison Avenue, New York, NY 10016,
United States of America

Library of Congress Cataloging-in-Publication Data
Kato, Daniel.
Liberalizing lynching : building a new racialized state / Daniel Kato.
p.   cm.
Includes bibliographical references and index.
ISBN 978–0–19–023257–3 (hardcover : alk. paper) —
ISBN 978–0–19–023258–0 (ebook) — ISBN 978–0–19–023259–7 (online content)
1. Lynching—Government policy—United States—History. 2. Lynching—Southern
States—History. 3. African Americans—Crimes against—History.
4. Federal government—United States—History. 5. United States—Race relations—History. I. Title.
HV6457.K37 2015
364.1'34—dc23
2015013633

1   3   5   7   9   8   6   4   2

Printed in the United States of America on acid-free paper

"How could America have combined such a substantial degree of popular domestic violence with such a high degree of political stability?"

—RICHARD HOFSTADTER, *American Violence: A Documentary History* (Knopf, 1970), xi.

"There can be a legal system that is nothing more than a means of terrorizing people."

—FRANZ NEUMAN, *Behemoth* (Harper and Row, 1963), 440.

Contents

Acknowledgments

AS I REFLECT on the process of writing this book, I am completely taken aback not only by how many people have helped me along the way, but also by the extraordinary quality of each person's generosity. This book began as a dissertation in the politics department at the New School for Social Research, and I have Victoria Hattam to thank for her leadership and guidance throughout what has been a nearly decade-long process. I could not have picked a better mentor. I am indebted to Ira Katznelson for giving me the language by which to explore. I also extend my sincere gratitude to David Plotke for believing in me when no one else did, and for continuing to do so ever since; Andrew Arato for pushing me to be as creative as possible and to think beyond disciplines; and Andreas Kalyvas for showing me that one can study politics without having to give up one's politics. I am also beholden to Ian Zuckerman, without whom this project would never have gotten started, and Alex Gourevitch, without whom this project would never have gotten finished. Both of you were there every step of the way and I could not have asked for better interlocutors, readers, or friends. A truly heartfelt thanks to Aziz Rana for not only being generous with his time, helpful with his comments, and supportive of my work, but also for his own work, which I find to be so inspiring. This book would not have happened if it were not for you.

Many have taken the time out of their busy schedules to help me—for which I am sincerely grateful. I thank Robert Mickey, whose comments were extensive, invaluable, and appreciated. I cannot say enough to Desmond King for reaching out to me at a point when I was not sure if this project was going anywhere. Your support confirmed that I was headed in the right direction. I also thank Christopher Waldrep, Sidney Tarrow, Dorian Warren, James Cone, Robert Kaczorowski, Eric Foner, Quinn Mulroy, Thomas Ogorzalek, Robert Tsai, and Janos Kis for their insights and comments.

I am very fortunate to have started this project at the New School for Social Research. I do not think I could have done this project at any other institution. Shout out to Jennifer Yvette Terrell for always keeping it real and keeping me on point. Big hug to Jorge Romero Leon for showing me how to find peace in the struggle. Muchas gracias to Carlos Yescas for allowing me to be his friend. A bow to Sarah Taylor for always making me feel like what I do is important. A toast to Jorge Sosa for being that person to whom I can totally relate and yet could not be more different. A nod to Matthew Gritter for always having my back. I owe Rosa Lim for keeping me sane. I also want to show love to Maya Joseph, Roberto Trad Hasbun, Nina Augustsson, Alvaro Espinoza, Robert Seyfert, Dorothy Kwek, Solongo Wandan, Aylin Topal, Claudia Heiss, Victoria Crespo, Petra Gumplova, Tsuya Yee, Rodrigo Chacon, Luis Herran Avila, Julie Fratrik, Molly O'Rourke, Samantha Morales, Alexandra Budabin, Amando Basurto, Marco Morales, Isaac Preciado, Carlo Invernizzi Accetti, Leslie Kawaguchi, Paule Cruz Takash, Molly Thompson, Alex Tom, Ingrid Benedict, Kimi Lee, George Nakasuji, Julian Osaki, Esther Castain, Curtis Young, Jay Betancourt, and Charles Jason Randolph.

I am honored to have finished this book at Barnard College, and thank the political science department for being so welcoming, and my colleagues who have been very supportive during the final stages of this process. I particularly want to thank Kimberley Johnson for showing me that it is possible to be successful and nice. I could not have asked for a better colleague. I am also extremely grateful to Kalamazoo College for giving me my first shot. In particular, I want to thank Arthur Cole, Christine Hahn, Shreena Gandhi, and Carol Anderson. Lest I forget, I thank Janelle Werner and everybody at TBL for all their help.

I am deeply honored that Oxford University Press took a chance on me. Angela Chnakpo is amazing. She believed in this project right from the beginning. I am also so grateful to Princess Ikatekit and Manikandan Kuppan for their expertise.

Last, I end where it all started—and that is with my family. My parents, Chizuko Kato and James Kato, have supported me more than I will ever know, and have inspired me more than they will ever know. Nancy, Amanda, and Chris have always been there for me, through thick and thin, although they hardly ever knew what I was doing or why I was doing it. Thank you Lindsey for being it all. I dedicate this book to you because none of this matters without you.

LIBERALIZING LYNCHING

Our Constitution is so simple and practical that it is possible
always to meet extraordinary needs by changes in emphasis
and arrangement without loss of essential form.[1]

—FRANKLIN D. ROOSEVELT

1

The Strange Career of Lynching

INTRODUCTION

On October 27, 1934, a mob lynched Claude Neal. The mob had removed Neal from
a Florida jail where he was awaiting trial for the murder of Lola Cannidy. After the
lynching, an observer described what had occurred:

> After taking the nigger to the woods about four miles from Greenwood [Flor-
> ida], they cut off his penis. He was made to eat it. They cut off his testicles and
> made him eat them and say he liked it. . . . Then they sliced his sides and sto-
> mach with knives and every now and then somebody would cut off a finger or
> toe. Red hot irons were used on the nigger to burn him from top to bottom.
> From time to time during the torture a rope would be tied around Neal's neck
> and he was pulled up over a limb and held there until he almost choked to
> death when he would be let down and the torture begin all over again. After
> several hours of this unspeakable torture, they decided just to kill him.[2]

This was all done in broad daylight, in front of thousands of people. Local newspapers had even advertised the lynching beforehand to make sure anyone who wanted
to come could attend.[3] How could such a seemingly brazen disregard for the law
have occurred so freely and openly?

One aspect to this question that has received scant attention is the federal government's role regarding lynching.[4] Most of the canonical work on lynching has been done by nonpolitical scientists.[5] This is, in part, a result of the commonly accepted belief that (un)civil forces in the South decided to take the law into their own hands.[6] Lynchings are commonly understood to operate outside the scope of the federal government. However, this formulation is problematic if only because the issue of lynching—and black rights more generally—was central to the very development of the federal government.[7] As Frederick Douglass stated, "this so-called but mis-called Negro problem is one of the most important and urgent subjects that can engage public attention."[8]

This book focuses on the federal government's role regarding lynchings; specifically, it examines those that occurred in the American South.[9] Contrary to previous explanations that either try to situate these lynchings outside the purview of the federal government or classify them as federally sanctioned acts, I argue that lynchings that occurred in the South between 1883 and 1966 were within the purview of the federal government but were not federally sanctioned. The term I use to capture this framework is *constitutional anarchy*. Constitutional anarchy is a modified version of the dual state, which was first introduced by Ernst Fraenkel. He is a German legal theorist who came up with the concept of a dual state to resolve how two contradictory political elements could, nonetheless, coexist simultaneously.[10] In this Americanized version of the dual state, constitutional anarchy resolves how the anarchic nature of lynch mobs and liberal democracy were able to operate in tandem with one another.[11]

This new political framing of constitutional anarchy provides a way of explaining how political actors could persist in thinking of themselves as liberal despite actively permitting extreme racial violence; it also illuminates how the federal government's inaction was actually part of a calculated set of judgments by an increasingly activist state. Although much of the literature surrounding the federal government and lynchings presumes the federal government lacked the capacity to intervene, constitutional anarchy provides insight into how the federal government could choose not to intervene while nevertheless maintaining its own sovereign authority. Instead of focusing on the variations in and across states, constitutional anarchy hence focuses squarely on how the federal government accommodated itself to local variation. Although federalism is not usually consonant with anarchy, there are conditions under which federalism does allow for it. In this instance, the federal government's choice not to intervene says as much—or even more than—when it actually did intervene.

More broadly speaking, constitutional anarchy is helpful in teasing out the ways in which legalism can sometimes enable lawlessness. Constitutional anarchy refers to a relatively stable arrangement of control that was predicated on how the three federal branches of government handled issues that each dreaded publicly, but approved of privately, thereby allowing the federal government the means by which it could deflect accountability while retaining authority. It situates negligence in a manner that operates squarely within the very ways federal powers are separated—and in so doing reveals how the separation of powers not only divides responsibility but can also obscure it.

HISTORICAL BACKGROUND

Lynchings are shrouded in mystery.[12] Legally speaking, lynchings do not exist. The *Corpus Juris*, the authoritative twentieth-century American legal encyclopedia, states:

> Lynching has no technical legal meaning. It is merely a descriptive phrase used to signify the lawless acts of persons who violate established law at the time they commit the acts. . . . The offense of lynching is unknown to the common law.[13]

Outside the legal realm, there is widespread disagreement regarding what constitutes a lynching, how many lynchings actually occurred, and whether lynchings were even particular to the American South.[14] The exact number will probably never be known.[15] The amorphous quality of lynching speaks to its elusive nature. The pervasive uncertainty surrounding lynchings contributed to its terror:

> It was not, in fact, at all clear what behavior would lead to mob violence, and it was this uncertainty that would have created terror within the black community. Blacks never knew when whites would interpret the most innocent or trivial of behavior—an impertinent glance, ill-advised stare, or surly word—as insolent or threatening and worthy of brutal retribution.[16]

Despite the graphic and public nature, lynchings nevertheless defy clarity, thereby enabling them to hide in plain sight.

Another reason why lynchings were able to hide in plain sight was because they were somehow both simultaneously too barbaric to comprehend and yet banal enough to overlook. For some, the barbaric nature of lynchings was paralyzing. Take, for example, the experience of W. E. B. Du Bois:

> Sam Hose had been lynched, and they said that his knuckles were on exhibition at a grocery store farther down on Mitchell Street, along which I was

walking. I turned back to the University. I began to turn aside from my work. I did not meet Joel Chandler Harris nor the editor of the *Constitution*. . . . Two considerations thereafter broke in upon my work and eventually disrupted it: first, one could not be a calm, cool, and detached scientist while Negroes were lynched, murdered and started; and secondly, there was no such definite demand for scientific work that I was doing.[17]

Unlike Du Bois, who was confounded by lynchings to the extent that he not only stopped what he was doing, but also questioned the significance of the very work to which he had devoted himself, others had the opposite reaction of refusing to infuse lynchings with any generalizable import. Lynching historian Arthur Raper posited that

> political scientists in the grip of consensus theory tended to treat episodes of mass violence in America as insignificant or aberrational—temporary exceptions to the norm of peaceful progress. . . . the effect not only of minimizing group violence in America, but of depriving it of political content.[18]

This claim of lynchings as aberrational would resonate had there been very few lynchings and they were all done in private, but lynchings were exceptional in that they happened so frequently and publicly to the extent that they resulted in a deranged pattern: the more they happened, the more the gruesome details became obscured.[19] Before going into the exact numbers, it is important to note that lynchings, as was the case with Claude Neal and Sam Hose, were sometimes very public events to which parents were encouraged to bring their children, and souvenirs were provided to mark the occasion. Amy Louise Wood describes certain lynchings as "carnivalesque entertainment."[20] But then, after a couple of days, the lynching would be forgotten. As Winthrop Sheldon noted in a piece written in 1906 titled "Shall Lynching Be Suppressed, and How?":

> Public indifference on the subject of lynching is almost universal the country over. The average American citizen, as he partakes of his morning roll and coffee and reads in his daily newspaper the sickening account of the latest lynching tragedy, is moved for the time being with a thrill of horror. He lays his paper aside, goes to his daily work, becomes absorbed in the business of money-making, and—that is the end of it. The incident is closed. It is only a few days' sensation and soon forgotten.[21]

The frequency and public nature of lynchings made them seemingly banal, thus obscuring their barbarity. Lynchings are thus confounding because they not only represented a level of barbarism that was unintelligible to many analysts, but also occurred frequently enough that they were seemingly commonplace to many Americans. The combination of barbarism and banality made lynchings something too horrible to examine and yet ordinary enough to dismiss.

Although a comprehensive account of lynching might, in fact, be impossible, nonetheless there has been extensive research to ascertain its general contours. Lynchings generally represent acts of violence initiated by an informal group of people who suspect another person or groups of persons of breaking a law and/or transgressing a social norm.[22] Lynching historian W. Fitzhugh Brundage identified four general categories of lynch mobs: (1) small terrorist mobs that acted in secret, (2) small private mobs that exacted vengeance for a wide variety of alleged offenses, (3) posses that claimed extralegal status, and (4) mass mobs that were public in nature.[23] In the American South, at least 2,400 black men were lynched between 1883 and 1966. The regional and racial differences led many to conclude there was something unique about the American South.[24] As W. Fitzhugh Brundage states: "Lynching, like slavery and segregation, was not unique to the South, but it assumed proportions and a significance there that were without parallel elsewhere."[25] These acts were not formally sanctioned and/or primarily administered by official authorities, but antilynching organizations, Southern newspaper editors, and academics all nevertheless seem to agree that lynchings were acts of violence that were "sanctioned by the community"[26] and "more or less ha[d] public approval."[27] According to lynching historian Christopher Waldrep, "lynching implied a killing carried out by a coherent community, an expression of localized popular sovereignty of the sort Southern white conservatives advocated."[28]

What is commonly understood as lynchings has not been chronicled extensively by political scientists, in part because lynchings have been labeled mistakenly as apolitical.[29] This book attempts to shine light on these more prevalent aspects of racial violence and to problematize its apolitical nature.[30] Although several hypotheses have been proffered for why Southern lynchings occurred, including the enforcement of social norms, suppression of political competition, and the stabilization of racial solidarity of whites, Stewart Tolnay and Elwood M. Beck found that the biggest factor was economic:

[E]conomic motives played an important role in mob violence against southern blacks . . . when the economic fortunes of marginal whites soured (e.g. because of shifts in farm tenure or swings in the price of cotton), violence against blacks increased.[31]

The fluctuating patterns of lynching correlated with the market turns of cotton prices. The greatest number of lynchings occurred during the late nineteenth century, otherwise known as the "bloody '90s," which corresponded to the falling price of cotton. There was a subsequent gradual decline in lynchings, except for a sharp upturn at the end of the 1910s and after World War I. The main cause for the decline in lynchings, according to Tolnay and Beck, was the mass exodus—otherwise known as *the Great Migration*—during which as many as six million African Americans escaped the South.[32]

In these accounts, however, the role of the federal government is muddled. Take Tolnay and Beck's portrayal of the criminal justice system:

> By failing to punish, or even indict, known members of terrorist gangs, the criminal justice system did little to ensure and protect the civil liberties of black citizens. This state-sanctioned terrorism sent a message to the African-American community that was as unambiguous as it was frightening.[33]

If the criminal justice system did little, how could terrorism then be labeled "state sanctioned?" To be state sanctioned, would it not have to had been the case that the state was the primary actor? Or at least endorsed such actions? What is the relationship between inaction and sanction? Although Tolnay and Beck were understandably more concerned with pinpointing the most determinative factors in lynching, the role of political institutions nonetheless requires further investigation.[34]

To this point, the federal government's culpability has led to conflicting interpretations, none of which has been resolved. This is somewhat understandable considering it hardly did anything.[35] Historian Thomas Sugrue suggests that federal inaction should not be mistaken as sanctioning because the "lack of federal intervention" was a result of "lack of administrative capacity."[36] But, others have couched governmental inaction not as capitulation, but as accommodation. As Desmond King and Stephen Tuck argue, through deliberate inaction, "federal officials did not just acquiesce in the Southern counter-revolution but promoted a nationwide order of white supremacy."[37] In other words, it was not an act of coercion in that Southern politicians forced the hand of Northern politicians as much as it was an act of Northern compliance with Southern racism. Government inaction provided the necessary license for lynchings to occur. This subtle distinction between being forced to acquiesce and choosing not to intervene is important because the former implies the federal government was taken hostage by Southern racists, thereby raising questions regarding sovereignty, whereas the latter implies the federal government's active decision to comply with southern racism, thereby raising questions regarding complicity.

LYNCHING AND SOUTHERN RACISM

When southern racism of the early twentieth century is examined, it is frequently done as if it were a solid mass that moved in a singular fashion. Terms such as the "Solid South" connote a degree of firmness and homogeneity.[38] Although recent research has problematized the solidity of racism among Southern whites, it is also important to parse out the different political reactions to Southern racism.[39] Not only did Southern whites have various opinions regarding racism and its manifestations, so too did the federal government. Unfortunately, most of the accounts that examine the federal government suggest that it approached Southern racism and all its manifestations in the same manner. Either the federal government sanctioned Southern racism explicitly or it was barred legally from doing anything about Southern racism. Segregation is an example of the former. In *Plessy v. Ferguson*, the Supreme Court justified segregation as consistent with equality before the law—separate but equal—and explains in part why it could be sanctioned positively as consistent with constitutional law.[40] But, to conflate the explicit approval by the federal government of segregation with all iterations of Southern racism—with lynchings, in particular—would be inaccurate both historically and conceptually.[41]

Although there is no denying the social and cultural imbrications of segregation and lynching, to conflate these two phenomena legally would be a mistake. Like segregationists, lynchers were seemingly "at liberty to act with reference to the established usages, customs and traditions of the people, and with a view to the promotion of their comfort, and the preservation of the public peace and good order."[42] But unlike segregation, lynchings consisted of acts that were never sanctioned formally. That is to say, segregation had been voted on, passed as law, and was enforced legally. There was no formal "lynch law" that outlined the crimes, trial mechanisms, and means of punishment. It is one thing to mandate different schools for blacks; it is altogether something else to sanction the murder of blacks. As Federal Circuit Court Judge Halmer Emmons noted, the "right of the negro to see the ballet dance" could be outlawed formally, whereas the right to "pillage and murder was more precious and beneficent privilege" and thus could not.[43] Thus, to link the state directly with lynching is not altogether accurate.

It is also important to distinguish the unique character of lynchings. Many regarded lynchings as representing an outright war, which necessarily involved the federal government. As Supreme Court Justice Joseph Bradley stated:

> The war of race, whether it assumes the dimensions of civil strife or domestic violence, whether carried on in a guerrilla or predatory form, or by private combinations, or even by private outrage or intimidation, is subject to the

jurisdiction of the government of the United States; and when any atrocity is committed which may be assigned to this cause it may be punished by the laws and in the courts of the United States.[44]

This "war of race" represented a frontal attack on American sovereignty. Unlike other aspects of Southern racism such as segregation, which had been rationalized away as "custom and tradition," the violence that lynchings epitomize went to the core of national sovereignty.[45] To kill without impunity struck at the heart of American jurisprudence so severely that it, necessarily, had to involve the complicity of the whole federal government. As U.S. Attorney Herbert Brownwell declared, "whenever mob violence is involved, that certainly comes within the federal authority."[46] President Dwight D. Eisenhower further expounded on Brownell's point:

[W]hen a State refuses to utilize its police powers to protect against mobs persons who are peaceably exercising their rights, the oath of office of the President requires that he take action to give that protection. Failure to act in such a case would be tantamount to acquiescence in anarchy and dissolution of the union.[47]

Southern lynchings represented a virulent form of racism, one that "requires" action of the federal government. Yet, as mentioned earlier, this "requirement" of federal intervention often went unheeded. What Justice Bradley aptly described as a "war of race" thus heightened the paradox of illiberal practices within a liberal polity in a way that extends beyond the insular narratives of federalism and focuses directly on the federal government's "failure to act."

This failure to act points to another reason why generalizing is problematic. Southern racism was more anarchic in nature and not administered directly by the federal government.[48] Some have tried to pin the blame solely on the federal government, and have analogized Jim Crow segregation with apartheid.[49] Maurice Evans, an Englishman from South Africa, had this to say about his experience traveling to the American South in the early part of the twentieth century: "[T]he very conditions I had left [in South Africa] were reproduced before my eyes, the thousands of miles melted away, and Africa was before me."[50] In his book comparing the United States, South Africa, and Brazil, political scientist Anthony Marx remarks how "the similarities in South African and U.S. rhetoric and practices of racial domination are striking, particularly in regard to segregation polices between the world wars."[51] Preeminent American historian C. Vann Woodward made a similar observation: "At the time of the First World War it had seemed that both regions [the Southern United States and South Africa] were going roughly the same way."[52]

Although the apartheid analogy seems, at first, to be fitting, it fails to take into account the localized nature of American racism. Both Marx and Woodward, whose receptivity to the apartheid analogy is evidenced by the previous quotes, were nevertheless quick to refute it. Woodward states that

> by the time the Second World War was over it was very plain that they [South African apartheid and American Jim Crow] were no longer traveling together. . . . The Jim Crow laws put the authority of the state or city in the voice of the street-car conductor, the railway breakman, the bus driver, the theater usher, and also into the voice of the hoodlum of the public parks and playgrounds. They gave free rein and the majesty of the law to mass aggressions that might otherwise have been curbed, blunted, or deflected.[53]

Marx makes a similar observation: "South African apartheid was more centrally imposed and pervasive than was Jim Crow segregation and exclusion in the more de-centralized post-Reconstruction United States."[54] Both Woodward and Marx's description of the contrast between the United States and South Africa highlights the de-centralized nature of American racism.[55] Lynchings, for the most part, appear to be acts during which those supposedly subject to the law somehow took it upon themselves to be the ones who enforced the law. The claim that the federal government somehow sanctioned and managed all the different iterations of Southern racism is thus historically inaccurate.

The other approach to framing the federal government's handling of Southern racism was that federal authorities were rendered impotent by the predominant role of states within a federalist structure. This is not meant to deny the long-standing tradition of implementing law enforcement at the local level. As William Novak notes, "nineteenth-century American governance remained decidedly local. Towns, local courts, common councils and state legislatures were the basic institutions of governance, and they continued to function in ways not unlike their colonial and European forebears."[56] But, the point of contention is the degree to which governance remained local, particularly after Reconstruction. To suggest that governance remained decidedly local is different than saying that governance remained exclusively local. The former provides for a limited role of federal intervention whereas the latter presumes no role for federal encroachment.

This claim of federal paralysis has been subsequently legitimated and perpetrated mainly through the state action doctrine. State action doctrine is often understood as locating private action as beyond the scope of the federal government. As stated in the *Civil Rights Cases*, "individual invasion of individual rights is not the subject-matter of the [Fourteenth] Amendment."[57] President William Howard Taft followed up on this sentiment in his inaugural address: "[I]t is not the disposition or within the province of the Federal Government to interfere with the regulation by Southern States of their domestic affairs."[58] Unless there was a provision in state law that sanctioned racial violence explicitly, it would seem to be the case that the federal government relinquished and/or delegated complete authority to combat racial violence to the states. Under this framing, federal prosecutors should have needed a qualitative shift in federal–state relations, either in the form of new legislation such as the Dyer antilynching bill or some sort of executive order to prosecute lynchers again.[59] However, this did not occur. Rather, in 1966, the Supreme Court ruled in favor of prosecuting private citizens who deprived other private citizens of the rights afforded to them by the Fourteenth Amendment.[60] The biggest explanatory deficiency of this concept that the federal government was too weak is its inability to explain the federal government's vacillation. Many of the comments, such as the one made by Taft, were in response to suffrage and the Fifteenth Amendment, not racial violence. The previously noted quote by Taft was preceded by the following:

> What remains is the fifteenth amendment to the Constitution and the right to have statutes of States specifying qualifications for electors subjected to the test of compliance with that amendment. This is a great protection to the negro. It never will be repealed, and it never ought to be repealed. If it had not passed, it might be difficult now to adopt it; but with it in our fundamental law, the policy of Southern legislation must and will tend to obey it, and so long as the statutes of the States meet the test of this amendment and are not otherwise in conflict with the Constitution and laws of the United States, it is not the disposition or within the province of the Federal Government to interfere with the regulation by Southern States of their domestic affairs. [61]

Karen Orren and Stephen Skowronek, leading scholars in American Political Development have alluded to this constitutional puzzle following Reconstruction: "[C]onstitutional changes that were all but dead-on-arrival, their paper persistence a mockery of democratic pretention, became important vehicles of transformation a century later, while leaving Reconstruction's own legacy no less clear."[62] The fact that essential federal laws could somehow go in and out of fashion in the span of approximately eighty years is not indicative of any particular characteristic of American federalism per se, but an indication of the will of a sovereign nation to enforce or not to enforce its own laws. The fact that it regained its "strength" after years of being "weak" lends credence to legal theorist Franz Neumann's claim that "the liberal state has always been as strong as the political and social situation and the interests of society demanded."[63]

Some have suggested that the United States was somehow both too strong and too weak. James Cutler, an economist who was one of the first to provide an in-depth analysis of lynching, first articulated this combination in 1905:

> In general, it may be said that the practice of summarily punishing public of-fenders and suspected criminals is found in two distinct types of society: first, the frontier type where society is in a formative state and the civil regulations are not sufficiently established to insure [*sic*] the punishment of offenders; and second, the type of society which is found in older communities with well-established civil regulations, the people of which are ordinarily law-abiding and conservative citizens. . . . In this country, however, all of these conditions exist side by side.[64]

Although there is credence in combining the two claims, it is unclear exactly how they can operate simultaneously. Many have hinted at it. Robert Dahl described it as "an active policy of non-enforcement."[65] Anthony Marx referred to it as "acting by withdrawal."[66] Ira Katznelson called it "willful federal inaction" and a "strategy of pragmatic forgetfulness."[67] Naomi Murakawa goes so far to say that lynching repre-sented the "law's logical extension, not law's abnegation."[68] But no one, as of yet, has provided any substantive analysis of exactly how this occurred.[69] A more historically accurate framework is needed—one that involves recognizing the complicity of po-litical authorities without necessarily implicating them, a theory that affirms the "strength" of the American state but not to the extent that it becomes totalizing, as was the case with South African apartheid. A framework of governance is thus needed that can account for how lynchings could exist as a tacitly accepted practice without being explicitly sanctioned by the law. We need what Leon Friedman de-scribed as a "framework of contrived anarchy."[70]

LYNCHING AND LIBERALISM

To flesh out a more historically accurate framework further, we also need to examine the implications of lynchings with respect to American liberalism. Partly at stake in this debate regarding the role of the federal government and lynching is the canoni-cal status of American liberalism.[71] To argue the United States was akin to apartheid would be a direct repudiation that the United States was liberal. To argue the United States was a "weak state" is an indirect critique of American liberalism in that it presumes the United States did not have the capacity to be liberal.

Rogers Smith confronts this question directly of how, if at all, racism relates to American liberalism. In his seminal article "Beyond Tocqueville, Myrdal and Hartz:

The Multiple Traditions in America," Americanist Rogers Smith postulated there are contradictory trends of liberalism and illiberalism operating concurrently in American political culture.[72] As critical as Smith is of liberalism, he nonetheless acknowledges that liberalism does "capture important truths."[73] Smith thus is reduced to providing an immanent critique of liberalism. He suggested two ways of framing these trends. His first argument was that these "multiple political traditions" coalesced into "competing racial institutional orders." The implicit premise was that these multiple traditions were very separate from one another, and the boundaries between the two were solid. [74] According to sympathetic critics like Ira Katznelson, this argument "flattens the history of liberal thought and practice" and, ironically, becomes a "conceptual mirror" of the very thing Smith is trying to argue against.[75] This then leads to Smith to revise his argument. In *Civic Ideals*, Smith stated that "liberalizing and democratizing changes have often created the conditions for the resurgence of inegalitarian ideologies and institutions."[76] This revised argument presumes a relationship between liberalism and illiberalism; somehow these two contradictory trends might not be so separate and might actually be imbricated with one another.

Also, in light of the recent deaths of Trayvon Martin, Rekia Boyd, Eric Garner, and Michael Brown, it is understandable why some have argued that the nature of racial violence has not changed over time. In response to the shooting of Trayvon Martin, journalist Ta-Nehisi Coates writes:

> When you have a society that takes at its founding the hatred and degradation of a people, when that society inscribes that degradation in its most hallowed document, and continues to inscribe hatred in its laws and policies, it is fantastic to believe that its citizens will derive no ill messaging. It is painful to say this: Trayvon Martin is not a miscarriage of justice, but American justice itself. This is not our system malfunctioning. It is our system working as intended.[77]

Although there is no denying a semblance of continuity of racial violence across time, these arguments are susceptible to critiques of determinism and hence disavow any element of political agency and autonomy. Historian Sean Wilentz's comment regarding the competing historiographies of Andrew Jackson that either characterizes him in completely glowing terms or completely derogatory ones seems particularly germane: "these admirable studies have generally submerged the history of politics in the history of social change, reducing politics and democracy to by-products of various social forces without quite allowing the play of politics its importance."[78] Although there are definitely elements of continuity when it comes to race/racism, as Marie Gottschalk points out, "it is important not to flatten out their differences, and the differences in the political, institutional, and economic context that created and sustained them."[79] In this regard, the central theme of sorting out relations of continuity and change within American Political Development can be extremely beneficial in unpacking how racial violence can be both ubiquitous and divergent across time.

These critiques of liberalism call for a qualification of liberalism.[80] This qualification of liberalism should come in the form of a framework that, to paraphrase Smith, concurrently allows for multiple traditions to exist. But, this framework should not settle for simple demarcations. It needs to imbricate these traditions with one another in a historically accurate manner that allows for change and continuity. Illiberal traditions, such as racism, might be ubiquitous, but the means by which that exclusion is administered, regulated, and legitimated within the broader rubric of American liberalism seems to change over time. With regard to lynchings, questions about the role of the federal government hence need to be rephrased. It is not about whether the United States was a liberal country or an apartheid country; rather, the question should be: How could the United States have characteristics of both? In respect to the weak state, the question should not be whether the United States was strong or weak, but how did the United States make itself weak with regard to lynching? The apartheid–liberalism nexus raises the issue of duality whereas the weak state–liberalism nexus raises the issue of an active process of withdrawal. When American liberalism is rearticulated and reconfigured, it is hence crucial to see not only how it affects how inequalities subsequently operate, but also how it sequesters what it abandons. With regard to lynchings, it is only within the interplay between the continuity of white supremacy and the historical changes after Reconstruction that the parameters of American liberalism can be found.

Racism in general and lynchings in particular call into question conventional understandings of liberal democracy and the rule of law. But, although abandonment of such concepts seems extreme, reconsideration is difficult. There is a double inversion that needs to occur to understand how something like lynchings were imbricated with American liberalism. The first has to do with inverting what is typically seen as irrelevant into something that is actually fundamental. The second inversion involves examining how emancipating policies can exacerbate inequality.

The excavation of racism oftentimes requires an examination of exclusion. Exclusion is often administered in a fashion that involves sequestering. The very act of sequestering is meant to negate any semblance of theoretical abstraction or significance. Because acts such as lynching do not comport with our general understanding, it is often marginalized as an unfortunate anomaly.[81] But, the historical ubiquity of racial violence to which Coates alluded suggests a level of continuity that demands a reconfiguration and reconsideration to the extent that shifts questions of racism from an exceptional oddity to a constitutive malady. Leonard Feldman refers to it as "constitutive exclusion"[82] and describes the process of "not simply being set outside the law but rather abandoned by it, exposed and threatened on the threshold in which life and law become indistinguishable."[83] In this regard, lynchings are not an aberration that bears no significance to American liberalism; rather, lynchings constitute the very basis by which American liberalism operates. The central premise is that it was only by abandoning the right to personal security for blacks could American liberalism work.

This constitutive abandonment is also complicated and obscured further by another inversion. The constancy of racial violence suggests a level of continuity that upends the conventional understanding of normalcy and crises. Political scientist Dara Strolovich expands on this upending: "bad things that happen to marginalized groups evade crisis framings and are instead normalized and particularized within dominant institutions."[84] In that same vein, lynchings emerged in part by the emancipating policies of Reconstruction, and also were normalized in a manner after Reconstruction that made it not a crisis.

In this regard, liberalism might then be its own worst enemy. In his book *Law and Irresponsibility: On the Legitimation of Human Suffering*, legal scholar Scott Veitch writes how "legal institutions are centrally involved in organizing irresponsibility." He goes on to note how "officials are able to rely on their legal obligations as a way of *evading* the very question of responsibility for their decisions and their consequences. The officials could, in effect, put themselves in a zone of nonresponsibility."[85] In other words, the very existence of liberalism deters from the further expansion of liberalism. At times, liberalism can be a "fighting creed" against itself.[86]

THESIS

When it comes to lynchings, the federal government did very little, and thus its role often goes underreported. However, inaction should not be underestimated. The ease of describing inaction obscures the complexity of conceptualizing inaction, and the primary concern with the federal government is how it did very little while nevertheless retaining the sovereign authority to act. How was the federal government able to have its cake and eat it too? How was it able to feign responsibility while maintaining authority? By bringing the federal government (which has commonly been in the background) into the foreground, the primary concern is conceptualizing governmental passivity. In so doing, the focus shifts from examining what the government did to conceptualizing how the government framed what it did not do.

Any conceptualizing needs to start with the Supreme Court because, as Karen Orren and Stephen Skowronek point out, "conflict with the Court presents the central issues of Reconstruction."[87] Unfortunately, the Supreme Court's role is often mistakenly overemphasized. Historians, such as Eric Foner, concluded that the Supreme Court "render[ed] national prosecution of crimes committed against blacks virtually impossible, and gave a green light to acts of terror where local officials either could not or would not enforce the law."[88] There has, however, been a significant upsurge of accounts by legal scholars that have subtly challenged this interpretation of state action and the Supreme Court's role during Reconstruction.[89] These revisionist accounts not only downplay the conventional narrative of judicial activism, but also—and more importantly—salvage a semblance of national sovereignty for the federal government.

Although any conceptualization needs to start with the Court, it cannot end there.[90] With regard to the federal government's role in lynchings, the judiciary is not the main protagonist in this story. Federal inactivity was justified on a false premise—namely, that the judiciary precluded federal rights enforcement. The judiciary, in fact, did not preclude federal rights enforcement; it simply accommodated federal nonintervention. The political branches are the ones that initiated federal involvement during the 1870s, federal withdrawal during the 1880s, and federal reengagement during the 1960s. The Court simply provided legal cover for political backtracking.

This legal cover was essential, however, and explains in part why the mischaracterization of judicial activism has persisted. Many politicians at the time found blaming the Court useful. Despite the fact that the federal judiciary never blocked federal rights enforcement when there was the political will actually to engage, much of the history of federal inaction nevertheless involves politicians hiding behind the parchment of legalese to obscure their own political desire not to engage in federal rights enforcement. Naomi Murakawa noted that "when confronted with racial violence, federal lawmakers sometimes invoked legal fictions that African-Americans enjoyed equal protection of the law, or they hid behind the cover of federalism."[91] As mentioned earlier, the 1966 Supreme Court rulings in *U.S. v. Price* and *U.S. v. Guest* proves there was no legal impediment stopping federal rights enforcement. By couching political inaction in terms of jurisprudential restrictions in a federalist system, political officials successfully mischaracterized what was actually a political arrangement made by politicians into a matter of state rights that was to be resolved by the courts. As legal historian Mark Graber notes in his article regarding legislative deference to the judiciary, "waving the banner of federalism," federal politicians oftentimes defers to the judiciary "to make controversial policies that political elites approve of but cannot publicly champion, and to do so in such a way that these elites are not held accountable by the general public, or at least not as accountable as they would be had they personally voted for that policy." Politicians can subsequently point "to their obligation to obey the law, while insisting that they disagree with the Court's holding."[92] In the case of lynchings, judicial "scapegoating" masked and thus empowered the political calculus of nonintervention.

Rather than challenge the political branches, the Court chose instead to operate in accordance with them by reacting to and accommodating what they were doing. With the political branches using legalese as cover, the bind that the Court was in becomes more clear. It contoured itself around two conflicting poles: the vacillating nature of the political and the duty of the Court to "secure a steady, upright, and impartial administration of the laws."[93] In these situations, the Court oftentimes strikes a balance between the two instead of simply siding with one pole over the other. The Court does not simply kowtow to the will of the other branches, nor does it attempt to coerce the political branches from doing something they do not want to do. Instead, the Court often strikes a middle ground that situates the political will in a manner that is consonant with the rule of law while simultaneously providing cover for political actors when there is insufficient political capital to act. The Court faces multiple pressures, all of which pull at it in different directions. It is simultaneously a mirror, a translator, and a punching bag.

The key to understanding the federal government is thus situating the dynamics across branches in a manner that neither collapses law entirely into politics nor presumes these two categories are completely distinct. As Judge Robert Katzmann notes, "the literature of political institutions tends often to concentrate on particular ones—studies of Congress, or of the White House, or of the Courts. But such a selective focus, although useful, tends to obscure the interrelationships and interactions of those institutions that account for the ebb and flow of decision making in our federal system."[94] Thus, a focus across the branches is needed that can illuminate the interdependency of both law and politics that is nevertheless predicated on the pressures these two facets have of being distinct from one another. Their interdependence functions only to the extent that it is understood as operating independently from each other. Interdependence thus requires both parties sometimes to work with each other and sometimes to work against each other. The Court contoured itself in such a way that threatened to compromise its own integrity. The political branches contoured themselves in such a way that threatened to compromise their own autonomy. Each contortion must be done with some delicacy because if it goes too far, it not only threatens its own legitimacy, but also the legitimacy of the other branches. Each branch is thus doing its own balancing act. There is a double move: the Court is working in abeyance to politics and obeisance to the law whereas the political branches are relying on judicial independence to mask their own unwilling-ness to act.

Recent work on interbranch dynamics has been especially useful in this endeavor. As Jeb Barnes and Mark Miller point out in their article on interbranch dynamics, "policymaking is best understood as a continuous dialogue among the institutions of government. The motivations of policymaking are complex, including ideology, strategic considerations and the desire to preserve institutional legitimacy."[95] It provides conceptual coherence to what has previously been understood as piecemeal, disparate elements by exposing how the national government can respond to societal actors via the relationship in and across branches.

Although there have been many accounts that chronicle the Court's decisions, what has not been understood extensively is the Court's rulings in light of such political vacillation and—more important—the implications of such as it pertains to the federal government as a whole. One-dimensional accounts of each branch, whether it is the executive, judicial, or legislative, have missed this coordination across the branches. The branches operated in a synchronous fashion. This matter of synchronicity is crucial in developing a critique that extends beyond any one branch and is levied more appropriately against American liberal democracy. Every branch was complicit in perpetuating a policy of nonintervention, which was based primarily on a misinterpretation of the law—namely, the state action doctrine. As such, the attention needs to shift from legal jurisprudence, which has been the focus traditionally, to that of sovereignty. Sovereignty is the rightful locus of study because nonintervention had more to do with the choice not to act across all three branches than the legal and/or institutional capacity to act. Questions about sovereignty often get mired in debates regarding federalism, separation of powers, and the Constitution. This is understandable, considering the framers' intent to divide sovereignty. But, when it comes to racial violence in the late nineteenth to the mid-twentieth centuries, it is appropriate to analyze the problem beyond any one branch because many of the elements that usually complicate matters of sovereignty converged to the point of collusion. The very fragments of sovereignty the American political system intended to be divisive was supportive of the decision for nonintervention—and, once it was established, no significant challenge emerged until the 1960s. The tremendous difficulties in reversing course had less to do with overturning a judicial decision than it had to do with upending and problematizing the calculus of nonintervention. Federal nonintervention became so entrenched that it took a crisis spurred by the civil rights movement to reverse course. The historical significance of the civil rights movement is not derived from its ability to correct a judicial misinterpretation as much as it was about ending a collusion of racism that persisted, in part, out of racist malevolence and lack of political courage, but also because of the policy of nonintervention that was perpetuated by all three branches.

The aim of this book is to structure lynchings with a historical focus on the dynamics in and across branches. This structure is constitutional anarchy. Building off one of the main premises of American Political Development that the character of political change is often fragmented and incomplete,[96] constitutional anarchy represents a sketchy patchwork of "a revolution but half accomplished"[97] wherein "American citizens in southern states where lynching prevails found themselves in the anomalous position of being residents in states which refused to guarantee them trial by due process of law when accused of crime and citizens of a government which confessed its inability to do so."[98] Without ever sanctioning or prohibiting lynchings, the federal government narrowed its attention to issues of containment. It exposes exactly how federal lawmakers were able to "invoke legal fictions" and "hide behind the cover of federalism" in the manner that Murakawa described.[99] Lynchings, for the most part, were situated within a constructed zone of permissiveness that was contingent, not upon the sanctioning of political authorities per se, but rather upon political authorities choosing to maintain an active policy of noninterference. Derived from Ernst Fraenkel's framework of the dual state, constitutional anarchy is a modified version of the dual state that allowed for legally bounded regions of lawlessness.[100]

Constitutional anarchy is a conceptual configuration of the federal government that epitomizes accurately the interplay between political vacillation and judicial accommodation as it relates to lynchings. It is a concept that is neither a strict theory of judicial interpretation nor an exclusive account of presidential or congressional decision making. Rather, constitutional anarchy is a theory of interbranch dynamics that hinges on law and politics being both independent and interdependent simultaneously. It schematizes how actors across all three branches of government were able to exclaim federal nonintervention without ever completely relinquishing federal authority for rights enforcement.

Constitutional anarchy derives much of its import from William Sewell's depiction of structure. As a political scientist and historian, Sewell best captures this meaning of structure:

> [A] proper understanding of the role of events in history must be founded on a concept of structure. A structural view of social action accounts for what I regard as an outstanding general characteristic of social life: that most social practices—whether international diplomacy, petty trade, or popular recreation—tend to be reproduced with considerable consistency over relatively extended periods of time. . . . When changes do take place, they are rarely

smooth and linear in character; instead changes tend to be clustered into rela- tively intense bursts. . . . Lumpiness, rather than smoothness, is the normal tex- ture of historical temporality.[101]

Sewell's definition neatly captures the "considerable consistency" of lynchings across the mid-nineteenth to mid-twentieth centuries, which are at the same time "book- ended" by the "intense bursts" of Reconstruction and the civil rights movement. So far, work on lynching has been piecemeal. There is a need to bring together material that has, to this point, been sporadic. Sewell's concept of structure should help bring these elements together in a coherent fashion.

Structuring lynchings in this manner requires a blending of history and theory. According to Sewell, "historians suffer from a kind of narrative overconfidence"[102] whereas theorists "need a serious infusion of historical habits of mind."[103] He calls for a compromise of the kind that Theda Skocpol did in her magisterial work *States and Social Revolution*:

> The problem with the historical strategy is that crucial causal processes tend to get lost in a muddle of narrative detail and are seldom separated out enough to make their autonomous dynamics clear. The trouble with the sociological strat- egy is that although it successfully specifies the causal dynamics of one factor, it tends either to conflate other causal factors with the chosen cause or to treat them as mere background. Skocpol's strategy is an inspired compromise. It ap- propriates the power of the sociological strategy but applies it to not one but several distinct causal processes.[104]

Although Skocpol's "compromise" runs the risk of not fully satisfying either strat- egy, she does point to the benefits that might be derived from combining the two.

This "compromise" is akin to what is often characterized as nonideal theory. Lynchings have often been marginalized by political scientists, in part because of their theoretical predilections.[105] The tendency to rely on theories that marginalize and hence depoliticize violence is emblematic of what political philosopher Charles Mills terms *ideal theory*: "[ideal theory] will abstract away from relations of struc- tural domination, exploitation, coercion, and oppression and will say little to noth- ing about actual historic oppression and its legacy in the present, or current ongoing oppression, though these may be gestured at in a vague or promissory way."[106] Sewell eludes to this point as well: "The typical strategy of dominant actors and institutions is not so much to establish uniformity as it is to organize difference. They are con- stantly engaged in efforts not only to normalize or homogenize but also to hierar- chize, encapsulate, exclude, criminalize, hegemonize, or marginalize practices and populations that diverge from the sanctioned ideal."[107] Mills then argues that a noni-deal approach, which operates on the assumption "that the natural and most illumi-nating starting point is the actual conditions of nonwhite" and is thus "better able to realize the ideals, by virtue of realistically recognizing the obstacles to their accep-tance and implementation."[108]

In an article titled "Political Philosophy and Racial Injustice: From Normative to Critical Theory," political philosopher Thomas McCarthy further collaborates Mills's argument for nonideal theorizing:

> [T]here are no theoretical means at hand for bridging the gap between a color-blind ideal theory and a color-coded political reality, for the approach of ideal theory provides no theoretical mediation between the ideal and the real.[109]

McCarthy then calls on political theorists to engage in more nonideal theorizing, which he takes to mean as getting "involved in just the sorts of interpretive-historical and social-theoretical disagreements that, in its self-understanding as normative theory, it hopes to avoid."[110] Although this kind of theorizing sacrifices a certain degree of criticality that comes with the "freestanding" character of normative theory, it can nonetheless provide a degree of illumination that comes with bringing order to a prevailing chaos of facts. By cleaning up the "messiness of political reality," this kind of "nonideal theorizing" that McCarthy is espousing can make explicit the "understandings, images, or models of society which are always at work, though usu-ally only tacitly."[111]

Nonideal theorizing epitomizes the kind of compromise for which Sewell argues in that it calls for theory to be more grounded historically while also recasting his-tory to be more cognizant theoretically. The goal of infusing each with the other is the hope of drawing on the strength of each approach to reposition lynchings from something insignificant or aberrational to something crucial to the development of the American state. To borrow the words of Billie Holiday, nonideal theorizing sees the "blood at the root."[112]

Theorizing of this kind is crucial if only for the sake of coherency. Although revi-sionist accounts of the judiciary during Reconstruction are limited mainly to a cri-tique of the dominant narrative of the judiciary, I am endeavoring to piece together a positive juridical–political framework for what was left after Reconstruction, when the judiciary signaled a suspension from federal rights enforcement. If the judiciary had not, in fact, completely dismantled federal rights enforcement during Recon-struction, then the question is raised of how and why this potential reservoir for federal intervention was not tapped sooner than it was. Why the *longue durée* of federal inactivity? A contingent framework of jurisprudence is needed to fill the conceptual void of how the federal government was able to feign responsibility for approximately eighty years while nevertheless retaining sovereign authority.

Constitutional anarchy is an example of nonideal theorizing in that it not only centers the experience of nonwhites as the starting point, but also it provides a conceptual category that neither completely collapses law into politics nor presumes these two categories are entirely distinct. With regard to lynchings, after Congress and the president no longer supported the federal government's involvement in the enforcement of rights for Southern blacks, the Supreme Court created a framework that relieved the federal government of any culpability for what might happen under its sovereign eye while simultaneously reserving to itself sovereign authority. The federal government deliberately stopped short of total jurisdiction, albeit with the proviso that it could, if it chose to, intervene. Because the bounding was self-imposed, the federal government could not only unbind itself whenever it wanted, but it could also set the line of where its jurisdiction started and stopped. Rather than upholding the prosecution of lynchers and/or the states that failed to deal with them, the Supreme Court instead decided to create "zones" wherein questionable activities such as lynchings could occur unhampered. These "anomalous zones" were, essentially, legally bounded regions of lawlessness that operated semi-autonomously under the overarching framework of a constitutional regime. These racialized spaces of exception served to insulate and "unadulterate" the norm from the vicissitudes that the lawlessness of the anomalous zone could and did engender. Race served two functions. With regard to segregation, race was reflected in the law in that it provided for the orderly differentiation for the separate-but equal doctrine. With regard to lynching, however, race formed the shadow demarcation that provided the contours or borders wherein an anomalous zone could emerge.

Constitutional anarchy was not necessarily a deliberate project of which everybody was necessarily conscious. Sewell's depiction of social structures is apt: "[S]ocial structures were objective and transpersonal patters or forces of which actors were at best incompletely aware and that tightly constrained their actions and thoughts."[113] The analytical strength of constitutional anarchy derives from its ability to discern rhetoric and capacity, between what was said and what was actually possible. Much of what was argued after 1883 was premised on the mistaken belief that the federal government stripped itself of the authority to intervene, when in fact it did not. The prevalence of this mistaken interpretation was grounded primarily on the instrumental value it provided to all three branches than its validity as a judicial principle. As many analysts have pointed out, constitutional interpretation is hardly ever definitive, and is mired constantly in conflicts and debates.[114] In that vein, rather than try to ascertain a singular definitive account of what the

Fourteenth Amendment *really* means, constitutional anarchy tries to make sense of how multiple interpretations can and have existed across time. Instead of figuring out which interpretation is more correct legally, constitutional anarchy reasserts the vacillating nature of political will-formation in understanding why and when one account prevails over others and how best to understand how interpretations shift over time. A central premise of constitutional anarchy is the malleability of the law that is able to contour itself around the political without necessarily losing its integrity as law. Rather than weighing in on which interpretation of the Constitution is correct, constitutional anarchy tries to explain how multiple interpretations could coexist simultaneously, and how certain interpretations can be deactivated and reactivated over time.

Because constitutional anarchy is an example of nonideal theorizing, this approach is less interested with being comprehensive and consistent, and more concerned with being determinate and accurate. In this regard, it is akin to methods associated commonly with historical institutionalism. Ronald Kahn and Ken Kersch describe the rigors of historical institutionalism:

> [H]istorical institutionalists rarely purport to arrive at timeless, strictly falsifiable conclusions. As such, historical institutionalist public law scholarship tends to be simultaneously descriptive, interpretive, and empirical, and its conclusions about laws of behavior are either modest or abstract.[115]

The modesty that Kahn and Kersch mentioned is reflected here in that I am not as concerned with establishing a comprehensive account of American history as I am with accurately politicizing what has often been ignored by political scientists.

Constitutional anarchy was not a preconceived, rigid idea waiting to be implemented, but rather an expedient measure taken by the Supreme Court to reconcile the accommodation of the federal government to Southern extremists after the dramatic legal transformations that occurred during Reconstruction. In that constitutional anarchy is a framework that makes allowances for the oscillation of the political will to enforce (or not to enforce) the law, it should not be regarded as a stable, ideal concept that can stand the test of time; rather, it should be regarded as an impromptu, legal act of improvisation that was context specific, politically contingent, and conceptually unstable.

To be clear, constitutional anarchy is a heuristic device intended to schematize a series of cases pertaining to lynching. As such, it is not meant to suggest that the Supreme Court justices had a deliberate project in mind. When justices decided cases, they were not necessarily concerned with the likes of constitutional anarchy. There is, however, a coherency to what has—until now—been deemed disparate and discontinuous decisions made by the Court.

Although I, like the historical institutionalists, do not strive for strictly falsifiable conclusions, there is nevertheless a degree of falsifiability to my claim for constitutional anarchy. Did the Supreme Court completely overturn Reconstruction legislation that pertained to lynchings? More specifically, did the Court ever make a ruling that stated that Section 6 of the Enforcement Act of 1870 and/or Section 1 of the Civil Rights Act of 1866 could not be used to prosecute lynchers? If the Court had done any or all of these things, then constitutional anarchy would be wrong. Constitutional anarchy hinges on the claim that the federal government always retained the authority to prosecute lynchers in the South, but at times chose not to wield that authority. If, in fact, the federal government somehow lost and/or never had the authority to prosecute lynchers in the South, then another theory is needed to explain the federal government's fluctuating role in relation to lynching. But, my research has led me to conclude the federal government did, in fact, retain the authority to prosecute lynchers. Even when the Court was making rulings that were detrimental to federal efforts to prosecute lynchers, the Court never repudiated and/or stripped the federal government wholly of its authority to engage in federal rights enforcement. Rather, the Court tended to dispose of lynching cases in a manner quite similar to the way legal historian Charles Mangum described the process by which the Court disposed of disenfranchisement challenges: "on some technical or subsidiary point, leaving the merits of the real issue untouched."[116] By sidestepping the issue, the Court never relinquished authority. Thus, it was never a matter of lacking the legal authority; rather, it was a matter of lacking the political will. The active policy of nonenforcement was more of a political agreement mired in comity than a legal principle of incapacity. In other words, the federal government's inaction regarding racial violence was less an institutional matter of resources or legal capacity and more of a sovereign decision not to act. Thus, it was not about what the law could have done differently—it always contained the seeds of an alternative doctrine—but that alternative was only available after the political branches were willing to act. Constitutional anarchy unpacks how the Court contoured the law to fit what the federal government was willing to enforce. More specifically, constitutional anarchy is meant to frame the federal government's fluctuating disengagement with the rights enforcement of blacks in such a way that accurately subordinates the legal complexities of such enforcement to the more pertinent question of political will formation. The ways in which the Supreme Court finessed this relationship between the law and the enforcement of the law are key to unlocking how laws can go in and out of fashion, as they did with lynchings.

In that I am focusing on legal cases, I make frequent references to the federal judiciary. At times, I refer to lower federal court decisions, but for the most part I examine Supreme Court decisions. When referencing the Supreme Court, I tend to focus on the majority opinion. By making such broad brushstrokes, I run the risk of portraying the Court as more of a unitary actor than it actually was. But, my brushstrokes are broad for a reason. Not only am I covering a span of one hundred years, but I am also focusing on situating the Court vis-à-vis the other branches. If this was focused solely on the Court, then a detailed analysis of the position of each Supreme Court judge might be warranted. But, my focus is on the federal government as a whole, with an analysis of how each branch of government acted, reacted, and fed off each other. I am more interested in unpacking the dynamics across branches than I am in delving into the dynamics within a single branch.

By no means should my focus on the federal government be taken as an attempt to exaggerate its role in stopping lynchings or to minimize the role of nonstate actors, such as the National Association for the Advancement of Colored People (NAACP) or Ida B. Wells, in reducing lynchings. Nor should it be mistaken as a causal mechanism to explain the variations of lynchings across states. There is already abundant literature examining the impact of antilynching organizations,[117] case studies of lynchings in particular states,[118] and attempts at formulating causal explanations for lynchings.[119] To reiterate, I am not as interested in understanding lynchings as I am in examining the federal government's allowance for lynchings. The analytical purchase of constitutional anarchy does not, therefore, hinge on its explanatory force as a causal mechanism for the variations of lynchings across states or, for that matter, the eventual decline of lynchings, but rather it focuses on the degree to which it schematizes accurately the federal government's response to lynchings in the South.

The strength of this book resides in the examination of interbranch dynamics and how theory is used to analyze the historical evidence, as well as how history is used to sharpen and contour the theoretical claims. To separate out any of these components would obscure the coordination and complicity across branches, as well as lose the kind of insight that comes from bringing together theory and history. This is not to say that work that looks exclusively at the Court or liberalism should not be done. It has been done and should continue to be done. But, the strength of this book derives from the insight that emerges from bringing together elements that are usually studied in isolation.

CHAPTER OUTLINE

Constitutional anarchy is predicated on certain presuppositions that need to be clarified beforehand. For example, it is necessary to establish the United States chose deliberately to be "weak" and was not forced to be weak. In so doing, the concern shifts from a question of sovereignty to an issue of institutional arrangement. It then was left to the judiciary to figure out an institutional arrangement in which the federal government could absolve itself of responsibility without sacrificing its own authority. The judiciary did so by using the dualistic framework of an emergency. When the social, political, and judicial matters are resolved, constitutional anarchy brings these matters together by arranging these elements into a coherent whole, and explains how a policy of nonenforcement was possible, sustainable, and removable.

A previous iteration of this book was sequenced chronologically, and in so doing it was incoherent conceptually. The case for constitutional anarchy was muddled. Constitutional anarchy is derived inductively in that it builds off the premises that the federal government chose an active policy of weakness and that the judiciary subsequently accommodated such policies in a manner that did not impinge on the sovereignty of the federal government. If either premise is incorrect, then constitutional anarchy is unwarranted. But, if both premises are indeed correct, then constitutional anarchy can describe aptly the entirety of the federal government. Building the argument in this manner solidifies what might otherwise seem to be a non sequitur. Hence, I decided to arrange my argument in a more conceptual manner wherein each chapter builds off the previous chapters.

Chapter 2 established the baseline after the Civil War, when Southern extremists were able to adjudicate a certain class of offenses and offenders. Although the initial emergence of the Klan might at first appear to contradict my account of the federal government, I go on to chart the development of the American state during the era when Southern lynchings prevailed and, in so doing, substantiate the first premise that the federal government chose an active policy of weakness as opposed to a forced position of weakness. Contrary to the standard interpretation that depicts the American state as having lacked the administrative and legal capacity to protect the lives of Southern blacks, this chapter unpacks a more pluralist conception of state weakness that characterizes the American state's behavior regarding racial violence as a more deliberate, calculated act of an active state choosing not to act. The state always possessed legal authority to prosecute lynch mobs, but the key determinant was garnering the political will to enforce the law. Examples gleaned from the presidential administrations of Ulysses Grant, Franklin Roosevelt, and Lyndon Johnson illustrate the American government's political vacillation to act and not to act. Examinations of two Supreme Court cases in 1966 highlight the political nature of federal rights enforcement. In light of the 1966 Supreme Court decisions in *U.S. v. Price* and *U.S. v. Guest*, the Court appears to have never repudiated or stripped the federal government of all of its authority to engage in combating racial violence. Although the Court clearly signaled, during Reconstruction, that it was not going to uphold claims of rights violations of blacks in the South, it did so without ever making a substantive decision on whether it could. Laws were, in effect, placed into suspended animation, and it was only when there was a political will to reengage with federal rights enforcement did the Court resuscitate these laws. In the parlance of the weak-state thesis, the American state did not lose its capacity to combat racial violence; it simply chose not to engage.

Having established in Chapter 2 that the American state maintained its capacity throughout, Chapter 3 delves into how the federal government framed such capacity. The federal government chose to wield its capacity by instituting an emergency. Emergencies tend to be associated with restricting rights, but there have been instances when emergencies led to the expansion of rights. During Reconstruction, racial terror was suspended temporarily and the radical practice of extending rights reserved previously for whites to former slaves was invoked. Chapter 3 focuses on the Supreme Court's handling of racial violence during Reconstruction to illuminate how the judiciary framed the unprecedented task of extending rights to blacks. Contrary to the standard account that depicts the Supreme Court as adamantly against federal rights enforcement for blacks, a close textual reading of the Reconstruction cases starting with Justice Miller's decision in *The Slaughter-House Cases*, indicates that the Supreme Court was amenable to federal rights enforcement for blacks. Framing these cases in the context of emergency, which the Court did, provides for a more coherent analysis that goes beyond the ideological proclivities of the justices and points to more structural concerns concerning the embedded nature of racism. The fact that an emergency was instituted to install rights for blacks not only illustrates a counterintuitive use of an emergency as rights enhancing, but also alludes to the difficulties of addressing racial violence during normal times. Developing the argument in this manner situates the judiciary as more accommodating than recalcitrant, which is what often occurs when examining the Court in isolation.

After situating how the judiciary accommodated the active policy of state weakness in Chapter 3, I then introduce constitutional anarchy in Chapter 4. An overall review of Supreme Court cases regarding racial violence suggests that, although the Court did rule in favor of acquitting lynchers of federal prosecution, it did not strip all authority for federal rights enforcement completely. Chapter 4 reassesses the Supreme Court's handling of racial violence and formulates a framework that can account for how lynchings could exist as a tacitly accepted practice without being sanctioned explicitly by the law. Initially, the chapter delves into how lynching emerged as a way of describing racial violence that differentiated it from previous incidents of racial violence, as well as from racial violence that pertained to voting. I then proceed to examine how, instead of cracking down on lynchers and/or the states that failed to deal with lynchers, the Supreme Court decided to create zones wherein questionable activities such as lynchings could occur unhampered. Lynchings, for the most part, were situated within a constructed zone of permissiveness that was contingent—not upon the sanctioning of political authorities per se—but rather upon political authorities choosing to maintain an active policy of noninterference. Drawing from Ernst Fraenkel's model of the dual state and Gerald Neuman's concept of anomalous zones, constitutional anarchy brings together how Southern extremists were able to carve out a degree of jurisprudential authority for itself, how the political branches of the federal government chose actively not to intervene in fighting Southern extremists, and, last, how the federal judiciary reconciled the dilemma of what seemed to be a challenge to national sovereignty.

Chapter 5 details the end of constitutional anarchy. In 1966, the federal government returned to combatting lynching. In many regards, the Court's switch in time upholding the prosecution of lynchers is eerily reminiscent to the Court's previous switch in time to allow for lynchings. As was the case after Reconstruction, the Court's reactivation of federal rights enforcement followed only when there were clear indications of support by the executive and legislative branches for federal rights enforcement. In other words, the Court was in the rearguard in providing for lynchings, and again found itself last in line when it came to stopping lynchings. By the time the Court reactivated federal rights enforcement with regard to lynchings, Congress and the president had already demonstrated their willingness to enforce the right of life for blacks in the South. It was the Court's ability to "reinterpret old statutes" when it deemed fit that constitutional anarchy is meant both to unpack and illuminate. I then conclude with some remarks about the change and continuity of racial violence across time and communities.

Although lynchings appear to represent the outright failure of liberal democracy to live up to even its most minimalist requirement, I hope to demonstrate how a liberal democracy dealt internally with this seeming contradiction. Not only does this new political typology of constitutional anarchy provide a way of reconciling the paradoxical coexistence of the enduring legacy of liberalism and racism, it also resituates how liberalism is defined and measured. The extent to which a polity is considered liberal should not be determined solely by the content of the law (e.g., freedom of speech, women's rights, due process); rather, it should also be determined by the scope of the law. To what extent is the United States liberal? Is it liberal everywhere for everybody? Constitutional anarchy adds the element of range to the discussion of what it means for a polity to be liberal.

The liberal state has always been as strong as the political
and social situation and the interests of society demanded.
—FRANZ NEUMANN[1]

Weak-state liberalism is not a formula for individual freedom
but a green light for the hawks to devour the sparrows.
—STEPHEN HOLMES[2]

2

Strengthening the Weak State: Politicizing the American State's "Weakness" on Racial Violence

⌒ ───

INTRODUCTION

The American state is "steeped in paradox and contradiction."[3] Nowhere is this more evident than in its troubled relationship with race, especially racial violence. After the national state emancipated blacks from the arbitrary power of slave masters, blacks eventually became subject to the arbitrary power of lynch mobs. It might be argued that there is no contradiction here, but simply a practical limit: the state lacked the administrative and political capacity to protect the lives of Southern blacks.[4] Such an assessment, however, not only fails to grasp the political dynamics underpinning racial violence, but also operates with an insufficiently theorized conception of state weakness. The standard interpretation of the American state's relationship with racial violence needs to be revamped. I argue for a more pluralist conception of state weakness. A differentiation can be made between states that are compelled to be weak and states that choose to be weak. The former presumes incapacity; the latter presumes autonomy.

This analytical distinction between different kinds of state weakness is especially illuminating for the study of lynchings, which involves extrajudicial illegal acts that cannot continue indefinitely without either tacit permission (the *choice* to be weak) or an inability to enforce the law (an *administrative* weakness).[5] Weakness in this one particular aspect runs counter to other developments that depict the state as growing stronger over time. Disentangling the different capacities of the state not only presumes a disaggregation of what constitutes a state, but also what constitutes weakness. Examining both sets as they relate to racial violence reveals an interdependency between "stateness" and weakness. By couching weakness as a legal principle of federalism, the federal government was able to relinquish responsibility while nonetheless maintaining authority. Weakness with respect to lynchings thus enabled the national state to pursue and strengthen other aspects of the state. By contextualizing inaction in a form of legalese, it undergirded inaction to the extent that it would take another revolutionary moment that was analogous to the period after the Civil War to reactivate federal rights enforcement.

This chapter examines how the federal government manipulated different aspects of the state to embed and obscure its complicity with white supremacy. In so doing, it attempts to intervene more broadly in the debates about American state development and weak-state theory.[6] First, I sketch the basics of weak-state theory, considering how it has been applied to the development of the postbellum American state in general and to the historical problem of racial violence specifically. With theoretical frameworks in place, it then becomes possible to analyze the political and legal history surrounding the strange career of federal rights enforcement regarding racial violence. Then, I examine the historical merits of the weak-state thesis, particularly as they relate to the initial emergence of Southern extremists after the end of the Civil War. Next, I analyze the federal government's initial response to racial violence under the Grant administration and document how the state was able administratively—but eventually withdrew from—enforcing the right of blacks to be protected against racial violence. I then shift to Franklin Roosevelt's era, during which attempts to create an antilynching bill were defeated, revealing the political calculus that continued to impede rights enforcement, and how this political problem was concealed by Roosevelt's claim that a new antilynching law was needed to engage in federal rights enforcement. I next contrast the 1966 Supreme Court decisions in *U.S. v. Price* and *U.S. v. Guest* against the landmark decision *Brown v. Board of Education* to show that the state always possessed legal authority to prosecute lynch mobs, and note the conundrum that was raised was about sovereignty. To conclude, I revisit works that reconcile this issue of sovereignty by elevating the concept of withdrawal as an action in and of itself. In sum, I argue that the relevant "weakness" that permitted the existence of lynching for nearly eighty years was not a matter of administrative capacity or state resources, but rather political choice and self-restraint by political officials and representatives.

WEAK STATE AND RACIAL VIOLENCE

Weak state is a relative term that tends to be contrasted with a strong society or a strong state.[7] Corresponding with Max Weber's ideal type of the state as an institution that enforces regulations, at least in part through a monopoly of the legitimate use of violence, weak-state theories provide an evaluative standard by which to measure how close states actually are to the ideal type. According to Joel Migdal, author of the landmark book on weak states, the relative strength of the state is measured by "the ability of state leaders to use the agencies of the state to get people in the society to do what they want them to do."[8] A weak state, then, is characterized by a "disjuncture between the state's rules of the game, as its leaders sought to establish the whole society as a single juridical whole and the actual operative dictates of behavior in society."[9] This disjuncture is often characterized as operating against the intentions of the state. Weak-state theories thus provide a nuanced approach that emphasizes the interdependent and dynamic relationship between state and society in a manner that complicates state autonomy and the interpenetration of societal actors as well as provides pluralist approaches to measuring and defining elements of statehood.

Political historian William Novak notes the once-prevailing view that the American state was weak:

> [T]he phrase "the American state" is seen as something of an oxymoron in a land of alleged "anti-statism" and "statelessness." When acknowledged at all, the American version of a state is viewed as something not quite fully formed—something less, something laggard, something underdeveloped compared to the mature governmental regimes that dominate modern European history.[10]

This claim for statelessness has recently been refuted across various aspects of the American state.[11] Although conventional accounts of the stateless nature of the American state have been widely discredited, it has nevertheless persisted in accounts regarding racial violence. At first blush, an analysis of the state's relationship to racial violence, especially lynching, seems to confirm conventional approaches that emphasize its weak capacity and legal fragmentation.

Sociologists Stewart Tolnay and Elwood M. Beck documented at least 2,400 black men that were lynched between 1883 and 1966.[12] Historian Robert Zangrando reported that "more than 99% of mob members escaped arrest, prosecution, conviction and punishment."[13] In the few instances when there were formal investigations, the conclusion was often "death at the hands of persons unknown."[14]

Easily obscured by the complexities of federalism, the national government is often portrayed as helpless to reign in the vicissitudes of lynch mobs.[15] Many analysts have argued that the federal government was hindered in combating lynchings because it lacked the legal authority and/or institutional capacity.[16] In general, political authorities—particularly at the federal level—are considered to have played a minor role in the regulation, administration, and eventual decline of lynchings.[17] To be sure, political authorities—particularly local law enforcement—were involved heavily in certain cases, often by abstaining from enforcing the law, but sometimes by direct participation in lynch mobs. In most instances, however, it was (un)civil forces that decided to take the law into their own hands.[18] These accounts presume that the state's failure to enforce the law was a result of incapacity rather than a decision about where, when, and how to exercise its power.

Although the American state appeared weak in relation to dealing with racial violence in the South, it nonetheless exercised strength in relation to other areas. In *Building a New American State: The Expansion of Administrative Capacities, 1877– 1920*, Stephen Skowronek details the expansion of national administrative capacities in other areas, such as the civil service, the army, and regulation of the economy.[19] This expansion occurred at the same time that the federal government's apparent weakness in relation to racial violence in the South remained constant. How can one particular aspect of the national state remain weak while other aspects of the national state were becoming strong? Answering this question implies a political rethinking about when and why a state might not want to enforce its laws fully.

Perhaps the very notion of "stateness" needs to be disaggregated. Instead of settling for a singular dimension of stateness, John P. Nettl outlines a multidimensional notion of stateness that provides for sector-specific investigations.[20] A state can thus be weak in some parts and strong in other parts. The discrepancy between quelling racial violence and other aspects of governance might then just come down to an issue of disaggregation. One way of reconceptualizing the state from this perspective is to sequester racial violence as an exception to general trends. Harry Scheiber's theory of federalism is an apt example. Scheiber categorizes federalism as five stages: (1) dual federalism from 1789 to 1861, (2) transitional centralization from 1861 to 1890, (3) accelerated centralization from 1890 to 1933, (4) cooperative federalism from the New Deal to World War II, and (5) creative federalism from the post-World War II onward.[21] Scheiber is, however, quick to note an exception to this schematization: "A residue of dual federalism from the antebellum era was evident in the area of civil rights, as Southern blacks were left virtually against private coercion, state action, and often terrifying violence."[22] Although Scheiber acknowledges the American state's (mis)handling of race, he makes no attempt to make it cohere to his general schematization. This strategy of separating out race from his overall framework is not atypical. According to Desmond King and Robert Lieberman, "many leading works of scholarship on core institutions of the American state overlook how race and segregation shaped their content and policy effects. This deficiency is one reason for singling out the segregationist dimension of the American state."[23]

This multidimensional approach has led some to conclude that viewing the state as a coherent, interconnected whole is impossible.[24] But, to presume analytically that the state is an incoherent whole is nonetheless to reaffirm the rigid categories by which that presumption is made. There is another way of reconceptualizing the state using Nettl's theory of disaggregation. Integrating the American state's relationship with race with other aspects is possible; but, to do so, weakness itself needs to be disaggregated. Although the dominant conception of weakness is that of incapacity, I venture another conception of weakness that is predicated on autonomy: there are times when the state is willing to be weak, rather than forced by lack of resources or capacity. This kind of weakness is premised as a positive choice made by the state. With regard to the military and American state building, Ira Katznelson notes "how a putatively 'weak' state in fact can be very capable."[25] It was through this governmental policy of weakness that the American state was able to get stronger in other aspects of governance. In this regard, weakness is not necessarily something to be avoided; rather, it can also be something to which to aspire. Weakness is thus not always a consequence of policy failure, but also it can stem from a policy being successful.

"Weakness" is a concept that should be disaggregated. It can refer to a relative scarcity of resources or lack of power, but it can *also* be seen as an explicit policy decision. In relation to racial violence, the American state deliberately pursued a policy of weakness. Weakness in this one particular aspect of stateness enabled it to pursue and strengthen other aspects of stateness. Although it did not have to be weak, the United States wanted to be weak. It pursued a policy of weakness by choice. In other words, the United States made itself actively weak with regard to a particular set of activities. We might say the most important issue here was not the *state* weakness of the new Union but the *political* weakness of groups disposed favorably to enforcing rights for blacks. The national state withdrew from prosecuting lynch mobs not because it did not have the wherewithal; rather, it withdrew to pursue other political ends.

I illustrate this subtle differentiation between being passively incapacitated and being deliberately inactive by resituating the American state's relationship with racial violence in wider political terms. Although many posit the Supreme Court as having impeded the federal government's ability to quell racial violence, after extensive research into four historical eras, I conclude that government inaction was the result of less the disabling nature of legal prohibitions on state action than of the political will not to act. Blaming the Court primarily for government inaction not only mischaracterizes what actually happened, but also relieves political authorities of the culpability that is due to them. By resituating state inaction in more political terms, the "weakness" of the American state in regard to racial violence is characterized more accurately as a deliberate, calculated act of an active state choosing not to act.

PROLOGUE AS PRETEXT

The weak-state theory is indeed persuasive, particularly as it relates to the initial emergence of Southern extremist groups such as the Ku Klux Klan.[26] The South plunged into chaos immediately after General Robert Lee's surrender at Appomattox.[27] Official reports gave vivid accounts of chaos in the South. Union Army General Carl Schurz reported that "in many districts robbing and plundering was going on with perfect impunity."[28] Although many reasons have been given regarding why the South plunged immediately into chaos after Appomattox, including the nature and intensity of the war[29] and the particularities surrounding the endgame of the war,[30] the lack of forethought on the part of the political authorities is often underestimated.

Although Congress and President Lincoln agreed on a plan in 1863, by 1864 they were very much at odds, particularly in light of Lincoln's pocket veto of the Wade–Davis Bill, along with his plan to reconstruct Louisiana using its old Constitution. Congress was in no hurry at this time to come up with a plan.[31] Problems associated with not having a preconceived postwar plan were compounded further by the tragic events that immediately followed Appomattox. Between strategizing and negotiating the endgame to the Civil War, dealing with the first-ever assassination of a U.S. President, coordinating the first-ever transfer of presidential power in a time of crisis, uncovering the conspiratorial plot that also included the attempted assassination of the Secretary of War and the Vice-President, coordinating a manhunt for the conspirators, investigating any other possible conspiracies, familiarizing the estranged Vice-President to the position of President, and, last, coming up with a plan for Reconstruction, it seems that all these events precluded the federal government from developing any sort of immediate plan for what to do with the occupied territories in the South. This series of events magnified the problem of not already having a postwar plan.

Issues concerning legal jurisdiction instantly became a problem after the war ended. In the South, there were as many as eight different types of courts operating simultaneously without any clear jurisdictional demarcations. The army had three types of courts: the court-martial, the military commission, and the provost court.[32] The Freedmen's Bureau had four of their own: single-judge courts with local agents in charge, single-judge courts with officers appointed specifically to act as judges, single-judge courts presided over by civilian magistrates, and three-judge courts.[33] Local civilian courts also operated in certain areas as well. Except for the court-martial, which dealt strictly with offenses committed by persons in the military,[34] questions concerning jurisdictional oversight arose constantly between and among these different courts of law.[35] Although the Freedmen's Bureau was instituted as a bureau of the War Department, it nevertheless faced problems inside the War Department. Disagreements arose because both the provost courts and the bureau courts wanted to try cases involving blacks.[36] In his report to the Senate, General Ulysses S. Grant stated: "The Freedmen's Bureau being separated from the military establishment of the country, requires all the expense of a separate organization. One does not necessarily know what the other is doing, or what orders they are acting under."[37]

Confusion surrounding jurisdiction was exacerbated after the Supreme Court came out with its decision in ex parte *Milligan*.[38] Ex parte *Milligan* stated that military tribunals could not claim jurisdiction if local courts were open and functioning. This decision appeared to run counter to the existing state of affairs operating in the South, in which the military courts were actively stripping jurisdictional claims of existing local courts.[39] When the decision first came out, Congressman Thaddeus Stevens decried that ex parte *Milligan* was "perhaps not as infamous as the Dred Scott decision, [it] is yet far more dangerous in its operation upon the lives and liberties of the loyal men of this country. That decision has taken away every protection in every one of these rebel States from every loyal man, black or white, who resides there."[40]

Although much of the analysis of the military courts has focused on lack of resources and instances of corruption, the question of who gets to decide which case fell under which court also played a prominent role in hampering the overall effort of meting out justice and added to the already chaotic situation facing the South during this time.[41] Because of the unclear definitions of jurisdiction, there were considerable amounts of irregularity and controversy. Some formal procedure and/or directive was needed to clarify these jurisdictional issues.

Only President Johnson, as commander-in-chief, could provide this clarity, but unfortunately he did not. After Appomattox, the army operated without specific guidance from Washington. Others had tried to rectify the situation, but without the sanction of the commander-in-chief, these efforts were in vain.[42] For example, Commissioner Howard of the Freedmen's Bureau formulated guidelines, but because President Johnson neither approved nor rejected Howard's proposal, "Howard soon had to tell his assistant commissioners to use their own judgment in adjudicating cases."[43] Congress tried to streamline the process, but its attempt was in vain as well. Congressmen John Bingham presented a bill that would have clarified the jurisdictional confusion. This bill passed both Houses easily, but the President never signed it.[44]

President Johnson became almost forthright about his indecisiveness. Take, for example, the case in Alabama in which citizens signed a petition calling for a constitutional convention. This petition was forwarded up the chain of command and ultimately found its way to President Johnson, who merely filed it.[45] In July 1866,

Louisiana Unionists, with the support of Governor Wells, convened a constitutional convention. Many predicted violence if they were allowed to assemble, so General Baird, the local commander, sent a telegram requesting advice:

> A convention has been called, with the sanction of Governor Wells, to meet here on Monday. The lieutenant governor and city authorities think it unlawful, and propose to break it up by arresting the delegates. I have given no orders on the subject, but have warned the parties that I should not countenance or permit such action without instructions to that effect from the President. Please instruct me by telegraph.[46]

General Baird received no reply and bloodshed ensued.

The "headless" nature of the occupation not only exacerbated the confusion regarding jurisdiction, but also it contributed to the debasement of the rule of law. The initial jurisdictional incoherency and subsequent executive indecision spawned crises of inconsistency, bias, and dysfunction. Stripped of formal procedures, bureaucracy, legal expertise, and democratic accountability, the rule of law quickly transformed from a responsibility the federal government was entrusted to maintain to a burden the government was struggling to retain.

Problems regarding jurisprudence inevitably emerged. Without guidance from Washington, the army went on to administer the South very haphazardly and inconsistently. To label the jurisprudential framework operating in the South as martial law would be somewhat of a misnomer, because martial law implies a certain degree of consistency, cohesiveness, and orderliness, which in fact did not occur in most of the South during this time.[47] In places such as New Orleans, the military allowed loyal citizens to govern themselves, albeit subject to military supervision.[48] In other places—Little Rock, for example—U.S. Army officers took a more direct role in regulating the affairs of the inhabitants. And in other places such as northern Georgia, the military commanders allowed Confederate officials to continue working at their respective posts.[49] In his annual report to Congress, Assistant Commissioner Jospeh B. Kiddoo pointed out that

> the judicial functions of the bureau had been conducted in a very irregular, though not necessarily illegal, manner.... Sub-assistant commissioners, having no uniform instructions, variously interpreted their powers and prerogatives, and often acted at variance with each other.[50]

This haphazardness should come as no surprise because most of the military commanders had little to no experience with reconstruction[51] and little to no extensive knowledge of the law.[52] Without dismissing the racist subtext that permeates much of the criticism levied against the occupation, some of the criticism regarding questionable legal practices seemed warranted.[53] Perhaps the most blatant act of mockery occurred in Major De Forest's courts:

> So informal were Major De Forest's courts that he thought that on ordinary occasions a sham officer could run them as well as himself. Indeed, one day when he was away a neighbor impersonated him and "tried" the case of a farmer and a Negro.[54]

This example illustrates how people with no legal training were making legal decisions based solely on their own discretion. It should then be of no wonder, then, why many Southern newspapers excoriated the military occupation for "exercising the most arbitrary and despotic power."[55]

Beyond matters of incoherency, inconsistency, bias, and possible corruption, there was also the basic issue of functionality. Although one may have presumed that the existence of so many courts would have resulted in an excess of legal activity, because of the confusion regarding jurisdiction, it actually led to a diminution of justice. Official reports from the field confirm this.[56] Two reasons have been given for why crimes went unpunished. Both are related to jurisdictional confusion. First, there was a general reluctance to spend time and resources on something that could be overruled at any moment.[57] Second, law enforcement officials did not want to risk being sued.[58] These disincentives only exacerbated the situation further.

Although many white Southerners would come to acquiesce to racist extremism, it was not a foregone conclusion. George H. Thomas, Major General of the U.S. Army, testified to Congress that "a great many of [Southerners] say that they failed in their attempt to gain their independence of the United States, and that they now wish to be quiet citizens of the country."[59] Joseph Stiles, a citizen from Virginia, confirmed this in his testimonial to Congress: "[Southerners] are anxious to see peace and quiet restored to the country."[60] Colonel Lewis Merrill observed, "in all my conversations with people, I have been met constantly with the palliative remark in regards to these [Klan] outrages—conceding that they are wrong and all that."[61] Congressional testimonials and military reports thus seem to suggest a strong proclivity against violence of any sort. This raises the question: Why were Southern extremist groups like the Klan able to garner such support among white Southerners after the Civil War?

Simple appeals to racism are insufficient.[62] Historian C. Vann Woodward argued persuasively in *The Strange Career of Jim Crow* against the inevitability of Southern extremists.[63] He pointed out that before the South capitulated to the doctrines of the extreme racists, there were three alternative philosophies of race relations vying for the region's support: liberal, conservative, and radical. Although there was no denying the "central theme" of racism, Woodward nevertheless made a convincing argument that racism was somewhat mutable and that the virulent form of racism espoused by white extremists was not preordained.[64]

To presume that white Southerners were completely aligned with Southern extremists also runs counter to their own testimonies. White Southerners were primarily concerned with procuring conditions conducive to securing their livelihood. A letter to President Johnson dated May 1, 1865, by the citizens of Chatham County, Georgia, is illustrative of the predicament facing many white Southerners at the time. It is striking to notice the paucity of their demands. There was no reference to white supremacy. Their only demand was a speedy recovery of government that could protect them:

> We have looked with deep interest upon the unsettled situation of our State, being without civil government and but partially protected by military rule, and thus exposed to repeated depredations and violence from bands of lawless men, whites and blacks, making raids and attacks upon the persons and property and comfort of quiet citizens in the country. . . . The daily increasing irregularities causing us to apprehend more extended depredations throughout the State, probably resulting in the abandonment and loss of the greater portion of the present year's crops, and subjecting the people of the State to the peril of famine and anarchy. . . . Believing, as we do, that unless our State be *speedily* [emphasis added] placed under a more systematic and efficient government the growing crops will be seriously endangered, a large portion of our population be lost to the State, and terminating in a destructive collision between the races composing our population, we, the people of Chatham County, speaking for ourselves, and in which we have reason to believe that our fellow-citizens of the other counties of the State will concur, invoke Your Excellency to protect our people.[65]

What makes this plea prophetic is that it predicts that, without federal assistance, dire consequences follow, including a "collision between the races." Although racism was prevalent at this time, it thus does not explain adequately the emergence and success of Southern extremism.

However, the federal government's actions, or lack thereof, seemed to push white Southerners into the extremist camp. The longer the federal authorities languished, the more resentful Southerners became and the harder it was for the federal government to enact reforms. The editor for the *Southern Cultivator*, a newspaper published out of Athens, Georgia, wrote in 1866 that so long as this course is continued, and human nature is unchanged, those who pursue it will be hated in peace even worse than they were hated in war; and the indignation and sense of outrage felt by each Southern man, will be more or less intense, as his perceptions of equality and justice are more or less clear.[66]

President Lincoln perhaps summed it up the best when he told Secretary of the Navy Gideon Welles that "here must be courts, and law and order, or society would be broken up. . . . and the disbanded armies would turn into robber bands and guerrillas."[67]

Historians, across the ideological spectrum agree on the nature of legal affairs that befell the South. George Bentley addresses the problem succinctly in the eyes of Southerners:

> With such conflicts of jurisdiction occurring quite often, and their stories being circulated in the southern press, and with army officers and Bureau officials themselves finding it necessary to issue orders cautioning agents against arbitrary arrests and needless assumptions of authority, the southern whites' original prejudice against courts shortly developed into absolute hatred. They railed at these courts for making "a mockery of all law," for their "irresponsible method of administering justice," and their "unlimited usurpation of judicial authority."[68]

James Cutler noted, "the foundation had been removed from the old legal system and no new system was established in the place of the old one which to any degree could cope with the condition of affairs."[69] Christopher Waldrep added that "the laws of the country were found wholly ineffectual for the punishment of individuals, and emboldened by impunity, their numbers and their crimes, have daily continued to multiply."[70]

Views at the time confirm this analysis. In a testimony to Congress, Dr. Pride Jones stated that "there was inefficiency somewhere and [Southerners] could not get protection."[71] Under these circumstances, as Assistant Commissioner Samuel Thomas pointed out in his letter to Union General Carl Schurz, "it is of no consequences what the law may be if the majority be not inclined to have it executed."[72] Even the majority leader of the Senate, William Pitt Fessenden, admitted to the precarious predicament placed upon white Southerners by the federal government: "They [Southerners] are not a people satisfied, or likely to be satisfied, with what we do . . . and I think it becomes us to look well that we give no proper occasion, and not only no proper occasion, but no plausible occasion, for accusations against us"[73]

Conditions were thus ripe for the Southern extremists. Southern extremists wanted to resist Reconstruction and subsequently took over groups such as the Ku Klux Klan, which were formed initially as a social fraternity organization, and then reconfigured them to function as temporary stopgap measures for what they regarded as a degenerative and corrupt legal system. The Ku Klux Klan was explicit about couching their actions in ways that addressed the primary concerns of white Southerners, which centered on the weakness of the federal government to administer the law effectively. Southern extremists were able to convince many white Southerners that a limited degree of extralegality was necessary to ensure a wider degree of stability. Although many Southerners regarded the actions taken by Southern extremists as deplorable, extremist groups were nevertheless able to garner the support of a majority of white Southerners because they appeared to be effective in restoring a semblance of stability and order.

The Ku Klux Klan's rapid rise occurred soon after it shifted its focus to restoring law and order. In spring 1867 the Ku Klux Klan made its transition from a social group to a band of regulators dedicated to curbing lawlessness. Its political reorientation was reflected in the Klan's revised and amended prescript. There was now a formal statement of character and purpose, where none had existed in 1866. It sounds like something out of a police handbook. Its purpose was "to protect the weak, the innocent, and the defenceless, from the indignities, wrongs, and outrages of the lawless, the violent and the brutal . . . and to support the United States Constitution and constitutional laws." There was also a series of ten questions, which every incoming member had to answer satisfactorily. Questions included whether prospective members favored maintaining the Constitutional rights of the South and whether they believed in the inalienable right of self-preservation of the people against the exercise of arbitrary and unlicensed power.[74]

This shift toward law and order was essential to the survival and success of the Klan because it enabled it to garner community support.[75] Support was difficult to acquire because many Southerners regarded the actions taken by the Klan as outrages. But, at the same time, the extremists were the only ones who had a viable strategy for restoring law and order immediately. Southern liberals had no answer; they relied solely on the "normal" legal order, and it was in a state of chaos. Southern conservatives had a long-term electoral strategy to "redeem" the South, but lacked any immediate plans to restore law and order. Only the extremists provided a plan (albeit for some) for restoring a degree of law and order immediately.

Not only was the Klan the only ones with a viable strategy for restoring law and order, they were also careful to depict their actions as temporary stopgap measures that could help the legal order get back on its feet. The Klan did not regard itself as law breakers but as law enforcers. This is clearly evident in the orders given by the leaders of the Klan. In fall 1868, the Grand Dragon of the Realm of Tennessee published General Orders No. 1:

> The Klan is not an institution of violence, lawlessness and cruelty; it is not lawless, it is not aggressive, it is not military, it is not revolutionary. It is essentially, originally, and inherently a protective organization. It proposes to execute law instead of resisting it; and to protect all good men, whether white or black, from the outrages and atrocities of bad men of both colors, who have been for the past three years a terror to society and an injury to us all . . . and will never use violence except in resisting violence. . . . We are striving to protect all good, peaceful, well-disposed and law-abiding men, whether white or black.[76]

This explains, in part, why the Klan had staged so many "mock trials"[77] or "extralegal trials"[78] immediately before killing somebody. These "trials" were a complete sham. There was no due process, no cross-examination, and not even any lawyers. The accuser usually confirmed the identity of the defendant without any corroborating evidence or cross-examination. Sometimes the defendant would deliver a tortured confession. However farcical these "trials" may have been, they nevertheless provided a patina of jurisprudence and legitimacy to the whole process. This notion of desperate times calling for desperate measures is perhaps best captured by Hubert Howe Bancroft, who wrote a book in 1887 titled *Popular Tribunals*. In this book, he writes in a fashion that is eerily similar to President Lincoln's speech, wherein he justifies his use of emergency powers:

> Omnipotence in rule being necessary, and law failing to be omnipotent, the element here denominated vigilance becomes omnipotent, not as a usurper, but as a friend in an emergency. Vigilance recognizes fully the supremacy of the law, flies to its rescue when beaten down by its natural enemy, crime, and lifts it up, that it may always be supreme; and if the law must be broken to save the state, then it breaks it soberly, conscientiously, and under the formulas of law, not in a feeling of revenge, or in a manner usual to the disorderly rabble.[79]

The Klan's claim of supplementing the law also reinforced the perception among many Southerners that it offered an effective tool for establishing and maintaining order.[80] This perception of effectiveness was based in part on reality and in part on exaggerated press reports. In the eyes of many Southerners, the federal authorities were making "a mockery of all law" and they felt that basic crimes such as murder, rape, and robbery were occurring on an unprecedented scale that would lead to complete and utter anarchy if they were not curbed. Although many of these claims of crimes were unsubstantiated, they were nonetheless exaggerated by Southern newspapers, politicians, and the Klan.[81]

This exaggeration had a twofold effect. It not only made the "primary" law enforcement agencies appear more inefficient than they actually were, but it also had the opposite effect of making the "supplementary" law enforcement agencies such as the Klan appear to be more efficient than they actually were. Although the primary law enforcement agencies were taking all the blame for the actual crimes, the Klan could take all the credit for the crimes that did not occur. As Eqbal Ahmad, noted scholar on guerrilla warfare states, "the guerrilla movement is believed to enjoy considerable advantage because its task is merely to destroy while the government must build and protect what it is building."[82] Exaggerated reports of crime thus not only furthered the perception of the ineffectiveness of the regular law enforcement officials, but they also furthered the perception that extralegal measures were needed. Amos Akerman, the first attorney general to head the Department of Justice, noted that "when panic arose, innocent acts were supposed to have criminal significance, and the mass of white people really believed themselves in danger. In this belief they were encouraged by a few demagogues who fanned the flame."[83] One could argue that the Klan was actively shaping and was actively shaped by its relation to the legal system.

Careful to avoid upsetting the delicate nature of the cost–benefit analysis by which white Southerners hinged their support, Southern extremists operated in such a way as to insulate most white Southerners from their extralegal actions, thereby ensuring white Southerners that the violent activities in which they engaged would be contained and would serve to supplement the legal order instead of destabilizing it. Klan members were adamant about depicting themselves "as not simply desperadoes whom society abhorred but could not control."[84] The Klan made sure to confine itself to "a certain class of offenders and a certain description of offenses."[85] Although the Klan maintained decentralized paramilitary units that did not adhere, for the most part, to any clear chain of command, it nevertheless was very consistent with regard to whom it targeted: blacks and Republican sympathizers. Assistant Adjutant General J. Warren Miller stated that "it is a remarkable fact that most of the outrages have been committed against colored people."[86] In other words, race became one of the markers to distinguish those immune to extralegal justice and those susceptible to the vicissitudes of extralegal justice. By focusing on "a certain class of offenders and a certain description of offenses," the Klan was able to reassure other Southerners that the terror would not extend outward to the entire South. It made the bitter pill of the Klan a little easier to swallow for many white Southerners. Although there was no limit to the kind of atrocities the Klan would commit, there was a limit to whom it would inflict those atrocities upon. In this regard, the anarchy was contained. It was not complete anarchy; it was only anarchic for a select, discernible few. In the words of Oliver Cox, "it is a special form of mobbing—mobbing directed against a whole people or political class."[87] Although concepts such as extralegality and exception tend to be temporal in nature, in this case, it is "Negroes who are extralegal, extra-democratic objects."[88] Thus, selective anarchy was regarded as a tactical goal for many of these paramilitary groups because it was seen as a necessary and successful expedient for "correcting" the North's miscues while simultaneously insulating white Southerners from the terror in which they were engaged.

However disinclined white Southerners might have been to violent conflict, Southern extremists were nonetheless able to curry their support. In his testimony, Major Merrill stated that

> it is certainly evident that nearly half in number, and much more than half in influence, are either in conspiracy against the law or conniving at the conspiracy. . . . In short, the conspiracy may be stated to have practically included the whole white community within the ages when active participation in public affairs was possible.[89]

During congressional testimonies, white Southerners rationalized the actions of the Klan as an unfortunate means to an orderly end. When asked whether the Klan was able to operate because people were afraid of it, Dr. Thomson replied,

> Although this [action taken by the Klan] is a terrible remedy, yet ultimate good will follow from it. . . . It is naturally likely that [the citizens of Union County] would not want to inflict punishment upon those who are willing to sacrifice themselves for the general good . . . I believe that these outrages have saved this community.[90]

Even those who were officially responsible for maintaining order agreed with this assessment.[91] Positing themselves as victims, white Southerners hence appeared to see themselves as torn between inept governance and violent extremism. When deciding between the two, it seemed to be the case that many white Southerners did not make their decision on purely racist grounds; rather, they sided with whichever element could best reestablish stability and order. Although the aforementioned quotes can be, justifiably, suspected of hyperbole, it is nonetheless interesting to note how, in their exoneration of Southern extremists, they were nonetheless explicit about dissociating themselves from such extremists. It is important to note the passive complicity of white Southerners. Historian Gunnar Myrdal perhaps summed it up the best: "[F]ew whites of the middle and upper classes in the South have expressed themselves as in favor of lynch justice. But equally few have pretended that they would take any personal risks to hinder a lynching, and they make no effort to punish the lynchers."[92]

The Klan emerged at a time when the legal order appeared to be lapsing into chaos. It was within this context that the Klan was able to embed a certain degree of exceptional and discretionary authority for itself under the discourse of law and order. For these Southern extremists, "restoring law and order" meant terrorizing select populations for the "sake of preserving peace and good order."[93]

PRESIDENT GRANT'S ADMINISTRATION: GOING FROM "STRONG" TO "WEAK"

If the story ended there, then the weak-state thesis would hold; but, when the federal government wanted to stop racial violence in the South, it could and did.[94] Between 1870 and 1872, the American state was active and effective in curbing racial violence in the South.[95] When the Department of Justice was first established, it was committed proactively to quelling racial violence. Amos Akerman was firmly committed to extinguishing the Ku Klux Klan.[96] One month after he took office, he issued a circular regarding the Enforcement Act of 1870 in which he stated that the statute "makes it your special duty to initiate proceedings against all violators of the act."[97] This task was seen by many as impossible for a host of reasons, including budgetary constraints,[98] difficulties in securing evidence,[99] lack of a detective force,[100] local resistance,[101] fear of witnesses to testify,[102] corruption,[103] and the highly talented defense lawyers that many Southern defendants were able to obtain.[104] The Department of Justice under Akerman was nonetheless central to curbing violence in the South in general and in taking down the Ku Klux Klan in particular.

Prosecution of Klansmen began in earnest starting in 1871.[105] In South Carolina, 600 suspected Klansmen were arrested,[106] leading to 390 indictments.[107] In Mississippi, 640 suspected Klansmen were arrested,[108] leading to 200 indictments.[109] In North Carolina, 763 indictments[110] resulted in 98 cases that involved 930 suspected Klansmen.[111] In Alabama, there were 130 indictments against suspected Klansmen.[112] In 1871, there were at least 190 criminal persecutions under the Enforcement Acts, leading to at least 108 convictions.[113] In 1872, 603 criminal prosecutions led to 448 convictions.[114]

Some have interpreted these numbers as indicating the federal government's incapacity to deal adequately with the Klan, since the number of arrests per the number of indictments is relatively low.[115] In the best-case scenario, the rate of indictment was barely more than half. For example, in Mississippi and South Carolina, 1,100 arrests led to 590 indictments only. If one compares the number arrested with the number actually convicted, the rate is even lower. For example, in South Carolina, U.S. Attorney Daniel Corbin had a 33% conviction rate, 26% acquittal rate, and 41% nolle prosequi rate.[116] For tried cases, his conviction rate dropped to 12% and his acquittal rate skyrocketed to 88%.[117] Because of this low rate of convictions, Akerman thought the Ku Klux Klan was "too much even for the United States to undertake to inflict adequate penalties through the courts."[118]

Low acquittal and conviction rates, however, do not necessarily mean the federal government was unable to dismantle the Klan. For example, Brigadier General Alfred Terry's letter to the Secretary of War declared:

[The Ku Klux Klan] is spread over so very large an extent of country that it is manifestly impossible to deal with it efficiently throughout all the states in which it exists at one and the same time. . . . Fortunately, it is not necessary, as I think, to attack the organization at every point. If in a single state it could be suppressed, and in that state exemplary punishment meted out to some of the most prominent criminals, I think that a fatal blow would be given everywhere.[119]

Legal historian Robert Kaczorowski confirms the effectiveness of Brigadier General Terry's strategy as set forth in this letter:

At the beginning of 1872, federal officers felt that they were on the verge of destroying the Klan. They also were heartened by the sharp curtailment of violence that had resulted from their efforts. The fear of prosecution not only restored peace, but it also motivated Klansmen to confess their crimes in the hopes of gaining leniency.[120]

There was also the military to consider. Although President Grant was reluctant to use the power granted to him by the Ku Klux Act of 1871 to suspend the writ of habeas corpus, he did dispatch federal troops to troubled areas in the South. Military historian James Sefton notes:

[I]n 1870 alone, more than 200 expeditions of federal troops were sent out at the request of state and federal civil authorities. In 1871, 160 operations were reported, not including those in South Carolina to suppress the Klan.[121]

Thus, the essential factor in breaking up the Klan was the federal government's resolve to declare war, although the war was waged rather inefficiently.[122]

Throughout the South, there were reports that confirmed the federal government's success in curbing violence in general and stopping the Klan in particular. In Alabama, U.S. Attorney John Minnis reported that the federal court "was demoralizing and carrying terror to these lawless K.K. Klans."[123] In South Carolina, U.S. Attorney Daniel Corbin believed that "only the prosecution of the leaders [of the Ku Klux Klan] was necessary to restore peace and order to the state."[124] Federal Circuit Court Judge Hugh Lennox Bond wrote to his wife: "[W]e have broken up the Ku Klux in North Carolina."[125] Allen Trelease, author of the preeminent book about the Ku Klux Klan, reports that, in Florida, "violence virtually ended by the end of 1871,"[126] whereas in Alabama, "Klan violence ground almost to a halt."[127] Major Lewis Merrill, who played a pivotal role in reducing the number of Klan members in South Carolina, reported that "the testimony is unanimous—the result was total suppression of the Ku Klux Klan."[128] In Tennessee, the birthplace of the Klan, historian Everette Swinney found that "the years of 1870 to 1873 [were] relatively free of Klan-type outrages."[129] Swinney even goes so far as to suggest that the enforcement acts were enforced less vigorously after 1874 because "the major objective which had occasioned their passage—the dissolution of the Ku Klux Klan—had been achieved."[130] In a study of Grant's Southern policy, historian Edwin Woolley writes:

> The result of the demonstration of force and determination in South Carolina, and of the vigorous arrest and prosecution of offenders elsewhere throughout the South, was that Kukluxism was practically extinct within a year.[131]

Although the federal government's "war" against the Klan was conducted with limited resources, and stopped short of doing complete justice to the past, these findings appear to indicate that it was nonetheless strong enough to dismantle the Ku Klux Klan.

Unfortunately, the political will to dismantle the Klan diminished quickly. In the 1874 midterm elections, Democrats gained ninety-four seats in the House, thereby giving them a 62% majority in the House. Democrats also gained nine seats in the Senate. Republicans lost ninety-six seats in the House and one seat in the Senate. Democrats also won nineteen of twenty-five gubernatorial races. Historian William Gillette called the Republican defeat in 1874 "the greatest upset in national politics since 1854. It was the first catastrophe in the Republican Party's twenty-year history and inaugurated an extraordinary shift in power."[132] A newspaper in New York remarked that "the election is not merely a victory but a revolution."[133] The Louisville *Courier-Journal* ran "Busted. The Radical Machine Gone to Smash."[134] Governor Ames of Mississippi perhaps summed it up the best: "a revolution has

taken place—by force of arms—and a race are disfranchised—they are to be returned to a condition of serfdom—an era of second slavery."[135]

It was around this time that President Grant reversed his stance on quelling racial
violence in the South. After suffering a barrage of criticisms for his decision to send
in federal troops after the Colfax Massacre,[136] President Ulysses S. Grant declared: "I
am tired of this nonsense. . . . This nursing of monstrosities has nearly exhausted the
life of the party. I am done with them, and they will have to take care of themselves."[137] There is no inkling here that he was forced to acquiesce; rather, his was a
politically calculated choice made for the sake of the party to which he belonged.
Grant subsequently forced Amos Akerman to resign as head of the Justice Department and appointed increasingly conservative attorneys general in his stead.[138]

It is important to note that the political will to stop racial violence in the South
did not simply disappear; rather, it was bargained away. In the presidential election
of 1876, there was a dispute with the electoral results between the Republican candidate Rutherford B. Hayes and Democratic candidate Samuel J. Tilden. To resolve
the dispute, a deal was reached—commonly referred to as *the Compromise of 1877*.
Hayes became President in exchange for withdrawing all federal troops in the South,
effectively "abandoning the cause of the Negro."[139] The compromise presumes that
Hayes did not necessarily have to abandon the cause of stopping racial violence.
How could he have bargained away a power he did not have? He used the threat of
continuing federal intervention as a bargaining chip that the Democratic Party was
all too willing to accept. The fact that the Republican Party used "abandoning the
cause of the Negro" as a bargaining chip, and that the Democratic Party accepted
this chip, suggest not only that the American state could have continued to quell
racial violence in the South, but also that the abandonment was more a result of political calculus than any inherent incapacity of the American state as such.[140]

Rather than simply asserting the American state was weak, a more fine-grained
analysis shows that this unraveling toward weakness emerged from a position of
strength. The American state was strong and then became weak, and this process of
"becoming weak" was more about bargaining among political actors than a mere
capitulation of the state to societal actors.

FDR'S "WEAK" EFFORTS

After Reconstruction, the federal government was seen as having essentially been
stripped of its legal authority to quell racial violence in the South. Beginning with
The Slaughter-House Cases in 1873 and followed by *United States v. Cruikshank,
United States v. Harris,* and the *Civil Rights Cases,* many regarded the Supreme
Court as having "rendered the attributes of national citizenship all but meaningless

to blacks."[141] Thus, for the American state to reengage in combating racial violence in the South, it would have to reconstitute the legal capacity to do so. This became apparent during the Franklin Roosevelt administration, when new legislation addressing racial violence came to the forefront. But, in fact, reconstituting the legal capacity was unnecessary.[142] No new law was needed for the federal government to engaging in stopping racial violence. Only the political will, an underlying alliance of political interests, was lacking.[143] As Arthur Kinoy pointed out in 1966, "new legislation is always helpful, but this is simply not the crux of the problem."[144] An analysis of antilynching politics under the Lyndon Johnson administration illustrates this point. Moreover, it shows how the key issues were political—especially the political conditions under which the state was willing to engage in rights enforcement.[145] This analysis moves between Supreme Court cases and political events to illuminate the limits of the classic variant of the weak-state thesis that claims it was the lack of legal authority that constrained the state in quelling racial violence.

Although no new law was needed, efforts were nonetheless made to establish new legislation. A total of 257 antilynching bills were introduced in Congress from 1882 to 1951. Three (1922, 1937, and 1940) reached a vote in the House. In 1922, the House vote was 231 for and 119 against with 85 abstentions (53%). In 1937, the House vote was 277 for and 120 against with 43 abstentions (64%). In 1940, the House vote was 252 for and 131 against with 52 abstentions (58%). NAACP President Walter White is reported to have counted seventy senators who had stated they would vote in favor of the 1937 antilynching bill if it were to come to a vote.[146] These votes would seem to indicate that there was majority support for new antilynching legislation. Unfortunately, none of these bills ever reached the Senate floor for a vote and hence did not become law.

Congressional debates surrounding new legislation confirm the political nature of nonintervention. Although many in Congress shared the belief that the Supreme Court had gutted any semblance of federal rights enforcement, their understanding of Supreme Court rulings was superficial at best. Claudine Ferrell characterizes the legal acumen of Congressman Leonidas Dyer, who was the author of one of the most prominent attempts at passing an antilynching legislation, as "rather weak and loose."[147] She goes on to describe other members of Congress as "lawyers with limited knowledge of constitutional realities [who] turned to friends for solutions to their dilemmas or mouthed pet phrases and made clichés out of disembodied judicial one-lines. Legislators over-simplified and generalized as they sought to discuss every probability and possibility, relevancy and tangential concern."[148]

A case in point is William Ford's 1948 article in the *Virginia Law Review* titled "Constitutionality of Proposed Federal Anti-Lynching Legislation."[149] Considered one of the more sophisticated defenses for the Southern position, Ford's main argument hinges on an analysis of *U.S. v. Cruikshank*, and he states "it was held not to be a crime within federal authority for two or more persons to conspire to deprive several Negroes of their right to vote by means of oppression and intimidation."[150] Ford's depiction of *Cruikshank* runs contrary to the majority decision written by Chief Justice Morrison Waite in which he stated explicitly: "[T]here is no allegation that this was done because of their race or color of the persons conspired against.... We may suspect that race was the cause of hostility, but it is not so averred.... Every thing essential must be charged positively and not inferentially."[151] Ford's racialized account of *Cruikshank* is thus not simply an oversimplification of the decision, but a gross mischaracterization.

But at least these members of Congress engaged in talks regarding the Constitution. When debate regarding the Dyer antilynching bill reached the Senate, few senators discussed specific case law at all. During the filibuster that was initiated by the Southern Democrats, Ferrell noted that proponents for lynchings would "manipulate or ignore legitimate arguments, analogies, and theories and ... avoid substantive issues that worked against local rule and white supremacy."[152] For example, adversaries of Dyer's bill never once questioned whether the Fourteenth Amendment reached state officers. Instead, Democrats filled their time during the filibuster by simply reading part of the congressional journal from the previous day to prevent discussion of the Dyer bill. Congress never dealt substantively with Supreme Court decisions in any comprehensive manner. Rather, Congress relied on oversimplifications or ignored the Court altogether.

This nonconfrontational view held by many congressmen is understandable considering the broader context of legislative deference to the Court at this time. Although it was stated explicitly by Senator Albert Cummins from Iowa that "the Supreme Court has more than once been a little vague in its decisions upon great public issues,"[153] Congress seemed content to settle on the belief that "the Court seems to intimate that there could be no such federal statute [to punish outrages by individuals upon colored people on account of the race] under the present constitution of the United States."[154] Assistant Attorney General R. R. Stewart goes on to note that the Supreme Court "has never been questioned since."[155] The legislative branch does not always acquiesce to the judiciary in this manner. Congress can combat judiciary rulings in a variety of ways. Political scientists Lawrence Baum and Lori Hausegger argue that "if the Court interprets a federal statute, Congress can override the Court's interpretation by revising the statute, propose a constitutional amendment, or enact a new statute to advance the same goal as the old statute within the limitations established by the Court's decision."[156] Political scientist Mark Miller continues this point by noting that "Congress determines the size of the Supreme Court, and of the lower federal courts, can remove judges through impeachment, remove certain types of cases from their jurisdiction, and restrict the powers of the federal courts."[157] There have been times when relations have been described as a "battle royale," and congressmen have been known to stand up to the Court. Miller points to the example of Congressman Tom Delay's response to *Newdow v. U.S. Congress*: "Congress is going to stand up in this particular case and fight the judiciary of the country and stop them from running amuck."[158] These counterinstances suggest that legislative deference is not inevitable, and that relations among the branches is more dynamic and contingent then it might first appear.

Going back to the antilynching legislation, the legislative deference shown to the judiciary at this time makes sense because of the underlying political divisiveness of federal intervention. Southern Democrats were adamantly against federal intervention and were willing to stage a filibuster in support of their own beliefs. As Senate Democratic leader Oscar Underwood from Alabama stated on November 28, 1922: "If the majority party insist on this procedure they are not going to pass the bill, and they are not going to do any other business."[159] The intransigence of Southern Democrats was matched by Republican apathy. The NAACP noted: "[H]ere was a group of men who committed mob violence on the floor of the United States Senate and the people of the North sit down tamely and accept the insolence of Underwood and his group without an audible protest against it."[160] Here is how the *New York Times* described the Senate stoppage: "The numerous record votes during the day seemed to indicate that many Republicans were not 'very angry' because of the filibuster. As a matter of fact, it is known that many of them are opposed to the [antilynching] legislation. If it can die as a result of the filibuster, these Republicans will shed no tears."[161] When the filibuster ended, the *New York Times* stated "the Republicans in the Senate were not sincerely and wholeheartedly in favor of the antilynching bill. Some of them would have had no stomach for a long fight on that issue. It was open to suspicion as a measure introduced mainly for partisan effect and election purposes."[162] According to NAACP Director Walter White, "Republicans were apathetic to the point of cowardice."[163] Historian Robert Zangrando states in his book chronicling the NAACP's efforts to end lynching: "[T]he antilynching bill was displaced by the indifference of its friends and the strategy of its enemies."[164] There is a difference between supporting a bill passively if it were to come up for a vote, and prioritizing a bill proactively and forcing a vote to occur. Although the numbers in the House suggest a wide breadth of support for new antilynching legislation, they do not indicate the depth of that support. Again, Robert Zangrando notes:

> [M]any congressmen treated antilynching as an expendable issue. They, their friends, and family were not the mob's targets, so the entire issue remained an

abstraction, constantly vulnerable to more expedient definitions of priorities. . . . The Association resented the fact that GOP leaders never made a serious effort to mobilize such cooperation, never tried to challenge or break a filibuster on an antilynching bill. . . . Despite periodic reassurances, the bill's fate remained in doubt. It always took a backseat, as NAACP strategists realized, to such items as the tariff, veterans' bonus, and ship subsidy bills, the rail strike and the disarmament conferences. [165]

Although many voiced concerns about the constitutionality of federal intervention, neither the Supreme Court's previous rulings nor the constitutionality of antilynching legislation was ever the primary issue. The underlying concern was the Southerners' adamant position to maintain white supremacy and the Republican Party's apathy to combat it. The failure of antilynching legislation and federal rights enforcement in general had more to do with personal, political, sectional, and racial biases than what was constitutional or not. Because of this, there was no incentive for Congress to provide a careful examination of Supreme Court decisions. If Southern Democrats were willing to filibuster new legislation, they assuredly would have blocked any political efforts to utilize previously made, but seldom used, legislation. The quest to pass new legislation was thus a barometer to see how far Congress was willing to go. Clearly, it was not that far, which signaled to the president what the political consequences would be for pursuing such actions.

In 1935, when the Wagner–Costigan antilynching bill was being filibustered by the Senate, President Franklin Delano Roosevelt told NAACP Secretary Walter White, "The Southerners by reason of the seniority rule in Congress are chairmen or occupy strategic places on most of the Senate and House committees. If I come out for the antilynching bill now, they will block every bill I ask Congress to pass to keep America from collapsing. I just can't take that risk."[166] This famous quote underscores my point that Roosevelt's silence on antilynching legislation had more to do with his not wanting to alienate his Southern base than it had to do with whether the constitutional authority existed. Roosevelt only went as far as the Southern Democrats would permit. Evidence of Roosevelt's dealings with the Southern Democrats regarding New Deal legislation bore this out. When New Deal legislation was being proposed, Southern Democrats were inclined to support the redress of existing patterns of economic distribution in the direction of more equality, but that support came to a quick halt when issues regarding the labor market and race relations began to be conjoined. Cognizant of this, FDR was thus careful to construct legislation accordingly. FDR's reluctance to engage with reconstituting the American state's ability to stop racial violence was akin to the "Compromise of 1877" in that it had less to do with the American state's incapacity to engage as much as reiterate the autonomy of political agents to not want to engage.[167]

In *U.S. v. Price* and *U.S. v. Guest*, the Supreme Court upheld federal rights enforcement for prosecutions regarding racial violence.[168] Although the Court's decisions in these cases were markedly different than its previous decisions, its decisions were nonetheless based on laws that existed since Reconstruction. By refusing to grapple with these inconsistencies, the Court's decisions in *Guest* and *Price* are mired in questions that point to the political nature of federal rights enforcement for blacks. Unfortunately, these questions are not even acknowledged, let alone answered. By turning a blind eye to what is going on beneath the surface, the Court appears to be trying to maintain some degree of legal consistency within the politically inconsistent world of federal rights enforcement.

On June 21, 1964, three Mississippi law enforcement officials and fifteen private individuals conspired and murdered three civil rights workers: Michael Schwerner, James Chaney, and Andrew Goodman. The conspiracy involved releasing the victims from jail at night; intercepting, assaulting, and killing them; and disposing of their bodies. The U.S. District Court sustained the substantive counts against the three law enforcement officials but dismissed the indictments against the fifteen private individuals. The case was then appealed to the Supreme Court. In *United States v. Price*, the Supreme Court reversed the dismissals against the fifteen private individuals.[169] Supreme Court Justice Abe Fortas delivered the opinion of the Court. The key to the decision was what constituted actions "under color of law." Fortas concluded that "to act under color of law does not require that the accused be an officer of the State. It was enough that he was a willful participant in joint activity with the State or its agents."[170] He then went on to argue for a broad interpretation of Section 241: "It is hardly conceivable that Congress intended 241 to apply only to a narrow and relatively unimportant category of rights."[171] Without delving into more recent applications and interpretations of 241, Fortas noted how "Section 241 was left essentially unchanged [from its original formulation] and neither in the 1874 revision nor in any subsequent re-enactment has there been the slightest indication of congressional intent to narrow or limit the original broad scope of 241."[172] Section 241 was taken verbatim from the Enforcement Act of 1870; Section 242 was taken from the Civil Rights Act of 1866. This, then, raises a question: If section 241 was originally broad in scope and has gone unchanged throughout the years, then why has it been interpreted so narrowly for so long? Why did the Court finally act against private individuals when it had failed to do so in previous cases?

Unfortunately, the Court never addressed these questions in *Price*. We have to look elsewhere for these answers—namely, in *U.S. v. Guest*.

Price was a watershed moment, according to legal historian Derrick Bell, because it "abandoned past doubts as to the constitutionality of section 241 and 242."[173] There had been some cases, most notably *United States v. Williams*, that cast some suspicion.[174] In *Williams,* four members of the Supreme Court—Frankfurter, Minton, Jackson, and Black—took the position that rights associated with the Fourteenth Amendment were not within the purview of Section 241. But, this was the dissenting opinion in *Williams*; it did not represent the views of the majority of the Court and could be regarded as not establishing a binding precedent. However, it was enough to raise doubts. *Price* quashed these doubts.

On July 3, 1964, Herbert Guest, Joseph Howard Sims, Cecil Williams Myers, and James Lackey shot and killed Lemuel Penn, a black citizen. On September 4, an all-white jury acquitted two of the Klansmen, Joseph Howard Sims and Cecil Myers, from any wrongdoing. The case then went to district court, and six private individuals were indicted under 18 U.S.C. 241 for conspiring to deprive Penn of the free exercise and enjoyment of rights secured to him by the Constitution and laws of the United States. These indictments were dismissed. The Department of Justice subsequently appealed the decision and the case went to the Supreme Court. In *United States v. Guest*, the Supreme Court reversed the district court ruling.[175]

Contrasting this case with the Court's overturning of segregation reveals not only why lynchings and segregation need to be disaggregated, but why lynchings represented such a legal conundrum for the Court. *Brown v. Board of Education* ruled segregation as unconstitutional. *Brown* has been hailed by many as a landmark decision that was truly unprecedented, if only because there was a long line of precedents upholding segregation as constitutional.[176] In *Brown v. Board of Education*, the Supreme Court is explicit that it is overturning *Plessy v. Ferguson*, which was the landmark case that accommodated segregation. Chief Justice Earl Warren stated: "Any language [347 U.S. 483, 495] in *Plessy v. Ferguson* contrary to this finding is rejected." Immediately after the *Brown* decision was publicized, Justice Jackson noted how "layman as well as lawyer must query how it is that the Constitution this morning forbids what for three-quarters of a century it has tolerated or approved."[177] Legal scholar Michael Klarman notes:

> *Brown* was hard for justices who approached legal decision making as Frankfurter and Jackson did, because for them it posed a conflict between law and politics. The sources of constitutional interpretation that they usually invoked—text, original understanding, precedent, and custom—seemed to indicate that school segregation was permissible.[178]

Although Jackson ruled in favor of banning segregation, he even admitted that he was "unable to justify the abolition of segregation as a judicial act" and agreed to "go along with it" as a "political decision."[179] Frankfurter went even further when he stated that "he would have voted to sustain school segregation in the 1940s because public opinion had not then crystallized against it."[180] Clearly, the Court took into account the political mood at the time and felt compelled to tailor its decision accordingly. In *Brown*, the Court addressed these concerns by framing the decision as "honestly arrived at, confidently espoused, and basically sound." In other words, it was imperative that the Brown decision appear to be "based upon law" and not politics.[181] This is one of the reasons why the *Brown* decision was unanimous. Klarman noted how "justices who disagreed with the outcome thus felt pressure to suppress their convictions for the good of the institution."[182]

Contrast *Brown* with *Guest*. In *Guest,* Justice Brennan makes a very similar statement akin to Warren's decision in *Brown* regarding the outright repudiation of previous case law: "the majority of the Court today rejects the interpretation of [section] 5 [of the Fourteenth Amendment] given in the Civil Rights Cases."[183] Although both *Brown* and *Guest* include statements that overturned precedent explicitly, there is a difference regarding the weight afforded to each. Although Chief Justice Warren's statement in *Brown* is made as part of a unanimous decision in which his was the only opinion given, Justice Brennan's decision in *Guest* was not the opinion of the Court, but one which concurred with parts and dissented with other parts of the majority opinion. Unlike *Brown*, which was unanimous and had only one opinion (written by Warren), *Guest* consisted of four opinions: Justice Stewart delivered the opinion of the Court; Justice Clark, with Justice Black and Fortas joining, provided a concurring opinion; Justice Harlan provided an opinion that concurred with parts and dissented in parts; and Justice Brennan, with the Chief Justice and Justice Douglas joining, also provided an opinion that concurred with parts and dissented in other parts. Belknap has argued the reason for the confusion in *Guest* is mainly political: "the ambiguity and confusion in the opinions was the result of judicial efforts to keep the Supreme Court from getting in the way of congressional attempts to combat racist violence in the South."[184] But, although the Court in *Brown* chose to mask the political dimensions by standing united, the Court in *Guest* chose to mask the political dimension by going in the opposite direction. If *Brown* was "honestly arrived at, confidently espoused, and basically sound," then one might argue that *Guest* was strangely arrived at, dividedly espoused, and highly questionable.

For example, take Justice Stewart's majority opinion. Contrary to Brennan's opinion that *Guest* overturned previous decisions, Justice Stewart clearly situated this case as working in accordance with the Court's previous decisions. Historian Michal Belknap makes this argument: "Rather than frontally assaulting the Court's past

construction, they endeavored to square their argument with the traditional interpretation."[185] Early on, Stewart states the cases that might at first appear to be in
direct contradiction with the Court's decision, such as *United States v. Cruikshank*,
United States v. Harris, and the *Civil Rights Cases*, and declares that "it [the Court's
view in these past cases] remains the Court's view today."[186] Right from the outset,
Justice Stewart is thus maintaining a degree of constitutional continuity for a case
that seemingly overturns past decisions.

Stewart continued: "[T]his is not to say, however, that the involvement of the
State need be either exclusive or direct."[187] This statement suggests that, rather than
confronting past decisions directly, Stewart instead found a circuitous route of by-
passing them. He did this first by lowering the threshold for what constitutes state
action. It is enough for the participation of the state to be "peripheral, or its action
was only one of several co-operative."[188] But even this formulation is unnecessary
because "this case requires no determination of the threshold level that state action
must attain . . . allegation of state involvement is sufficient."[189] Stewart goes on to
refer to a minority opinion in *Bell v. Maryland* that stated that "a private business-
man's invocation of state police and judicial action to carry out his own policy of
racial discrimination was sufficient."[190] Stewart's reference to Justice Douglas and
Goldberg's opinion in *Bell* is puzzling for two reasons. First, it implies a highly questionable and unique conception of state action that does not take into account state
actors at all; second, it is derived from a minority opinion with which three other
members of the Court strongly disagreed, and on which three others expressed no
opinion. Law Professor Alfred Avins argues this point: "[T]he United States Supreme Court has turned history inside out . . . the *Guest* case is so wide off the mark
that it would be necessary to burn all the Congressional Globes in the nation to
support it."[191] Avins's critique is most evident when Justice Stewart acknowledges
that "the allegation of the extent of official involvement in the present case is not
clear."[192] Stewart's opinion, which served as the opinion of the Court, thus seemed
concerned primarily with maintaining constitutional continuity, even if it came at
the expense of coherency and accuracy.

The other opinions took a more radical and broad interpretation of the federal
government's authority with regard to rights enforcement. In a concurring opinion
with Justice Black, and Justice Fortas joining in, Justice Clark stated that "it is, I believe, both appropriate and necessary *under the circumstances here* [emphasis added]
to say that there now can be no doubt that the specific language of [section] 5 [of the
Fourteenth Amendment] empowers the Congress to enact laws punishing all
conspiracies—with or without state action—that interfere with Fourteenth Amendment rights."[193] Justice Brennan, with the Chief Justice Earl Warren and Justice
Douglas joining in, went the farthest: "A majority of the members of the Court

expresses the view today that [section] 5 [of the Fourteenth Amendment] empowers Congress to enact laws punishing all conspiracies to interfere with the exercise of Fourteenth Amendment rights, whether or not state officers or others acting under the color of state law are implicated in the conspiracy."[194]

But, these interpretations raised their own questions. Clarks's statement raised the question of what "the circumstances here" consists, because previous decisions pointed out emphatically the importance of state action when evaluating conspiracies. Unfortunately, Clark did not expound further on the subject. Although Stewart's formulation of state action is confusing because of the highly tenuous basis for such a formulation, Clark's disregard for the necessity of state action is even worse because it seems, clearly, to contradict previous cases. Justice Brennan's comment about what the majority of the Court expresses is dubious because, if this were the case, then why did Justice Stewart deliver the opinion of the Court in which he stated clearly that the stance taken in the *Civil Rights Cases* "remains the Court's view today."[195] Although many in the Court seemed willing to make a clean break from the past, the opinion of the Court, as articulated by Stewart, continued to be in lockstep with what the Court had decided previously. Had the Court made a clean break, then it would not have to reconcile how and why it maintained such a narrow version of Section 5 for approximately eighty years. But, by making constitutional continuity a priority, the Court's decision raised more questions than answers. Although *Brown* and *Guest* both represent a conflict between law and politics, the Court in *Brown* chose to resolve the conflict under the guise of unanimity and clarity whereas the Court in *Guest* chose to resolve it under the guise of plurality and ambiguity. The *Brown* decision was meant for the front page; the *Guest* decision was meant for the back page. Each strategy was trying to resolve the conflict between law and politics, but in its own way.

The comparison between *Brown* and *Guest* also illustrates the different problems each faced. The main concern with *Guest* was how it was able to argue for constitutional continuity despite the seemingly radical departure from precedent, whereas the primary problem with *Brown* was how it was able to argue for constitutional disruption in the face of a long tradition of legal precedent that suggested otherwise. The "situatedness" of the political was also different. Although the political will to enforce the law preceded *Guest*, the political will still had to be mustered with *Brown*. The *Guest* Court was thus operating in the rearguard whereas the *Brown* Court was nudging the political to act. In this regard, it seems apt to characterize *Brown* as legally radical and more politically controversial, whereas *Guest* was legally incoherent but politically moderate.

It is also unclear whether the Court in *Guest* could have done what the Court in *Brown* did. For *Guest* to have overturned precedent as occurred in *Brown* would have meant that the federal government had relinquished sovereign authority. Although segregation can and was accommodated within a system of federalism, lynchings represented a direct repudiation of American sovereignty. As Judge Emmons notes, the "right of the negro to see the ballet dance" could be formally outlawed, whereas the right to "pillage and murder was [a] more precious and beneficent privilege" and thus could not.[196] Questions emerged constantly regarding why the United States was able to exercise its sovereign authority in other matters but not stop lynchings. Unlike segregation, which centered on more ethical and sociological concerns, questions regarding lynchings raised questions regarding the sovereign capacity of the United States.[197] Although failure to act against segregation amounted to a lack of moral turpitude, failure to act against lynchings "would be tantamount," according to President Eisenhower, "to acquiescence in anarchy and dissolution of the union."[198] Although the federal government did, in fact, fail to act for approximately eighty-three years, for the Court to have acknowledged that failure as an explicit legal category that needed to be overturned would have amounted to a formal recognition that the federal government was somehow not sovereign during that time. The Court backed off on making such a claim, in part because it was not true and in part because it did not need to.

Going off of Stewart's opinion, if in fact it was the case that state action remained broad in nature this whole time, then there is a need to revisit the Supreme Court cases at the end of Reconstruction. After Reconstruction, when the federal government provided white Southerners the autonomy to manage racial affairs in the South, the Supreme Court responded accordingly—through cases such as the *Slaughter-House Cases, United States v. Cruikshank, United States v. Harris*, and the *Civil Rights Cases*—that it was going to rule negatively on issues relating to federal rights enforcement for blacks in the South.[199] But, in light of the rulings in *Price* and *Guest,* the Court appeared to have never repudiated or stripped the federal government of all its authority to engage in combating racial violence. I revisit these Reconstruction cases in the next chapter. For now, however, suffice it to say in the parlance of the weak-state thesis, the American state did not lose its capacity to combat racial violence; rather, it simply chose not to engage.

ACTING BY WITHDRAWING

In terms of sovereignty, the Supreme Court decisions in *Guest* and *Price* illustrate that the federal government never relinquished its sovereign authority. The federal government might have relieved itself of any culpability for what happened under its sovereign eye while simultaneously reserving to itself sovereign authority. It deliberately stopped short of total jurisdiction, albeit with the proviso that it could, if it chose to, intervene. Because it was a self-imposed bounding, it could not only change itself whenever it wanted, but it could also set the line of where its jurisdiction started and stopped. Unlike segregation, which was delegated mostly to the respective states to regulate and was couched in liberal terms, the federal government never relinquished the authority to combat racial violence completely nor did it provide a coherent, consistent answer to why it did not intervene.

Part of the difficulty in ascertaining the federal government's compliance with racial violence is schematizing negligence. In comparing South Africa apartheid and Jim Crow segregation, political scientist Anthony Marx observed the distinctively American pattern of an "active" withdrawal:

> [In the case of the United States,] a decentralized state of limited capacity was held together by allowing for local variation. Rather than exert its authority, the central state acted by withdrawal, consolidating its authority as best it could by avoiding further conflict.[200]

Picking up on Marx's concept of acting by withdrawal, Desmond King and Stephen Tuck specifically point out the "deliberate inaction" of Congress and the Republican Party:

> [C]ongressional behavior was marked by several decades of deliberate action and deliberate inaction—in response to the rising tide of white supremacy across the country. . . . By choosing not to act, the [Republican] party fanned Southern exclusions and gave added legitimacy to mistreatment and racism in the North and West.[201]

To act by withdrawal can, at times, be obscured because of the difficulties in describing the implications of not acting.

As mentioned previously, this inaction was often couched mistakenly in terms of weakness. If the federal government had, in fact, relinquished complete authority to combat racial violence to the states, then it would have needed new legislation to bequeath the federal government the authority to do so, but it had not. When the federal government wanted to combat racial violence, it simply resurrected old laws that were always there but rarely used. Thus, the unwillingness of political actors to act has been mischaracterized as weakness when it should have been an explicit decision by the state—namely, the decision of "whether one will have access to

political and legal protection and recognition or will be excluded from it."[202] Robert
Dahl describes eloquently how this exclusion is related to racial violence:

> Suppose that x is existing policy, and y is an alternative to it requiring govern-
> mental action, e.g., x is a policy of non-interference by the federal government
> in lynching cases and y is legislation requiring the federal government to inter-
> vene. . . . If no governmental action is taken, then in fact x is government
> policy.[203]

Dahl purposefully describes it as a "policy of non-interference" to emphasize the
explicit choice not to act. The active policy of nonenforcement was more of a political agreement mired in comity than a legal principle of incapacity. In other words,
the federal government's inaction regarding racial violence was less an institutional
matter of resources or legal capacity and more a sovereign decision not to act.

Building off of Dahl's reference to lynching as an "active policy of noninterference," it is imperative to see how each branch of the federal government
colluded in the establishment, perpetuation, and maintenance of such an active
policy. Although passage of the Civil Rights Act of 1866 and the Enforcement Act
of 1870 provided federal authorities authority to prosecute lynch mobs, political
opposition was such that it precluded legal officials from using these laws. This pre-
clusion was not preordained by law; rather, it was effectively blocked by political
brinksmanship. Federal rights enforcement for blacks required a degree of political
fortitude that was very hard to establish, let alone maintain. To say that the federal
government maintained legal authority and neglected to use that authority was not
an act of willful neglect on behalf of enforcement officials, but was more reflective
of how powerful the political opposition was. As Timothy Stanley and Alexander
Lee point out, "while law may structure society, it is only the will of governors and
people that gives it character and force."[204] Claiming that it was a purely legal issue
allowed actors to obfuscate their responsibility and accountability.[205] By couching
political inaction in terms of jurisprudential restrictions in a federalist system, the
federal government successfully mischaracterized what actually was a political arrangement made by politicians into a matter of state rights that was to be resolved
by the courts. Disentangling the political nature of federal inaction from the legal
principle of federalism provides the conceptual pivot by which we can distinguish
the (in)actions of sovereignty from actual challenges to that sovereignty. Collapsing
the political into the legal provided a way for the federal government to evade responsibility without actually abdicating its authority. In other words, in matters
regarding racial violence, the law stayed constant; it was the political will to enforce
the law that varied.[206]

Couching nonintervention in political terms is not meant to suggest that it was somehow any less formidable. Federal rights enforcement for blacks required a degree of political fortitude that was very hard to establish, let alone maintain. Federal reengagement required an extraordinary act of political will. As Amos Akerman points out succinctly, combating the Klan "amounted to war, and cannot be effectually crushed on any other theory."[207] The war metaphor is poignant because it not only highlights the extraordinary challenges associated with such an ordeal, but also it alludes to the kind of political solidarity that is needed to place the country on such a war footing. Although it might appear somewhat paradoxical that something akin to war was needed for the enforcement of rights, it nevertheless speaks to the propensity of American political institutions to facilitate racism. It is thus understandable why presidential leadership—ranging from Grant's vacillation, Roosevelt's acquiescence, and Johnson's steadfastness—was the primary determinant for the (re)activation of federal rights enforcement for blacks. According to political philosopher and legal jurist Carl Schmitt, the onus on presidential leadership is appropriate considering the exceptional nature of federal rights enforcement for blacks. According to Schmitt, "sovereign is he who decides the exception."[208] In this case, it is the president, whose duties include taking "care that the laws be faithfully executed," that decides when the exception of federal rights enforcement for blacks is activated.[209]

CONCLUSION: DISTINGUISHING WEAKNESS AS AUTONOMY FROM WEAKNESS AS INCAPACITY

A weak state denotes a sense of incapacity, specifically in terms of resource scarcity or lack of authority. But the aforementioned examples of engagement and nonengagement do not mesh well with these characterizations of the weak state.[210] Against Migdal's definition of a weak state as the inability to get people in the society to do what the state wants them to do, I have endeavored to illustrate another conception of a weak state in which the state chooses not to engage society at all. The former presumes incapacity; the latter presumes autonomy. The federal government—from 1870 to 1872, and in 1966—illustrates the American government's capacity to act; the Grant and FDR examples are evidence of choosing not to act. Thus "weakness" is a concept that should be disaggregated. It can refer to a relative scarcity of resources or lack of power, but it can *also* be seen as an explicit policy decision. To borrow the words of legal theorist Franz Neumann, the federal government was "as strong as the political and social situation and the interests of society demanded."[211] Although it did not have to be weak, the United States wanted to continue being weak. It pursued a policy of weakness by choice. It was politically convenient for

Roosevelt to push the responsibility on Congress to pass new legislation, and it was legally convenient for Congress to presume the Court had, effectively, dismantled federal rights enforcement. Federal actions against lynching were a hot potato everybody was trying to pass. In other words, the United States made itself actively weak with regard to a particular set of activities. We might say the most important issue here was not the *state* weakness of the new Union but the *political* weakness of groups favorably disposed to enforcing rights for blacks. The national state withdrew from prosecuting lynch mobs not because it did not have the wherewithal; rather, it withdrew to pursue other political ends. As Desmond King and Stephen Tuck argue, through deliberate inaction, "federal officials did not just acquiesce in the Southern counter-revolution but promoted a nationwide order of white supremacy."[212]

Shall we be citizens in war, and aliens in peace?[1]

—FREDERICK DOUGLASS

The tradition of the oppressed teaches us that the "state of emergency" in which we live is not the exception but the rule.[2]

—WALTER BENJAMIN

3

The Tragic Legality of Racial Violence: Reconstruction, Race, and Emergency

INTRODUCTION

Chapter 2 focused on demonstrating the federal government's capacity to intervene; this chapter examines how that capacity was exercised. The federal government chose to wield its capacity by instituting an emergency. Emergencies tend to be associated with the restriction of rights, but there have been rare instances when emergencies have nevertheless been instituted to expand rights. Such was the case with Reconstruction. Reconstruction, the era immediately after the Civil War, marked the transition from a slave society and represented a brief period during which the federal government engaged in rights enforcement for blacks. This engagement was premised on this concept of emergency. Unlike typical emergencies that call for a reduction of civil liberties under the aegis of security, during Reconstruction, the ubiquity and banality of racial terror was suspended temporarily and the radical practice of federal intervention into rights enforcement was invoked.

This chapter primarily looks at the Supreme Court's handling of racial violence during Reconstruction to illuminate how the judiciary framed the unprecedented task of extending rights to blacks. This move was unprecedented not only because blacks previously "had no rights which a white man was bound to respect,"[3] but also because of the predominant role of states in rights enforcement in American federalism. The Fourteenth Amendment was, initially, meant to be a revolutionary tool in defense of interceding normal practices of law. It was a means of securing social transformation that inaugurated a degree of centralization that interjected the federal government into the enforcement of rights.[4] But, as the commitment to racial justice waned and the transformative project of Reconstruction lost political traction, the Court's interpretation of the Fourteenth Amendment subsequently morphed from being something that operated alongside normal law into something that infused itself within normal law. The juxtaposition of emergency as rights reinforcing is counterintuitive if only because we tend to associate emergencies as rights limiting. However, the counterintuitive use of emergency during Reconstruction highlights how—in the words of Frederick Douglass stated in the chapter opening— blacks were citizens in war and aliens in peace.

Contrary to the standard account that depicts the Supreme Court in general and Justice Samuel Miller in particular as adamantly against federal rights enforcement for blacks, a close textual reading of the Reconstruction cases starting with Miller's decision in *The Slaughter-House Cases*, indicate that the Supreme Court was, in fact, amenable to federal rights enforcement for blacks.[5] The reason for such divergent interpretation has to do with the failure to take into account the contingent and temporal nature of the emergency. Framing the Reconstruction cases, which include, *The Slaughter-House Cases*,[6] *U.S. v. Cruikshank*,[7] *U.S. v. Harris*,[8] and *The Civil Rights Cases*[9] in the context of an emergency, which in fact the Supreme Court did, provides for a more coherent analysis that goes beyond the ideological proclivities of the justices and points to more structural concerns concerning the embedded nature of racism.

I first outline the concept of emergency and how it was applied during Reconstruction, then map out the complex political terrain surrounding congressional Reconstruction that provided the backdrop for the Supreme Court's first foray into interpreting the Fourteenth Amendment. From there, I segue to an in-depth examination of *Slaughter-House* and how Justice Miller racialized the concept of emergency to reconcile the radical implications of federal rights enforcement. Next, I examine *U.S. v. Cruikshank* and illustrate not only how the judiciary was able to expound further on Miller's racial emergency, but also how it used the emergency to evade the controversy surrounding federal rights enforcement. After my study of *Cruikshank*, I then analyze *U.S. v. Harris* and *The Civil Rights Cases* to detail how the Court was able to skirt responsibility without necessarily relinquishing authority. Last, I conclude with remarks regarding the tragic consequences of framing racial violence as an emergency and the subsequent structural impediments of addressing racial violence during normal times.

BRIEF TYPOLOGY OF EMERGENCIES

Typically, emergencies correspond to existential threats that demand immediate action. We often associate them with foreign attacks and civil war. During these types of emergencies, civil liberties tend to be suspended temporarily. Eric Posner and Adrian Vermeule refer to it as a tradeoff thesis:

> The tradeoff thesis holds that governments should, and do, balance civil liberties and security at all times. During emergencies, when new threats appear, the balance shifts; government should and will reduce civil liberties in order to enhance security in those domains where the two must be traded off.[10]

This tradeoff thesis resonates in most instances of emergencies, including the Civil War, World War I and World War II, and the war on terror.[11]

Generalities, however, should not be mistaken for prerequisites. Although it might appear clear initially what an emergency is and what it entails, many analysts have noted that the term *emergency* is a very "elastic concept."[12] Legal analyst Jane Perry Clark tried to ascertain what, exactly, constituted an emergency and concluded, "the recognition of the emergency depends in each situation upon the judgment in particular circumstances of the executive, the legislative and above all, the judicial authorities. All three seem successfully to have evaded any definition."[13] She goes on to say that this evasiveness is possibly a result of their realization that *the doctrine is of necessity vague and amorphous* [emphasis added]."[14]

The elasticity of what constitutes an emergency is perhaps best evident by Franklin D. Roosevelt and the New Deal. Expanding the notion of crisis to include economic matters, Roosevelt invoked emergency powers to implement his plan to restore economic stability.[15] This was the first time in American history that an emergency was declared to address an economic crisis. This example suggests that the concept of emergency can be extended to cover a variety of issues that go beyond traditional understandings of war and security.

Although the Roosevelt example illustrates executive appropriation of what constitutes an emergency, judicial authorities also have an interest in declaring an emergency. Contemporary legal analyst Oren Gross picks up on Clark's depiction of emergency as a vague concept and how it can benefit the judiciary. Gross notes how the ability of an emergency to accommodate shifting and expanding powers can lend legitimacy to what might otherwise be illegitimate:

> The concept of emergency powers invokes images of short-term transient measures that are designed to respond to a particular emergency and then

be removed as soon as, or shortly after, that emergency has been met successfully. The sense that emergency measures, which may deviate from what is normally acceptable within the confines of a legal system in ordinary times, are to be temporary and are not to affect the legal and political terrain for years to come makes the draconian nature of such measures easier to accept.[16]

In other words, declaring an emergency is an effective way to bide time during periods of legal and political uncertainty. It is akin to putting up a legal firewall that insulates the norm. Without such a firewall, the Court is compelled to make drastic decisions that could possibly set new norms or transform permanent values.[17] By instituting an emergency, the Court can make radical decisions without necessarily altering traditional standards of jurisprudence. An emergency provides a way for the Court to respond to political fluctuations while maintaining a nonpolitical façade, providing the Court a degree of interpretive leeway in which it can maintain independence from the other branches without having to confront the other branches directly.

There have also been recent calls to reexamine the racialized and gendered nature of what constitutes a crisis. In a 2013 article titled "Of Mancessions and Hecoveries: Race, Gender and the Political Construction of Economic Crises and Recoveries," political scientist Dara Strolovich problematizes the conventional understanding of normalcy and crises: "[B]ad things that happen to marginalized groups evade crisis framings and are instead normalized and particularized within dominant institutions."[18] In her examination of the New Deal, Strolovich observes that "the very policies that helped to alleviate the economic crisis of the Great Depression and to offer citizens a 'New Deal' in fact reflected, reinforced and reconstituted these patterns of inequality. It is not just that some women or people of color were 'left out' by these policies that included the National Labor Recovery Act, Fair Labor Standards Act and the Social Security Act. Rather, inequalities were rearticulated and exacerbated by precisely those policies that are typically viewed as the most emancipatory and redistributive."[19] The unequal consequence of emancipatory policies serves to "normalize some bad things while constructing others as crises"[20] and hence sheds light on the quote by Walter Benjamin, which prefaces this chapter, that reconfigures the state of exception as the rule when it comes to oppressed groups. In this vein, I will argue that lynchings emerged in part by the emancipatory policies of Reconstruction and also were subsequently normalized in a manner that made them not a crisis.

SITUATING THE LEGAL AND POLITICAL CONTEXT
OF RECONSTRUCTION

Because of the transformative intent, political volatility, and ambiguous nature of Reconstruction, it is understandable why the Supreme Court would consider Reconstruction an emergency. Historians Charles and Mary Beard referred famously to Reconstruction as the second American revolution: "seldom, if ever, before had there occurred in the affairs of a nation a revolution so drastic ... the so-called Civil War was a social war, ending in the unquestioned establishment of a new power in the government."[21] This "new power" to which the Beards were referring was the emergence of a powerful central government. Before the Civil War, the chief distinguishing characteristic of the American political system was "that there was no state,"[22] and what Reconstruction aimed to do was, according to political historian Bruce Ackerman, "to redefine We the People of the United *States* as We the People of the *United* States."[23]

The transformative nature of Reconstruction was nonetheless complicated by the political volatility of Reconstruction. During and after reunification, radical reconfigurations of party coalitions, impeachment, and widespread violence characterized the intra- and interparty disputes during this period. Initially, the antebellum framework of federalism seemed clear. In March 1866, Republican Congressman John Bingham stated in Congress:

[W]ith the restoration of those States to their constitutional relations, and the establishment of courts of justice therein, our powers in the premises cease, and under the Constitution of the country freedmen and refugees alike are dependent for justice and their rights upon the civil administrators of the law within those respective States. . . . But when peace is restored; when the courts of justice are opened; when her white-robed ministers take the golden scales into their hands, justice is to be administered under the Constitution, according to the Constitution, and within the limitation of the Constitution.[24]

According to abolitionist Wendell Phillips, to declare peace is to "put a fence between the Federal Government and the State Government. . . . Put up the fence and the [national] law runs to it, not over it."[25] The end of war connoted restoration of constitutional normalcy, and the Constitution gave the federal government very limited authority to interfere with issues regarding the rights of citizens.[26] Hence, it would appear to be the case that the perceived antebellum relationship between the federal government and the states precluded the federal government from becoming involved in the rights enforcement of citizens in general and blacks in particular.[27]

With regard to civil rights, legal historians Harold Hyman and William Wiecek wrote that "in their nineteenth-century sense, civil rights were primarily factors of a person's state and community."[28] Republican Senator Oliver Morton from Indiana follows up on this sentiment:

> [T]his [federal] Government has no right, and it has no power, to impose a fundamental condition on any State by which that State parts with any right which it has under the Constitution of the United States. A State cannot alienate her rights under the Constitution of the United States any more than a man can alienate those great natural rights that belong to him . . . and if a State has a right under the Constitution of the United States that right cannot be alienated, bartered, or compacted away.[29]

To have direct federal intervention, changes needed to be made.

Presidential Restoration

The events that transpired during the Presidential Restoration made it clear to many Republican congressmen that peacetime changes were needed to ensure blacks' right to life. *Presidential Restoration* refers to the period after Lee's surrender at Appomattox and the midterm elections of 1866. This was when President Johnson had virtually sole power to dictate the federal government's policy regarding the ex-Confederate states. As Chief Justice Salmon Chase wrote in a letter to President Johnson, "Everything now, under God, must depend on you."[30] Although Johnson's decisions do not lend themselves to being arranged in any sort of coherent plan, considering how inconsistent, sporadic, and contradictory they were, he had stated on several occasions that he wanted the states to restore themselves. When a delegation from South Carolina visited the White House, President Johnson was quoted as saying, "[W]e must deal with the question of restoration and not reconstruction. I suspect that I am a better States-rights man than some of those now present. . . . Let each State judge of the depositary of its political power."[31] According to historian Eric Foner, President Johnson's central assumption was "that the Southern states could be trusted to manage their own affairs without federal oversight."[32] In that vein, many white Southerners began to pass a series of state laws that were known as *black codes*. "Intended to define the freedmen's new rights and responsibilities,"[33] these black codes nevertheless resulted in "getting things back as near to slavery as possible"[34] by "putting the state much in the place of the former master."[35] Combined with other factors, including the elections of many ex-Confederate officers[36] and the disturbing rise of white-on-black violence,[37] the intransigence of white Southerners seemed clear.[38]

Congressmen seemed, for the most part, to agree that Presidential Restoration was not protecting the rights of freedmen adequately. In response to the black codes, Senator Lyman Trumbull from Illinois stated:

> Since the abolition of slavery [via the Thirteenth Amendment], the Legislatures which have assembled in the insurrectionary States have passed laws relating to the freedmen, and in nearly all the States they have discriminated against them. They deny them certain rights, subject them to severe penalties, and still impose upon them the very restrictions which were imposed upon them in consequence of the existence of slavery, and before it was abolished.[39]

The respective states could not be entrusted to reconstruct themselves.

The tipping point for many reluctant congressmen appeared to be the New Orleans Riot of 1866. In lieu of the growing political power of former Confederate officers, in particular the reelection of Mayor John T. Monroe, Governor Wells convened a constitutional convention on July 30, 1866, to establish a new state government. Those opposed to this "radical" plan formed a mob outside the building where the convention was being held and the scene quickly degenerated into what General Sheridan called "an absolute massacre."[40] Thirty-four blacks and three whites were killed, and well more than hundred people were injured. Many have attributed the riot to President Johnson's lenient policy of Presidential Reconstruction. Although the local army commander had telegrammed Washington, expecting violence might occur, and was in a position in which he could have prevented much of the bloodshed if given permission, Johnson failed to give the order. Johnson even went so far as to tell the Louisiana lieutenant governor that the convention could be dispersed.[41] General Holt wrote that Johnson's leniency had unleashed "the barbarism of the rebellion in its renaissance."[42] According to Eric Foner, "the events in New Orleans discredited Presidential Reconstruction."[43] According to historian Michael Les Benedict, "Johnson's activity in the Louisiana crisis was probably the most important factor in his abandonment by the state-rights-oriented Democratic wing of the Republican party."[44] With respect to the rights of freedmen, Congress thus came to the conclusion that changes were needed.

But, few Republican congressmen wanted a complete break from the past.[45] Most wanted as little change as possible. Through scale analysis, Benedict aptly demonstrated that "more Republican Senators scaled consistently conservative than radical. . . . The groups that support radical legislation never made up 50 percent of either house of Congress, constituted the majority of the Republicans only half the time, and never controlled an overwhelming majority of the Republican votes."[46] The Boston *Daily Advertiser* observed that "while he held his position as "Leader of the House," Thaddeus Stevens, one of the most radical congressmen in the House, "no man was oftener outvoted."[47] Charles Sumner, perhaps the most radical Senator, wrote, "[H]ow few here sympathize with me! I sometimes feel that I am alone in the Senate."[48] He also stated in Congress that "most of those about me have a different opinion."[49] The federal government would have to assume some responsibility for the rights of freedmen. Many, if not most in Congress wanted to turn federalism on its side rather than on its head. In other words, Congress wanted to increase the power of the federal government without necessarily usurping the sovereignty of the states.

Congressional Reconstruction: Stage 1

Congress went about changing federalism in three phases. During the initial phase, the federal government bestowed upon itself the legal authority to ensure federal rights enforcement for blacks. During the second phase, the federal government established institutional capacity as well as garnered the political will and got actively involved.In the last phase, Congress began the process of retrenchment.

Congress passed two laws that provided the federal government the legal authority to protect blacks' right to life. The first was the Civil Rights Act of 1866; the second was the Fourteenth Amendment.[50] The Civil Rights Act was introduced into the thirty-ninth Congress on January 5, 1866, and was ratified April 9, 1866. It was passed by virtue of Congress's power under Section 2 of the Thirteenth Amendment. There are two key provisions I would like to point out. Section 1 of the Civil Rights Act of 1866 states

> that all persons born in the United States and not subject to any foreign power, excluding Indians not taxed, are hereby declared to be citizens of the United States; and such citizens . . . shall have the same right, in every State and Territory in the United States . . . and to full and equal benefit of all laws and proceedings for the security of person and property, as is enjoyed by white citizens, and shall be subject to like punishment, pains, and penalties, and to none other, any law, statute, ordinance, regulation, or custom, to the contrary notwithstanding.[51]

Section 3 states:

> that the district courts of the United States, within their respective districts, shall have, exclusively of the courts of the several States, cognizance of all crimes and offences committed against the provisions of this act, and also,

concurrently with the circuit courts of the United States, of all causes, civil and criminal, affecting persons who are denied or cannot enforce in the courts or judicial tribunals of the State or locality where they may be any of the rights secured to them by the first section of this act.[52]

These two provisions bestowed a degree of rights enforcement to the federal government. To what extent had yet to be determined.

Three months after ratifying the Civil Rights bill, Congress proposed the Fourteenth Amendment. The Fourteenth Amendment was very similar to the Civil Rights Bill of 1866. Section 1 of the Civil Rights Bill was proposed initially to be Section 1 of the Fourteenth Amendment. After several modifications, here is the final draft of Section 1 of the Fourteenth Amendment:

All persons born or naturalized in the United States, and subject to the jurisdiction thereof, are citizens of the United States and of the State in which they reside. No State shall make or enforce any law which shall abridge the privileges or immunities of citizens of the United States; nor shall any State deprive any person of life, liberty, or property, without due process of law; nor deny to any person within its jurisdiction the equal protection of the laws.[53]

The Fourteenth Amendment was proposed June 13, 1866 and ratified July 9, 1868.

These two laws were riddled with ambiguities and many questions and concerns were raised regarding the scope, intent and details of the federal government's authority.[54] However, both pieces of legislation passed—a fact that should not be taken lightly, if only because it was the first time in American history that Congress enacted a major piece of legislation over a President's veto. The Civil Rights Act of 1866 and the Fourteenth Amendment inaugurated a new chapter in federalism. To what extent they transformed federalism would remain unclear for years, but it did represent the opening salvo of Congress's attempt at providing the federal government the authority to protect the rights of citizens.

Although relations between President Johnson and Congress were amicable initially,[55] tensions arose after Johnson vetoed two congressional bills.[56] His veto of the two bills came as a shock to most of Congress, and would mark the beginning of a historically unprecedented feud between Congress and the president that would ensue throughout the remainder of Johnson's tenure, eventually ending in an impeachment process that fell one vote short of its goal. The major disagreement Johnson had with Congress was the involvement of the federal government in rights enforcement. Simply put, Congress wanted to expand the federal government's ability to enforce rights whereas President Johnson favored antebellum notions of federalism. Not only was Johnson trying to block congressional legislation through his use of the veto, but also he was impeding the enforcement of the legislation that Congress was able to pass despite his vetoes. When the 1866 Civil Rights bill became law, Johnson actively went out of his way to impede its enforcement. Legal historian Robert Kaczorowski notes:

> [T]he president's opposition to federal law enforcement was more than passive. He appointed legal officers who shared his opposition to national authority and nullified the efforts of conscientious legal officers by pardoning prisoners who had been convicted of violating federal laws. Combined with the exponential increase in federal case loads after the Civil War, racism, the strong support for states' rights and the expense and inconvenience of bringing a case to a federal court, it should then be of no wonder why so little effort was exerted by federal legal officers to enforce civil rights during the 1860s.[57]

He goes on to note:

> [T]he posture taken by the attorney general in his correspondence with United States attorneys and United States marshals inhibited their active involvement in civil rights issues. . . . The attorney general consistently refused to instruct subordinate legal officers as to their responsibilities under the Civil Rights Act or to answer their questions concerning the meaning and scope of federal civil rights enforcement authority, "believing that to be entirely a judicial question." Federal officers were left to act on their own, but, in light of the president's known opposition to civil rights enforcement, politics and self-interest were powerful inducements toward inaction.[58]

The feud between Congress and the President came to a hilt during the midterm elections of 1866. Because the election occurred between the proposal and ratification of the Fourteenth Amendment, it would prove to be a bellwether regarding the electoral support for congressional Reconstruction in general and the proposed Fourteenth Amendment in particular. During the midterm elections of 1866, historian Eric McKitrick, author of the landmark biography of Andrew Johnson, notes "there was an extraordinary absence of vagueness and ambiguity."[59] Ackerman elaborates this point further:

> As the election of 1866 reached its climax, voters were being asked to confront a truly constitutive question. Stripped down to essentials, it was simply this: which was more fundamental to the American Union—racial identity or

political identity? Doubtless, many voters would have preferred to avoid such a probing question; many would have been happy to suppose that Reconstruction could proceed without their having to wrestle with their souls. But the American system did not give them this choice. For good or for ill, they would have to cast a ballot one way or the other. They could vote for a party of a white Southerner who did not disguise his racism but who insisted on its compatibility with loyalty to the Union. Or they could vote for the party of the Fourteenth Amendment, asserting that "all persons born or naturalized in the United States . . . are citizens of the United States," and that "no State shall abridge the privileges or immunities of citizens of the United States."[60]

Although the Congressional Republican campaign platform centered around the ratification of the Fourteenth Amendment and further reconstruction, the president's platform centered on its rejection and immediate restoration. To garner more support for Presidential Restoration, Johnson's sympathizers launched a "grand national organization" for the purposes of "giving the death blow to the radicalism which has proved so disastrous to the reunion and prosperity of the States."[61] The National Union movement was not "trying to establish a new national party, but called for the election of Congressmen who would support Johnson's policies,"[62] which consisted of "calling for reconciliation between North and South, affirming the loyalty of Southern whites, and arguing that suffrage requirements should be left to the states."[63] The creation of the National Union movement represented a distinct break between Johnson and the Republican Party, thereby facilitating a subsequent political realignment. This break with the party was made evident in Johnson's "swing around the circle," in which he "kept saying the same things over and over and denouncing Congress for opposing what had now become a derisive Republican byword: 'My Policy.'"[64] The congressional Republicans won a resounding victory. Republicans not only outnumbered Democrats and Johnson conservatives, but also they got well above the two-thirds majority required to override a presidential veto. McKitrick noted that "the sweeping character of the Republican victory in the 1866 fall elections had represented, in effect, a final mandate for unfettered radicalism."[65] After the elections, President Johnson became the epitome of a lame duck president.

Congressional Reconstruction: Stage 2

In 1868, the Republicans ran on a platform of stability, peace, and sectional concord, whereas Democrats ran on a platform of disruption bordering on revolution. The resounding victory for Republicans in 1868 not only provided their party with legitimacy, but also seemingly extinguished any hope for those who may have wanted to avert or halt Reconstruction. Republican presidential candidate Ulysses S. Grant garnered 214 of a total 294 electoral votes to beat Democratic presidential candidate Horatio Seymour to become the eighteenth president of the United States. Republicans increased their control over the Senate by gaining five seats, which meant that Republicans held fifty-seven of the sixty-six seats. The Democrats did, however, manage to gain twenty seats in the House of Representatives. That said, the Republicans still maintained a commanding majority in the House, with 174 of 243 seats.

The 1868 election results forced the Democratic Party to reassess its strategic thinking. After 1868, the Democratic Party abandoned direct political confrontation and adopted a more conciliatory and flexible attitude toward Reconstruction in the hope of gaining the support of disaffected centrists and conservatives within the Republican Party. Although this more conciliatory approach, otherwise known as *the New Departure*, was widely criticized by many Southerners, it was nonetheless supported by Southern luminaries such as former Confederate Senator from Arkansas Augustus Garland, former Vice-President of the Confederacy Alexander Stephens, and former Governor of North Carolina Zebulon Vance.

For Republicans, although they won a resounding victory in 1868, many believed their victory would be short-lived. Four states—Virginia, Mississippi, Texas, and Georgia—had yet to be readmitted into the Union.[66] In the seven states that had been readmitted in time for the 1868 elections, restrictions were placed on former Confederate soldiers that prevented them from voting. There was also the issue of black suffrage. Although many Republican leaders acknowledged that extending suffrage to blacks was necessary to win in the South, they were nonetheless hampered by the electoral results of 1867. In 1867, voters in Ohio, Pennsylvania, New York, and New Jersey rejected state referendums to extend suffrage to blacks. It thus seemed to be the case that what was best for the long-term interests of the party (extending suffrage to blacks) was not necessarily what was best for the short-term interests of Northern politicians (getting reelected).

After the 1868 elections, both parties felt a course correction was needed. Although the Republicans won a resounding victory in 1868, they were still potentially a minority party and felt like they needed to increase their vote, particularly in the South, if they were to retain their majority. Having lost resoundingly in 1868, the Democrats were, in fact, the minority party and felt they needed to increase their vote if they were ever to regain prominence. Both parties subsequently began to compete for the political center. Republicans targeted Southern Whigs and Democrats targeted conservative Republicans. This electoral strategy to capture the center would play out in the 1872 elections. For Republicans, this strategy—and the subsequent results in the 1872 elections—pushed the party toward the right, away from the radical demands of the left. For the Democrats, it revealed how any conciliatory strategy was doomed to fail, thus pushing the party away from moderates and toward the radical demands of the right. The ideological shifting to the right of both parties later proved to have a devastating impact on blacks' right to life.

On March 4, 1869, Ulysses S. Grant became the eighteenth president of the United States, handily beating the Democratic candidate, Horatio Seymour.[67] During Grant's tenure as president, Republicans were able to maintain a majority in both houses. He was able to appoint four Supreme Court Justices: William Strong (1870–1880), Joseph Bradley (1870–1892), Ward Hunt (1873–1882), and Morrison Waite (1874–1888). Andrew Johnson never got the opportunity to appoint a Supreme Court justice. Also during Grant's tenure, only three justices had not been picked by either himself or Lincoln: Samuel Nelson (1845–1872, appointed by Tyler), Robert Grier (1846–1870, appointed by Polk), and Nathan Clifford (1858–1881, appointed by Buchanan). It thus seems safe to conclude that the Republican Party prevailed over all three branches of the federal government during Grant's tenure as president.

No longer shackled by the need for a supermajority to override the anticipated veto of the president, Congress immediately passed a series of legislation that specifically addressed the racial violence occurring in the South. There are three pieces of legislation that particularly stand out: the Enforcement Act of May 31, 1870; the Enforcement Act of April 2, 1871 (otherwise known as *the Ku Klux Act of 1871*); and the Act to Establish the Department of Justice.

The Enforcement Act of 1870 became law on May 31 of that year. It consisted of six sections, which added up to a general civil rights statute designed to protect freedoms guaranteed by the Fourteenth and Fifteenth Amendments. Sections 6, 12, and 13 are particularly relevant. Section 6 states:

> That if two or more persons shall band or conspire together, or go in disguise upon the public highway, or upon the premises of another, with intent to violate any provision of this act, or to injure, oppress, threaten, or intimidate any citizen with intent to prevent or hinder his free exercise and enjoyment of any right or privilege granted or secured to him by the Constitution or laws of the United States, or because of his having exercised the same, such persons shall be held guilty to felony, and, on conviction thereof, shall be fined or imprisoned, or both, at the discretion of the court.[68]

Section 12 states "that the commissioners, district attorneys, the marshals, their deputies, and the clerks of the said district, circuit, and territorial courts shall be paid for their services."[69] Section 13 states "that it shall be lawful for the President of the

United States to employ such part of the land or naval forces of the United States, or of the militia, as shall be necessary to aid in the execution of judicial process issued under this act."[70]

On April 2, 1871, the 42nd Congress (1871–1873) passed the Ku Klux Act, which expanded on the Enforcement Act of 1870. Section 2 of the Act spells out twenty-two specific practices of conspiracy, including the conspiracy of "depriving any person or any class of persons of the equal protection of the laws, or of equal privileges or immunities under the laws."[71] Section 3 made it "lawful for the President . . . to take such measures . . . as he may deem necessary for the suppressions of such insurrection, domestic violence, or combinations . . . that obstruct or hinder the executions of the laws, thereof, and of the United States, as to deprive any portion or class of the people of such State of any of the rights, privileges, or immunities, or protection, named in the Constitution."[72] Section 4 made it "lawful for the President . . . to suspend the privileges of the writ of habeas corpus" whenever unlawful combinations are "organized and armed and . . . set at defiance the constituted authorities of such State or when the constituted authorities are in complicity with, or shall connive at the unlawful purposes of, such powerful and armed combinations."[73]

These acts expanded dramatically the authority and power of the federal government. *The Nation* asserted that these acts "not only increase the power of the central government, but they arm it with jurisdiction over a class of cases of which it has never hitherto had, and never pretended to have, any jurisdiction whatever."[74] Although this expansion of federal jurisdiction can be said to follow in the same spirit and logic of the Civil Rights Act of 1866 and the Fourteenth Amendment,[75] several congressmen who voted for the Civil Rights Act of 1866 and the Fourteenth Amendment found this new expansion of federal jurisdiction as having gone too far.[76] Democrats delivered the expected opposition. Democratic Congressmen William E. Arthur from Kentucky stated:

> [U]nder the pretext of protecting the people, the people are being enslaved; under the pretext of establishing order, liberty is being overthrown; under the pretext of securing the rights of the voter, the voter is disfranchised; under color of maintaining the manhood of man in the political equality of the colored man, the manhood of man is denied in the political degradation of the white man.[77]

What was somewhat surprising, however, was the number of Republicans who also voiced opposition. Prominent Republicans such as Lyman Trumbull, who co-authored the Thirteenth Amendment and was vocal in his support of the Fourteenth Amendment, insisted "the states were, and are now, the depositories of the rights of the individual against encroachment" and to interfere with these depositories "would then be an annihilation entirely of the States."[78] Although Trumbull believed the Fourteenth Amendment "has not extended the rights and privileges of citizenship one iota," he did regard the Ku Klux Act of 1871 as extending it in ways that were not consistent constitutionally.[79] Carl Schurz, the former Union army general who toured the postbellum South and reported an overwhelming number of atrocities and violence occurring in the South, also considered the Ku Klux Act unwarranted and characterized it as "insane."[80] Although the Enforcement Act of 1870 and the Ku Klux Act of 1871 passed, they portended, according to Eric Foner, "a major breach over Southern policy, which would culminate in the Liberal Republican movement of 1872."[81] These acts not only hinted at a split in the Republican Party, but also foreshadowed the congressional strategy of handing the reigns of Reconstruction over to the judiciary. According to Robert Kaczorowski, "Congress attempted to put down this armed insurrection in the South through the federal judicial process. . . . Legislation aimed at Klan activity inescapably thrust the federal courts into the administration of criminal justice on a massive scale."[82]

In 1872, Republicans appeared to be in good shape. President Grant was reelected with more electoral college votes and popular votes than he had in 1868.[83] Republicans increased their majority in the House of Representatives by sixty-three seats and many ex-Confederate states were still under Republican control.[84] In response to the Republican success in the 1872 elections, the *Alabama State Journal* concluded that the "Democratic party . . . was so effectually defeated that it can never rally again. Its career is ended." In South Carolina, the *Columbia Daily Union* stated that "the South is largely Republican."[85]

Congressional Reconstruction: Stage 3

But in many regards, the 1872 election was a pyrrhic victory for Southern blacks. During Reconstruction, different wings of the respective parties jockeyed for control; therefore, to assume the party maintained a unity of ideals, strategies, and goals would be a mistake. Although it might appear that support for Reconstruction was solid in 1872, because the Republican Party was formally in control of both houses and the presidency, a closer examination of what was occurring in each party suggests otherwise. The year 1872 was a time of intense intraparty struggle. Although Reconstruction in general and federal rights enforcement in particular were tied intimately with the Republican Party, what exactly Reconstruction entailed and the extent to which federal rights enforcement were actuated was a debate that had as much to do with what occurred within parties as it did across parties.

Closer examination of the 1872 elections reveals that claims regarding Republican ascendancy and Democratic despondency were overblown. In the Senate, the Republicans lost nine seats in the 1872 elections. In North Carolina, the Republican majority slipped from Governor Holden's 20,000 in 1868 to a slim 1,000 for Tod Caldwell in 1872. In Texas, the Democrats had already taken over the legislature in 1871, and continued retention of the governorship for Republicans seemed highly unlikely. The gubernatorial races in Louisiana and Arkansas, and the legislative election in Alabama were so close that the opposition was threatening to gain control by challenging the returns. Republican ascendancy thus seemed tenuous at best.

In addition, the victories Republicans did obtain in the 1872 presidential and congressional elections had more to do with the weaknesses of the opponents' campaigns than it had to do with the strength of Republican campaigns. Horace Greeley, the 1872 Democratic presidential candidate, was not terribly liked by Democrats. Democratic Congressman Michael Kerr from Indiana wrote that campaigning for Greeley "is the bitterest pill of my whole political life."[86] John Mosby, former Confederate general from Virginia, was perplexed by the choice: "Why should the South array itself on the side of Greeley, her unrepentant life-long enemy against General Grant, when Greeley justified and approved every one of the president's acts that was odious to us?"[87] Greeley split the Democratic vote and in so doing ensured the reelection of Grant.[88] Thus, the reelection of Grant was as much as or even more so about the unpopularity of Greeley than it was about the support of Grant.

If Republicans hoped to have any chance in the South, they would have to recruit more white Southerners because blacks comprised the majority in only three Southern states: South Carolina, Louisiana, and Mississippi. The Republican Party thus set out to reach out and capture a segment of the Southern white vote. According to historian Michael Perman, this new strategy of the Republican Party would be "the most absorbing and volatile feature of southern party politics after 1868."[89] In their efforts to capture a segment of the Southern white vote, Republicans chose to target Southern Whigs. Although the Whig Party dissolved in 1856, many members were still alive and had, according to Perman, "never really given up their partisan identity."[90] Whigs seemed like a natural target for Republicans because they had opposed secession from the start, and their reputation was that of moderation and harmony.[91] The courting seemed to work. According to Perman, thousands of Whigs affiliated with the Republicans during this period. In North Carolina, three of every four native white Republicans had been a Whig. In Mississippi, the Republican Party reportedly drew its Southern white voters from antebellum Whigs.[92]

The active recruitment of Southern Whigs helped the Republicans carry the South in the 1872 elections, but this victory had come at a price—namely, a deemphasis on federal rights enforcement. Although helping Republicans maintain their majority, the increasing prominent Southern Whigs nonetheless pushed the Republican Party to the right, away from the radical position. Historian Eric Foner notes this shift:

> Instead of uniting Republicans in a struggle for survival, the question of violence further exacerbated the party's internal discord. . . . Alabama Gov. William H. Smith declared reports of violence exaggerated and insisted that local officials bore the primary responsibility for law enforcement. . . . The governor's caution undermined his credibility among many rank-and-file Republicans and strengthened black support for his rival. Mississippi Gov. James L. Alcorn proved as reluctant as Smith, [who] proposed to establish a seven-man Secret Service—hardly a force capable of suppressing violence. Georgia's Republican administration declined even to organize a militia, and although Florida Gov. Harrison Reed did recruit a mostly black force, he never sent it into action against the Klan.[93]

Although the 1868 elections affirmed the policy of seeking stability via the nationalization of rights, the 1872 elections affirmed the Whiggish policy of seeking stability through conciliation. In this new Whiggish Republican Party, rights enforcement became identified as a radical issue that had to be deemphasized if Republicans wanted to stay in power. In this light, the Enforcement Act of 1870 and the Ku Klux Act of 1871 reflect the last-ditch effort by radicals to retain their vision of Reconstruction, rather than the slowly progressing culmination of their efforts. Gillette sums up this point adeptly:

> [T]he most far-reaching reconstruction measures of a national political character had been undertaken precisely when support for reconstruction was on the wane; the federal government had undertaken these bold innovative programs at a time when Republicans were losing their power and purpose.[94]

Although on paper it might appear that the fate of Reconstruction was as yet secure as a result of the fact that Republicans controlled both houses in Congress and the executive branch, in fact the Republicans were only able to remain in power by being more equivocal on Reconstruction.

The year 1872 would not only mark a shift in the stance of the executive branch on federal rights enforcement, but also it would denote a subtle yet definitive shift in party politics and strategy. In 1872, a discernible rightward shift occurred in both parties. For the Republicans, the 1872 elections validated the rightward shift they had made to accommodate the Whiggish interests of Southern whites. For the

Democrats, the 1872 elections invalidated their centrist shift to accommodate conservative Republicans and invoked a course correction that would spawn a shift to the right. In addition, a new party, the Liberal Republican Party, entered the fray. In May 1870, Republican Senator Carl Schurz from Missouri launched the Liberal Republican Party in response to the reports of corruption associated with the Grant administration, mounting criticism and exhaustion with Reconstruction, and a growing desire to put economic and administrative reform front and center.[95] This new party attracted disaffected Republicans and Democrats. The party rose to prominence when its nominee for President, Horace Greeley, was eventually endorsed by the Democrats. Perman sums up adeptly the events leading to the 1872 election:

> The fusion of the Liberal-Republicans and the Democrats in the national election of 1872 marked the culmination of the politics of convergence. The intention of the New Departure strategy, which had initially been inaugurated in the South and then later adopted by the Democratic party as a whole, had been to defuse the issue of Reconstruction and thus clear the way for lukewarm Republicans to join with the Democrats. To this end, a split and subsequent secession from the ranks of the Republicans was exactly what the party in the South had been trying to engineer by means of the New Departure lure.[96]

But, this conciliatory strategy backfired. Gillette analyzed the 1872 election returns as follows:

> Dissatisfied Republicans failed to defect in large numbers, and many disgruntled Democrats refused to vote. The whole character of the campaign was borne out by the patterns of voting and nonvoting: Greeley succeeded in nothing but in uniting the Republicans and dividing the Democrats.[97]

After the elections, Southern newspapers ran several articles reporting the inordinate amount of people who did not vote. The Atlanta *Constitution* reported "a great deal of Democratic apathy." The Raleigh *Sentinel* detected that "there is a fearful apathy present. . . . All over the state there was an unaccountable and inexcusable indifference manifested." The *Sentinel* reported 56,000 registered voters failed to vote and another 41,000, most of whom were probably white, had not even registered. In a state that Grant carried by only 20,000, the *Sentinel* calculated there were at least 30,000 who opposed his candidacy but failed to vote.[98] Compared with the off-year election of 1870, the numbers seemed low. In Alabama, the total vote for Democrats was 1,000 less than in 1870. In North Carolina, the party's choice for attorney general in the off-year election of 1870 got 1,641 more votes than its gubernatorial nominee in 1872. In South Carolina, the gubernatorial candidate in 1872 got 15,000 fewer votes than in 1870. Compared with the 1876 presidential election, the 1872 presidential election garnered two million less votes.

Like the defeat in 1868, the Democratic defeat in the 1872 presidential elections triggered yet another change of direction in the party's strategic thinking. For Democrats, the 1872 presidential elections illustrated the failure of a conciliatory strategy. Perman summarizes expertly the Democrats' analysis of the 1872 elections:

> During the 1872 campaign, they had observed that the party's problem was not that it was failing to gain new adherents and broader support but simply that it was not capitalizing on the electoral assets it already possessed. Vast numbers of its supporters were just not being mobilized but, instead, were withdrawing and refusing to vote.[99]

If anything, the 1872 elections illustrated how little the Democrats needed to depend on attracting additional support. Instead of trying to gloss over differences and pitch themselves as a nonpartisan, nonsectional, broad-based coalition, this new strategy, which came to be known as the *"straight-out" basis*, focused on accentuating contrasts and distinctions.

Based on the electoral returns, Democrats concluded that sectional reconciliation and party realignment were not necessary for electoral victory. The massive number of abstentions led many Democrats to believe they needed to spend their time courting their own constituency instead of courting disaffected Republicans. In response to voter apathy, Senator Samuel B. Maxey of Texas commented, "[W]e had better solidify our own ranks."[100] Because voter apathy was seen as the primary problem, the antidote needed to be dramatic. As former Texas Governor James Throckmorton stated, "[O]nly live coals can bring them out of their shells."[101] In addition, the fact that no Northern state voted for Greeley led many Democrats to conclude that no amount of conciliation would ever satisfy Northerners and thus their opinions could be ignored. For Southerners, sectionalism apparently was as much a Northern choice as it was a Southern preference. Southern Democrats also concluded from their analysis of the 1872 election returns that race needs to be in the forefront. As Perman points out so eloquently: "White supremacy was not merely an asset the [Democratic] party was foolish to squander, it was a reality most unwise to overlook."[102]

As mentioned, 1872 marked a rightward shift in both parties. Both shifts worked to the detriment of blacks because each shift called for diminished support for Reconstruction in general and federal rights enforcement in particular. But, like

President Grant's change in stance, it was still unclear what the durability, extent, and depth of this shift would be. How long would they last? How deep were they? It took subsequent elections, starting with the 1874 midterm elections, to answer these questions.[103] Unfortunately, the Supreme Court could not wait until then and had to make crucial decisions regarding Reconstruction.

Congress's Plan for the Judiciary

Although there were dramatic changes occurring in Congress throughout this period, Congress was nonetheless focused on extending and broadening the power of the federal judiciary. From 1863 to 1876, Congress passed a series of legislation that vastly expanded the jurisdictional scope of the federal courts, including the 1863 Habeas Corpus Act, the 1866 amendment to the 1863 Habeas Corpus Act, the Internal Revenue Act of 1866, the Separable Controversies Act of 1866, the Local Prejudice Act of 1867, the 1871 Voting Rights Act, and the Jurisdiction Removal Act of 1875. All these Acts allowed special provisions in which federal courts could remove suits from state courts. Legal historian William Wiecek argues that "in no comparable period of our nation's history have the federal courts, lower and Supreme, enjoyed as great an expansion of their jurisdiction as they did in the years of Reconstruction, 1863–1876."[104] Combined, these acts of legislation led Wiecek to conclude that "Congress had determined to expand the power of the federal courts, sometimes at its own expense, more often at the states', to make them partners in implementing national policy."[105]

In line with the notion that Congress wanted to expand the power and authority of the federal judiciary to be able to hand it the reigns of Reconstruction, Congress also passed legislation establishing the Department of Justice. One month after the Enforcement Act of 1870 was enacted, the Department of Justice was established. The Act to Establish the Department of Justice not only enlarged the authority of the attorney general's office, but also it centralized the legal business of the national government. Congress established the Department of Justice to make the handling of the nation's legal affairs more efficient and effective.

Before the Department of Justice was established, the federal judiciary was in disarray. Not only was the attorney general unpaid, but also scarce resources were allotted and the attorney general had very limited authority over the federal attorneys and marshals. The scattered district attorneys and marshals remained all but completely independent.[106] Congressmen Thomas Jenckes, who introduced the bill to create a Department of Justice, noted how the hiring of government lawyers in Washington had grown reckless, with each department hiring its own lawyers, and each providing different and often conflicting legal advice.[107] Bills to strengthen the attorney general's office had appeared before Congress in 1819, 1822, 1829, 1845, 1854, 1855, and 1866, but none became law, mainly because of fears that it would centralize and aggrandize federal authority. Also, U.S. attorneys prior to the Civil War gave only passing attention to the enforcement of federal criminal laws. In light of the anarchic status and limited activity of federal legal officers, Congress's reliance on them is puzzling and somewhat surprising. According to Robert Kaczorowski, "the protection of persons and property from violence was a radically new function Congress thrust upon federal legal officers for which they were ill prepared institutionally and professionally."[108] However, because Congress decided to respond to Southern violence through the federal judicial process, the Department of Justice was crucial to protecting blacks' right to life by not only providing the necessary resources, but also by streamlining the federal judicial process in such a way that something programmatic could be instituted.

In addition to passing laws for the explicit purpose of broadening and expanding the scope of judicial authority, Congress also delegated wide discretionary power to the federal judiciary by passing vague legislation. Historian Eric Foner notes how Congress was purposefully vague, in part to provide the judiciary "maximum flexibility":

> Moderate Republicans preferred to allow both Congress and the federal courts maximum flexibility in implementing the Amendment's provisions and combating the multitude of injustices that confronted blacks in many parts of the South.... Indeed, as in the Civil Rights Act, Congress placed great reliance on an activist federal judiciary for civil rights enforcement.[109]

There were three reasons why Congress wanted to cede power to the federal judiciary: (1) the presence of irreconcilable differences within Congress,[110] (2) the anticipated fear of what Southerners would do when they were allowed back into Congress,[111] and (3) the changing mood and concerns of the electorate.[112] Taken together, these three reasons illuminate why Congress would expand the scope and authority of the judiciary branch voluntarily, even if it was done at the expense of its own power.

Not only did Congress aggrandize the authority of the judiciary, but also Congress made it difficult for the judiciary to adjudicate. When Congress reconvened in December 1865, one of their priorities was to figure out the status of the rebellious states vis-à-vis the federal government.[113] There were five distinct theoretical positions posited at this time regarding the status of the rebellious states: (1) the Southern theory, which the Northern Democrats defended persistently; (2) the presidential theory, on which President Johnson insisted; (3) the theory of forfeited rights that was formulated by Congressman Samuel Shellabarger and was shared by many moderate Republicans; (4) the theory of state suicide espoused by Senator Charles Sumner; and (5) the conquered-province theory championed by Congressman Thaddeus Stevens.[114] Each position staked out a claim on three crucial issues: the status of the ex-Confederate states vis-à-vis the Union, the appropriate body for judicial oversight, and the legal process by which Reconstruction was to occur. The theory of forfeited states had the most support among those in Congress and was the one the Supreme Court affirmed.

With regard to whether the rebellious states ever technically "left" the Union, the theory of state suicide and the conquered-province theory argued that the states had left the Union. This was the position many radical Republicans staked out. The Southern theory, which garnered the support of most of the Democratic Party, and the theory of forfeited rights, which garnered the support of many moderate Republicans and hence the majority in Congress, argued that the states did not leave the Union. The presidential theory was the basis of Johnson's Restoration plan and wanted to strike a compromise between these two positions; it argued that the rebellious states somehow "remained asleep in suspended animation."[115]

All but the theory of forfeited rights provided a simple answer to resolving the jurisprudential anarchy plaguing the South. Under the theory of state suicide and the conquered-province theory, there was no real conflict between military courts

TABLE 3.1

Congressional Theories of the Status of the Ex-Confederate States

Theory	Primary Advocate	In/Out of Union	Jurisdictional Oversight	Normal/ Martial Law
Southern	Northern Democrats	In	Civilian courts	Normal
Presidential	President Johnson	In/out	President	Martial
Forfeited rights	Congressman Shellabarger	In	Congress	???
State suicide	Senator Sumner	Out	Military courts	Martial
Conquered province	Congressman Stevens	Out	Military courts	Martial

and civilian courts because the civilian courts were no longer legitimate; they were no longer part of a "state." The Southern theory followed the same logic in that it agreed that there was no real conflict between military courts and civilian courts, but unlike the previous formulations, the Southern theory asserted that this was because the states never ceased to exist as states. Hence, it was the military courts that were illegitimate. Under the presidential theory, the President is the sole authority on reconstruction, and thus all conflicts regarding jurisprudence were his responsibility.

Although it was the most convoluted legally, the theory of forfeited rights nevertheless garnered the most support in Congress. The theory consisted of three claims: (1) no state ever was or could be out of the Union, (2) a state could be a state and still be capable of having lapsed from a Republican form of government, and (3) if the state did "lapse," there was a "constitutional obligation to guaranty each State a republican form of government . . . and it is the right of Congress, under the Constitution, to take jurisdiction and decide."[116] To make his case for the theory of forfeited rights, Ohio Congressman Samuel Shellabarger, the theory's primary architect, quoted the opinion of Chief Justice Taney in *Luther v. Borden*:

> Under this article of the Constitution it rests with Congress to decide which government . . . is the established one, for as the United States guaranties to each State a republican government, Congress must necessarily determine what government is established in a State before it can decide whether it is republican or not.[117]

Shellabarger's use of *Luther v. Borden* is interesting because, in that decision, the Court ruled that cases involving the guarantee clause were nonjusticiable because they inherently raised political questions—in other words, there was no fair, neutral way to decide issues concerning the guarantee clause.[118]

This theory of forfeited rights thus made the legal status of Reconstruction somewhat murky. The other theories demarcated a clear separation between the "normal" law of local/civilian courts and the "martial" law of military courts. Under the Southern theory, "martial" law was eliminated and "normal" law prevailed. Under the theory of state suicide, the conquered-province theory, and the presidential theory, "martial" law was used exclusively; "normal" law was never touched. It was only the theory of forfeited rights that upheld the simultaneous operation of normal law and martial law, and left it to Congress to determine how these two legal frameworks were to coexist. The Court was thus granted more power with vague provisions and complicated resolutions.

The Lower Federal Court's Rulings during the Era of Congressional Reconstruction

Congress, under the auspices of Republicans, ceded control to the judiciary in the hopes that the judiciary could protect and advance Reconstruction. The Supreme Court, however, was hesitant to make decisions that were permanently binding. The Court's reluctance to lead became clear when examining the discrepancy between the decisions made by the Supreme Court justices while riding circuit and the decisions made as the Supreme Court. The level of support for Reconstruction was markedly different across the different echelons of the judiciary. There were four cases on which Supreme Court justices decided while riding circuit that dealt with the Civil Rights Bill of 1866 and/or the Fourteenth Amendment: *U.S. v. Rhodes*,[119] *re Turner*,[120] *Live Stock Dealers and Butchers Association v. Crescent City Livestock Landing and Slaughterhouse*,[121] and *U.S. v. Hall*.[122] In *U.S. v. Rhodes*, Supreme Court Justice Noah Haynes Swayne, while riding circuit, upheld the constitutionality of the Civil Rights Act.[123] Swayne opined that the Reconstruction legislation "reversed and annulled the original policy of the constitution"[124] and "in the future it throws its protection to every one . . . and will continue to perform its function throughout the expanding domain of the nation, without limit of time or space."[125] In 1867, Supreme Court Chief Justice Samuel Chase, on his Maryland circuit, expressed similar views. Chase granted Elizabeth Turner, a former slave, a habeas writ. Like *United States v. Rhodes*, this case was applied to a private act that did not involve the state at all.[126] In the circuit court of Louisiana in 1870, Supreme Court Justice Joseph Bradley ruled, in what would later be coined *The Slaughter-House Cases*, that the federal courts had primary authority to protect civil rights because these rights were recognized and secured by the U.S. Constitution as rights of American citizenship.[127] In 1871, federal district Judge William Woods, who would later become the first Southerner appointed to the Supreme Court since 1860, decided in *U.S. v. Hall* that the federal government had both a right and a duty under the Thirteenth and Fourteenth Amendments to reach into states to inhibit the actions of state officials or individuals intended to deprive citizens of First Amendment rights. Woods concluded that every American citizen was entitled to the enforcement of the laws for the protection of his fundamental rights, as well as the enactment of such laws.[128]

Although Supreme Court justices were willing to make substantive decisions in support of the Reconstruction legislation while riding circuit, there was clear apprehension to carry that support over to the Supreme Court.[129] In *Georgia v. Stanton*, the Supreme Court dismissed disputes concerning the constitutionality of the Reconstruction Acts passed by Congress because it deemed those disputes to be political in nature and thus nonjusticiable.[130] In *Mississippi v. Johnson*, the Court refused to enjoin presidential execution of the Reconstruction Acts.[131] In Ex parte *McCardle*, the Supreme Court declined jurisdiction after Congress repealed the relevant statute.[132] The most positive spin was perhaps provided by legal historian Stanley Kutler who concluded that these three cases illustrated how "the Court legitimated the congressional program by indirection."[133]

The Court's support for Reconstruction was more explicit in *Texas v. White*, in which the Court affirmed the basic premises of mainstream Republican opinion: the seceded states and their people were out of their proper relation to the Union, that their reconstruction constituted a political question, and that it therefore had to be resolved by the legislative, and not the judicial, branch of the national government.[134] Kutler states that "*Texas v. White* is often seen as the high-water mark of respectability for the Republican program."[135] This high-water mark is not only evidence of the Court's reluctance to lead the federal government's efforts in Reconstruction, but also its support for congressional-led plans for Reconstruction. All the Supreme Court cases up to this point favored Reconstruction as, primarily, a political program, and as such it was the primary responsibility of Congress to articulate and advance what Reconstruction was and would be.

Even when the Court was seemingly curtailing Reconstruction, it was still nevertheless defending Congress' leadership role in advancing and articulating Reconstruction. On the surface, *ex parte Milligan* appears to be a clear repudiation of Reconstruction. A close examination, however, reveals that it was a very focused attack against only one form of Reconstruction, not necessarily a repudiation of Reconstruction as a whole. In *Milligan*, the Court voided the wartime conviction of an Indiana man by a military tribunal on the grounds that civilian courts had been functioning at the time of his trial. According to Hyman and Wiecek, the Milligan case "raised serious doubts about the Freedmen's Bureau and Civil Rights laws, and obscured the meaningfulness of the Thirteenth Amendment's enforcement clause."[136] Immediately after the ruling, Secretary of War Edwin Stanton wrote to Johnson that he "was unable to determine what cases, if any . . . can be acted upon by military authority."[137] When the decision first came out, Congressman Thaddeus Stevens decried that ex parte *Milligan* was "perhaps not as infamous as the Dred Scott decision, [it] is yet far more dangerous in its operation upon the lives and liberties of the loyal men of this country. That decision has taken away every protection in every one of these rebel States from every loyal man, black or white, who resides there."[138] Stevens' worry was verified when President Johnson used *Milligan* to cancel military trials in the South, which tended to protect the newly enshrined rights of freedmen, and to reinstate the civilian courts, which tended to favor the racist inclinations of the antebellum status quo.[139] *Milligan* would also later be the basis by which Southern lawyers dismantled congressional Reconstruction.[140]

Although the Court struck down the use of military trials, in the concurring o-
pinion written by Chief Justice Samuel Chase and Justice Miller, on which Swayne
and Wayne signed off, the anterior right of Congress to act was defended explicitly:

> We cannot doubt that, in such a time of public danger, Congress had power,
> under the Constitution, to provide for the organization of a military commis-
> sion, and for trial by that commission of persons engaged in this conspiracy.
> The fact that the Federal courts were open was regarded by Congress as a suffi-
> cient reason for not exercising the power; but the fact could not deprive Con-
> gress of the right to exercise it. Those courts might be open and undisturbed in
> the execution of their functions, and yet wholly incompetent to avert threat-
> ened danger, or to punish, with adequate promptitude and certainty, the guilty
> conspirators.[141]

This defense of Congress is in line with letters Miller wrote. In a letter dated February 6, 1866, Miller noted, "the Republican Party is the only one from which I can
have any hope for the country."[142]

During the early stages of Reconstruction, the Supreme Court supported a
congressional-led plan for Reconstruction, but it was unclear exactly what Congress
wanted. Congress wanted the Court to lead, but could only provide vague principles. Both branches were reluctant to lead, and thus fundamental questions emerged
regarding which branch should lead, how each branch should lead, and when each
branch should lead. But, as we will see, every decision by the Court nonetheless
contributed to a kind of mission creep. *Mission creep* refers to the expansion of a
project beyond its original goals. In this situation, every time the Court made a decision in support of congressional-led Reconstruction, it was taking on more and
more of a leadership role. What were intended to be acts of deferral were, in fact,
guiding acts of policy.

During the early stages of Reconstruction, the Court focused on narrowing its
support to congressional-led plans for Reconstruction as opposed to presidential-
led plans for Reconstruction. As Reconstruction rolled on, not only did political
volatility in Congress increase, but also Congress' desire for judicial leadership. In
trying to retain Congress' maneuverability amid such extreme political volatility, the
Court would apply the concept of emergency. As political winds stabilized and the
Congressional will to engage in federal rights enforcement dissipated, the Court
would eventually distort the emergency to accommodate the political resolution to
disregard the plight of Southern blacks. In so doing, the Court took what was meant
to be a weapon to combat racial violence and turned it into an enabler of racial
violence.

SLAUGHTER-HOUSE CASES: INSTITUTING THE EMERGENCY

This judicial reluctance to lead prevailed even when the Supreme Court took on its first case regarding the Fourteenth Amendment. *Slaughter-House* was the Court's first interpretation of the Fourteenth Amendment.[143] In this case, the Court began the process of parsing out different aspects of race and, based on those differing aspects, conjured up different schemas for action. However pivotal it might have appeared initially, the Court made sure to couch this parsing out in a way that was in line with the transformative intent of Reconstruction, the ambiguous nature of the Reconstruction legislation, and the political volatility swirling around during that time. By framing Reconstruction in general and the Fourteenth Amendment in particular as a racialized emergency, Justice Miller instituted a schema, which later justices picked up, that provided a way for the Court to make decisions in accord with the immense and swirling pressures it was facing at the time.

The case involved the constitutionality of an 1869 statute passed by the state legislature of Louisiana that attempted to bring sanitary reform to New Orleans by centralizing all slaughtering and butchering to one location. This facility was to be maintained by a private corporation. A group of butchers felt this statute deprived them of the ability to pursue their chosen occupation, depriving them of the "privileges and immunities" outlined in the Fourteenth Amendment. They further believed this constraint on their occupational choices relegated them to the status of involuntary servitude, which was deemed unlawful by the Thirteenth Amendment.[144] The lower federal courts had ruled the Slaughterhouse Act unconstitutional. But, in April 1873, the Supreme Court overturned the lower federal court ruling and sustained the Louisiana statute. The decision was five to four. Justice Samuel Miller wrote the majority opinion, which was joined by Justices Nathan Clifford, William Strong, Ward Hunt, and David Davis. Justice Stephen Field's dissenting opinion, which was joined by three other justices—Chief Justice Salmon Chase, Justice Joseph Bradley, and Justice Noah Swayne—would later become influential in its reading of the due process clause. This is not to imply that Miller's decision was irrelevant; it is simply to note that all did not embrace Miller's inventive decision.

It is also important to highlight the irony surrounding this case. The first case involving the Fourteenth Amendment, an Amendment mired in the history of slavery and racism, involved the civil rights of Southern white butchers. John Campbell, counsel for the white butchers, was former assistant secretary of war for the Confederacy and a staunch advocate of states' rights who was now calling for an expansive interpretation of rights, privileges, and immunities to be protected as never before by the federal courts. Thomas Durant, counsel for the racially integrated Reconstruction government in Louisiana, was arguing for a narrow interpretation of the Fourteenth Amendment.

In the majority decision, Miller's argument is divided into three major components: police powers, race, and privileges and immunities. He related each back to the overarching framework of federalism. Unfortunately, Miller did not schematize his arguments in any orderly fashion. In many ways, Miller's opinion reads like a shopping list, and it is unclear whether these components are interrelated or if they are completely separate. For example, it is uncertain whether his argument regarding police powers should take precedent over and/or is even related to his argument regarding race or privileges and immunities. It is also unclear whether Miller's argument hinges on any one aspect or if it should be read as one big mélange. The lack of synchrony between the three components of Miller's argument is most likely a result of a difference of opinions among the justices who sided with the majority.

In the majority decision, Miller argued that the Louisiana statute was within the purview of the police powers of the state of Louisiana. He also disagreed with the plaintiffs that the statute violated their privileges or immunities. The literature evaluating and contrasting Miller's conception of police powers, and privileges and immunities with the dissenting opinions is exhaustive and needs no further explication here.[145] But what has gone underanalyzed is exactly what is relevant to the issue at hand—and that is Miller's conception of race as it relates to the Fourteenth Amendment.[146] By focusing on Miller's conception of race, this by no means should be connoted as privileging Miller's conception of race as being more important than the other components of his decision. Rather, I focus on race because it factors into Waite's subsequent conception of race in *Cruikshank*, in addition to shedding light as to how Woods was later able to come up with a different formulation in *Harris*.

Those who have focused on Miller's comments on race have tended to regard *Slaughter-House* as the case that set the stage for dismantling Reconstruction, and they hold Justice Miller, author of the majority opinion, primarily responsible. The standard account is that Miller renounced federal rights enforcement for blacks and that subsequent Reconstruction cases, including *Cruikshank, Harris*, and *The Civil Rights Cases*, simply followed suit.[147] Recently, however, some legal scholars have subtly challenged this interpretation of Miller's decision.[148] These revisionist accounts argue that Miller sidestepped the issue of federal rights enforcement for blacks.[149] Although the revisionist account delves more into the content of Miller's decision than the prevailing view, both the standard and revisionist accounts are mistaken because each share the view that Miller did not provide a way for the federal government to engage in rights enforcement for blacks. Miller did, in fact, preserve the revolutionary potential of the Fourteenth Amendment. He did so by establishing a racialized emergency.

With regard to the Thirteenth, Fourteenth, and Fifteenth Amendments, Miller wrote the following in the majority decision:

> No one can fail to be impressed with the one pervading purpose found in them all, lying at the foundation at each, and without which none of them would have been even suggested; we mean the freedom of the slave race, the security and firm establishment of that freedom, and the protection of the newly-made freeman and citizen from the oppressions of those who had formerly exercised unlimited dominion over him . . . in any fair and just construction of any section or phrase of these amendments, it is necessary to look to the purpose which we have said was the pervading spirit of them all, the evil which they were designed to remedy.[150]

With the exception of blacks, the Fourteenth Amendment had not altered the traditional pattern of federalism. Had Miller positioned himself closer to a more expansive reading of the Fourteenth Amendment, it would have led him down a road that he found unjustifiable. In the majority decision for *Slaughter-House*, Miller asked,

> Was it the purpose of the 14th Amendment, by the simple declaration that no state should make or enforce any law which shall abridge the privileges and immunities of citizens of the United States, to transfer the security and protection of all the civil rights which we have mentioned, from the States to the Federal government?[151]

Miller went on to conclude that this interpretation "would constitute this court a perpetual censor upon all legislation of the States, on the civil rights of their own citizens"[152] and "we are convinced that no such results were intended by Congress which proposed these amendments nor by the States which ratified them."[153] He thus concluded:

> [W]e do not see in these amendments any purpose to destroy the main features of the general system. . . . Our statesmen have still believed that the existence of the States with powers for domestic and local government, including the regulation of civil rights—the rights of persons and of property—was essential to the perfect working of our complex form of government, though they have thought proper to impose additional limitations on the States, and to confer additional power on that of the Nation.[154]

Fearing a complete overhaul of federalism, Miller wanted to limit the applicability of the Fourteenth Amendment. One way in which Miller envisioned this limitation was by instituting an existential demarcation. Miller overturned the lower court ruling in part, not because of what the butchers were doing, but because of who the butchers were racially.

Comparing Miller's opinion with the dissenting opinions reinforces this claim that Miller was, in fact, trying to racialize the applicability of the Fourteenth Amendment. In addition to criticizing Miller's understanding of police powers, and privileges and immunities, the dissenting justices clearly disagreed with Miller's argument for the racialized application of the law. Bradley postulated a contrasting view of congressional intent that sanctioned the establishment of a new normal that went radically beyond antebellum conceptions of federalism. Bradley stated explicitly: "They [persons of the African race] may have been the primary cause of the amendment, but its language is general, embracing all citizens, and I think it was purposely so expressed."[155] Bradley elaborated further in more detail:

> The mischief to be remedied was not merely slavery and its incidents and consequences; but that spirit of insubordination and disloyalty to the National government. . . . The amendment was an attempt to give voice to a strong National yearning for that time and that condition of things, in which American citizenship should be a sure guaranty of safety, and in which every citizen of the United States might stand erect on every portion of its soil, in the full enjoyment of every right and privilege belonging to a freeman, without fear of violence or retribution.[156]

In the dissent, Swayne fully embraced this concept of a new normal. He was even more blunt than Bradley:

> The language employed [in the Reconstruction Amendments] is unqualified in its scope. . . . No distinction is intimated on account of race or color. . . . The protection provided was not intended to be confined to those of any particular race or class. . . . The construction adopted by the majority of my brethren is, to my judgment, much too narrow.[157]

This last statement by Swayne is instructive in that it refuted and thereby confirmed that Miller was, in fact, using race to limit the scope of the Reconstruction amendments.

Although Bradley and Swayne had a historical disagreement with Miller regarding congressional intent, Field had a more principled disagreement with Miller regarding equality and justice. Field was perhaps the most sympathetic to Miller's conception of race: "I was not prepared, nor am I yet, to give it the extent and force ascribed by council."[158] If Field stopped there, then it might have been more apropos for him to write a concurring opinion. But he did not. Field went on to say that "it is not confined to African slavery alone. It is general and universal in its application."[159] This is in line with Bradley's dissent. But, Field went on to argue that any selectivity was inherently discriminatory. He hearkened back to the congressional floor debates surrounding the Civil Rights Act of 1866, which is the direct antecedent to the Fourteenth Amendment. He quoted Senator Trumbull: "I take it that any statue which is not equal to all, and which deprives any citizen of civil rights, which are secured to other citizens, is an unjust encroachment upon his liberty."[160] According to Field, any differentiation, even if it is on behalf of an oppressed race that had been targeted selectively to be slaves, is discrimination.[161] If Congress had intended the amendments to be racially selective, Field argued that selectivity was inherently unconstitutional. Differing from and going beyond Bradley's argument for congressional intent, Field was addressing and critiquing directly Miller's conception of the racialized application of the law.

Miller was clearly advocating for a more selective approach than the dissenting justices. The dissenting justices provided a model of federalism that was more in line with the previous lower court decisions in establishing a new normal of centralizing power within the national government. Operating under such broad auspices, race was submerged within the broader rubric of centralization. In racializing who was eligible under the new Reconstruction amendments, Miller was trying to finesse federalism in such a way as to be aligned with the framers' intent of the Reconstruction amendments while also avoiding the kind of radical transformation for which the dissenting opinions were advocating. Although each dissenting justice critiqued Miller on different grounds, all seemed to agree that Miller was, in fact, arguing for a framework of selectively applying the law based on race.

It is important to note here that, although Miller was against completely unending federalism, he was not against all forms of federal intervention. In a letter dated February 6, 1866, Miller evinced support for a qualified degree of federal intervention:

We cannot in the face of the events that have occurred since the war trust the South with the power of governing the negro and Union white man without such guarantees in the federal Constitution as secure their protection. . . . Show me the first public address or meeting of Southern men in which the massacres of New Orleans or Memphis have been condemned or any general dissent shown at home at such conduct. You may say that there are two sides to those stories of Memphis and New Orleans. There may be two sides to the stories, but there was but one side in the party that suffered at both places, and the single truth which is undenied that not a rebel or secessionist was hurt in either case, while from thirty or fifty negroes and Union white men were shot down precludes all doubt as to who did it and why it was done.[162]

Justice Miller regarded the racial violence befalling the South during Reconstruction as something that could be squelched by the Republican Party in a short period of time. As one Republican supporter observed succinctly, "we never contemplated when we took the freed blacks under the protection of the North that the work was to be for an unlimited time."[163] Miller supported a temporary framework that gave Republican political officials exceptional powers. Although he was short on details, Miller did, in fact, articulate a legal framework that could accommodate these characteristics. He did so by conceiving of Reconstruction as a kind of "racial emergency."

Referring to the Fourteenth Amendment, Miller wrote in the *Slaughter-House* decision that "it is so clearly a provision for *that race and that emergency* [emphasis added], that a strong case would be necessary for its application to any other."[164] Emergency, in this regard, served as a boundary concept that delimited an extreme case in which the authorization of federal intervention was distinguished from politics as usual. In other words, the emergency signified the boundary where federal intervention into rights enforcement stopped and started. Miller's framing of the emergency regarded state enforcement of rights as the norm and the federal rights enforcement for blacks as the emergency.

To understand Miller's formulation of how this emergency worked, we need to delve further into his opinion in *Slaughter-House*. In the majority decision in *Slaughter-House*, Miller stated:

> [I]t is quite clear, then, that there is a citizenship of the United States, and a citizenship of a State, which are distinct from each other, and which depend upon different characteristics or circumstances of the individual.[165]

Many read this passage as a theory of dual citizenship. The concept of dual citizenship, which is also known as *dual federalism*, refers to the idea that there are rights proffered to citizens qua their status as Americans and that there are other rights proffered to citizens qua their status as New Yorkers, Californians, Alabamans, and so on. Critics of Miller regard this dual citizenship as a misnomer, because they interpret Miller as ranking the rights of citizens qua their status as members of a state so much that he rendered national citizenship meaningless.[166] Those less critical of

Miller regard him as simply providing a framework for dual citizenship without delineating the content of each.[167]

Most tend to disregard the last phrase of this famous passage regarding the different characteristics or circumstances of the individual.[168] But if we connect this last phrase with a previous statement he made about "that race and that emergency," a different interpretation emerges of what kind of dual citizenship Miller envisaged. Miller's use of the term *emergency*, in addition to his statements regarding two distinct citizenships, suggests a dualistic framework of jurisprudence that pivots on race. The dualism that I am extrapolating from Miller's decision is different from what most analysts have derived. Contrary to his critics, Miller was not stripping federal citizenship of any and all content. Contrary to more sympathetic analysts, Miller was not simply providing a framework for dual citizenship either. Rather, Miller was laying out a dualistic framework of jurisprudence for normal conditions and the emergency of race. His reference to race as an emergency hints at how this dualistic framework of jurisprudence was to operate. Although nonemergencies were to be handled by the traditional framework of state rights jurisprudence, the emergency of race triggered the activation of another framework of jurisprudence— namely, federal rights enforcement as outlined in the newly passed Reconstruction legislation. By treating race as an emergency, Miller regarded the Fourteenth Amendment like an emergency decree, bequeathing extraordinary power to the federal government that was to be used solely for the emergency of race.[169]

Miller's association of race with emergency is crucial in understanding how Miller could retain a conservative notion of American federalism along with a federal government strong enough to remedy the "evil" of racial oppression.[170] Although the normal state of affairs dictated a states' rights-centered theory of American federalism, Miller thought that this normal state of affairs should not constrain how an emergency functioned and is regulated. The "evil" of oppression that stemmed from slavery signaled an emergency that rendered the normal state of American federalism inoperable for a certain range of activities. Miller drew this distinction racially. If race was involved, then the federal government could possibly step in right away. According to Miller, if race was not involved, then "a strong case is necessary" for the federal government to intervene. By racializing the Fourteenth Amendment, Miller was able to retain a racially radical project while simultaneously preserving federalism and containing the power of the federal government to involve itself in all aspects of American lives.

Miller's conception of an emergency was similar to the one expounded in 1851 by Chief Justice of the Supreme Court Roger Taney in *Mitchell v. Harmony*.[171] The case involved the Doniphan raid during the war with Mexico. The plaintiff was a trader, whose wagons, mules, and goods were seized by the defendant, a lieutenant colonel of the U.S. Army. The Court upheld the jury's decision that found for the plaintiff. In the majority opinion, Taney wrote:

> It is impossible to define the particular circumstances of danger or necessity in which the power [of emergency] may be lawfully exercised. Every case must depend on its own circumstances. It is the emergency that gives the right, and the emergency must be shown to exist before the taking can be justified.[172]

Using a very similar logic as espoused by Taney, Justice Miller in *Slaughter-House* decided that an emergency was not shown to exist and thus ruled against the butchers. Had the butchers somehow related their case back to the "evil," which the Fourteenth Amendment was designed to remedy, they would have been more successful in activating the "provision for that race and that emergency." However, they were obviously unable to do so because they were white. In framing federal rights enforcement for blacks under this rubric of emergency, Miller provides the Court a degree of interpretive leeway that was in line with the revolutionary intention of Reconstruction, but is nevertheless flexible enough to stay in accord with the volatile political conditions surrounding Reconstruction at the time.

CRUIKSHANK: EXPANDING ON AND SUBSEQUENTLY EVACUATING OF THE RACIAL EMERGENCY

The judicial maneuverings in *Cruikshank* expounded on and subsequently confirmed the racialized emergency instituted by Miller in *Slaughter-House*, albeit in a way that exonerated judicial evasion egregiously. Although Justice Bradley, in his circuit court decision of *Cruikshank*, provided much-needed specification of Miller's racialized emergency, Justice Waite in his Supreme Court decision evacuated the racialized emergency of any substantive meaning while nevertheless retaining the structure instituted by Miller. By upholding Miller's framework of a racialized emergency, the Supreme Court in *Cruikshank* was able to close its eyes to racial violence while simultaneously paying lip service to it.

U.S. v. Cruikshank was in response to the Colfax Massacre.[173] The Colfax Massacre of 1873 occurred in Colfax, Louisiana, after the escalation of a series of incidents following the failed coup made by the Fusionists against the Republicans in the 1872 elections. Tensions heightened to the point where a few white Republicans and many blacks occupied a courthouse in Grant Parish to prevent another coup. A mob consisting largely of Confederate veterans attacked the courthouse on April 13. The mob surrounded the occupied building and not only hunted down and shot blacks who tried to retreat, but also the mob shot blacks who were waving white flags of surrender. Three whites and anywhere from sixty-two to eighty-one blacks died. General Sheridan described the event in Colfax as an act of "terrorism."[174] On June 16, 1873, the federal grand jury in New Orleans indicted ninety-seven defendants. Each defendant was accused of 32 violations of the Enforcement Act of 1870. Of the ninety-seven defendants, nine were selected to go to trial. The jury acquitted one and failed to reach a verdict on the rest. The remaining eight were retried; three were found guilty and five were acquitted.

In his circuit court opinion in *Cruikshank*, Justice Bradley upheld Miller's framework of racial emergency. Bradley not only picked up on Miller's dualistic framework, but also provided further specification regarding what aspects of race should be under federal protection. With regard to the Reconstruction amendments, Bradley stated:

> The war of race, whether it assumes the dimensions of civil strife or domestic violence, whether carried on in a guerrilla or predatory form, or by private combinations, or even by private outrage or intimidation, is subject to the jurisdiction of the government of the United States; and when any atrocity is committed which may be assigned to this cause it may be punished by the laws and in the courts of the United States; but any outrages, atrocities, or conspiracies, whether against the colored race or the white race, which do not flow from this cause, but spring from the ordinary felonious or criminal intent which prompts to such unlawful acts, are not within the jurisdiction of the states.... Unless this distinction be made we are driven to one of two extremes— either that congress can never interfere where the state laws are unobjectionable; however remiss the state authorities may be in executing them, and, however much a proscribed race may be oppressed; or that congress may pass an entire body of municipal law for the protection of person and property within the states, to operate concurrently with the state laws, for the protection and benefit of a particular class of the community. This fundamental principle, I think, applies to the amendments.[175]

The dualistic distinction Bradley made between the war of race and ordinary felonies is further specification of what Miller had introduced in *Slaughter-House*. Bradley not only provided confirmation that Miller was, in fact, instituting a dualistic framework of jurisprudence that was predicated on race, but also Bradley built on it in the hope of making it more viable. Although Miller instituted the racialized emergency, Bradley specified what racialized acts were to be within the proviso of this emergency. Bradley divided the racialized acts into two major categories: "ordinary felonies" that fell under state jurisdiction and activities associated with "the war of race" that activated federal intervention.[176] By building on and further elucidating what Miller meant by "that race and that emergency," Bradley not only validated that the Supreme Court was, in fact, treating the Fourteenth Amendment as an emergency decree with respect to federal rights enforcement for blacks, but also he provided a further firewall that distinguished the exception from the norm.

Attorney General Amos Akerman shared a very similar sentiment with Bradley. Akerman was the head of the Department of Justice from 1870 to 1871. He considered the actions of the Klan to have "amounted to war, and cannot be effectually crushed on any other theory."[177] Akerman believed that "unless the people become used to the exercise of these powers now, while the national spirit is still warm with the glow of the late war . . . the 'state rights' spirit may grow troublesome again."[178]

Bradley's circuit court decision was subsequently appealed to the Supreme Court. The Supreme Court, under the auspices of Chief Justice Morrison Waite, reversed Bradley's circuit court opinion based primarily on its interpretation of the Fourteenth Amendment. The Chief Justice himself delivered the opinion of the Court, thereby adding further confirmation that the Supreme Court supported this decision. Waite made three general criticisms regarding the charges made against the defendants: (1) the charges fell under the jurisdiction of state governments, (2) the charges were too vague to be indictable, and (3) according to the Fourteenth Amendment, the federal government is primarily involved when individual states deny rights to citizens, not of "one citizen against another."[179]

If Waite stopped there, then the conventional wisdom that Waite simply narrowed the conception of state action would be correct. However, he then went on to note, "[T]here is no allegation that this was done because of their race or color of the persons conspired against."[180] This begs the question: If the Fourteenth Amendment does not cover private action, why even bring up the matter of race? Is not any and every action of one citizen against another, even if it involves racial discrimination, outside federal jurisdiction? In the next paragraph he hinted at why he brought this up:

> No question arises under the Civil Rights Act of April 9, 1866 (14 Stat. 27), which is intended for the protection of citizens of the United States in the enjoyment of certain rights, without discrimination on account of race, color, or previous condition of servitude, because, as has already been stated, it is nowhere alleged in these counts that the wrong contemplated against the rights of these citizens was on account of their race or color.[181]

It was this reference to the Civil Rights Act of 1866 that Waite left the possibility open for the federal government to have jurisdiction over private action if rights were deprived on account of race or color. Thus, it would seem to be the case that the Civil Rights Act of 1866 has a broader understanding of state action than that under the Fourteenth Amendment. Waite did not attempt any reconciliation of this difference, nor did he conclude that one negated the other. He was not compelled to because it was extraneous to the case at hand. By distinguishing the Civil Rights Act and the Fourteenth Amendment without reconciling the differences between the two, Waite was thus able to make a narrow decision regarding state action without necessarily foreclosing the possibility of a broader, racialized interpretation of state action.

Waite then went on to acknowledge one aspect in which the federal government has expanded its power:

> The right to vote in the States comes from the States but the right of exemption from the prohibited discrimination comes from the United States. The first has not been granted or secured by the Constitution of the United States, but the last has been.[182]

Unfortunately this was all for naught, according to Waite, because this "right of exemption" was not explicitly articulated by the prosecutors: "We may suspect that race was the cause of hostility, but it is not so averred. . . . Every thing essential must be charged positively and not inferentially."[183] The connotation of this quote was that race was an essential legal category and, had it been averred, the Court might have ruled differently. According to legal historian Pamela Brandwein, "it is plausible to conclude from [Waite's] statements that he would permit prosecution on racial motive, as long as that motive could be established."[184]

Further evidence supporting this reading of Waite's decision can be found in his letters to Hugh Bond. After *Cruikshank*, Circuit Judge Hugh Bond teased Waite for making a "Dred" decision in the enforcement case, referring to the infamous *Dred Scott* case in which Chief Justice Taney ruled that people of African descent could never be citizens of the United States.[185] In response, Waite wrote, "Sorry for the 'Dred,' but to my mind there was no escape."[186] In other words, Waite was apologizing for making a racist decision that the Court would probably later regret. Yet he justified his decision by saying that his hands were tied. In an ironic twist of fate, because race was not mentioned, he had no other choice but to make a *Dred*-like decision.

His obfuscating remarks regarding the Civil Rights Act of 1866 and "the right of exemption from prohibited discrimination" suggested that there might have existed a loophole for private acts that were predicated on racial discrimination. If Waite had not made those remarks regarding race, then that would have meant that his comments regarding private action covered all acts of one citizen against another. By mentioning race, he made an exception out of it. Parsing out Waite's argument illuminates the ways in which he made very definitive statements regarding constitutional interpretation while nonetheless subtly leaving open the possibility of federal action if there was racial intent. Although he did not indicate exactly what and how federal action would look like, he nonetheless did provide the possibility for it when it came to issues regarding racial animus.

In this regard, Waite did not repudiate directly Bradley's circuit court opinion regarding the racial emergency, although he overturned it. Rather than address Bradley's circuit court opinion directly, Waite chose instead to attack the presumptions made by Bradley. Bradley's concept of race might have been correct if the prosecutors had made the charges "positively and not inferentially." However, because—according to Waite—they had not, he was able to reverse the circuit court decision and still provide for the framework proffered by Bradley in his circuit court decision. In sidestepping the issue of federal intervention when it comes to matters of race, Waite thereby provided for it.

Although *Slaughter-House* was evaluating the constitutionality of a statute and *Cruikshank* was, primarily, examining the scope of federal jurisdiction, each nonetheless conceptualized race in a very similar way. Both treated specific racialized acts as an exception to normal operating procedure. This dualistic framework within which each was operating does not preclude constitutional interpretation, but it did require constant provisos regarding to which framework they were referring. For the most part, judges have been concerned primarily with what constituted the standard measures of jurisdiction, and allude only briefly to the exceptional framework that was predicated on "that race and that emergency." However brief, these allusions were nonetheless important because they acknowledged a different set of standards by which certain matters of race were to be adjudicated. The consistent nature of these allusions across cases indicated they were not casual, insignificant passages that could be dismissed easily. Rather, they were essential statements regarding the non-inclusion of a specific range of activities. Although questions regarding exactly what this range of activities was, how the activities were to be adjudicated, and how they related to all other matters were unsettled, the unresolved tenor was not indicative of the triviality of such matters. In fact, it was the very opposite.

U.S. V. HARRIS AND THE CIVIL RIGHTS CASES: ENDING THE RACIAL EMERGENCY

U.S. v. Harris and *The Civil Rights Cases* reflect a jettisoning of the racialized emergency based on the premise that the emergency was over and "normal" jurisprudence

had returned. Although Justice Woods's opinion in *Harris* and Justice Bradley's o-
pinion in *The Civil Rights Cases* might at first appear hypocritical, considering their
previous respective opinions in *Hall* and *Cruikshank*, in light of the framework of a
racialized emergency, it extended the criticism beyond individual hypocrisy and
raised a deeper structural issue of how to address racial violence during "normal"
times. Linking racial violence with emergency made such acts as lynchings that
occur during normal times as beyond the pale of normal jurisprudence.

In *U.S. v. Harris*, the Court reached a similar verdict as in *Cruikshank*, but for different reasons.[187] The case involved Roosevelt Harris, who led an armed mob that
included at least 19 people. The mob broke into a Tennessee jail, captured four black
prisoners, and subsequently beat all four of them, lynching one. They were indicted
under the Ku Klux Klan Act of 1871, otherwise known as the Force Act of 1871.
Writing the majority opinion, Justice William Woods threw out Section 2 of the Ku
Klux Klan Act of 1871 because "the section of the law under consideration is directed exclusively against the action of private persons, without reference to the laws
of the states, or their administration by the officers of the state, we are clear in the
opinion that it is not warranted by any clause in the fourteenth amendment to the
constitution."[188] He cited previous cases such as *Slaughter-House* and *Cruikshank* as
precedent, but he did so in a way that was out of context. Woods's references to these
cases were limited to statements that alluded to the normal operations of federalism
without ever mentioning the references that described the emergency framework of
race. The only time he mentioned race was in reference to voting and the Fifteenth
Amendment, thus ignoring the distinction that Miller made between "that race and
that emergency," and that Bradley made between the "war of race" and "outrages
against the colored race that spring from ordinary felonious or criminal intent."
Woods never even entertained a racialized reading of the Fourteenth Amendment,
and thus left the dualistic framework created by Miller and expounded by Bradley
untouched.

With regard to *Harris*, the fact that Woods wrote the majority opinion in *Harris*
is particularly telling because he penned the decision in *U.S. v. Hall*.[189] Woods's o-
pinion in *Hall* is completely counter to his opinion in *Harris*, in which he states,
"the only obligation resting upon the United States is to see that the states do not
deny the right. This the [fourteenth] amendment guaranties, and no more."[190] The
fact that Woods could pen both *Hall* and *Harris*, cases that seem at odds paradoxically, suggests that the inconsistency does not lie in the differential makeup of the
court and/or the ideological proclivities of the judges per se, but rather in the political context in which these cases occurred.

That same year, the Supreme Court decided on *The Civil Rights Cases*. Like Justice
Woods in *Harris*, Justice Bradley in *Civil Rights Cases* made a decision that seems to

run contrary to his previous stance. Here it became clear that, not only had there been a racial emergency, but that it was now over. The *Civil Rights Cases* struck down the public accommodations provisions in the Civil Rights Act of 1875 because they were regarded as invalid under the Fourteenth Amendment. In the majority o-pinion, Justice Bradley stated:

> [T]here must be some stage in the process of his elevation when he [the Negro] takes the rank of a mere citizen, and ceases to be the special favorite of the laws, and when his rights as a citizen, or a man, are to be protected in the ordinary modes by which other men's rights are protected.[191]

What Bradley seemed to be alluding to was his circuit court opinion in *Cruikshank* in which he referred to "the war of race and how that is subject to the jurisdiction of the government of the United States, and is different than ordinary felonious or criminal intent."[192] Before *The Civil Rights Cases,* blacks were "the special favorite of the laws" in the form of being afforded federal protection when the "war of race" broke out. No longer. After *The Civil Rights Cases,* the war of race effectively col-lapsed back into ordinary jurisprudence.

The four Supreme Court cases that are being examined here coincide with crucial elections, each of which signaled a directional shift in the political support for Re-construction. *Slaughter-House* followed the 1872 elections, which signaled the period of political uncertainty when the fate of Reconstruction was unclear; *Crui-kshank* followed the 1874 elections, which indicated the period of backtracking when the political will to continue Reconstruction was waning but not yet extin-guished; and *Harris* and *The Civil Rights Cases* followed the fateful 1876 elections, which marked a period of political surrender when it became clear there was very little political will to fight racial violence. Throughout it all, the Court maintained its position for a congressionally led plan for Reconstruction. In light of the political volatility surrounding Reconstruction, the Supreme Court wanted to create a frame-work that could adjust accordingly, and thus rendered Reconstruction an emer-gency that made race an "essential" factor in interpreting the Reconstruction amend-ments. As mentioned earlier, an emergency tends to be politically activated, and the contents, borders, and scope tend to be relegated to the judiciary to decide. In this particular emergency, the boundaries were, in part, drawn racially. More specifically, it had to do with whether race should play a factor in interpreting the Reconstruc-tion amendments. Following this logic, after the emergency was lifted, then race was no longer "essential" and judicial decision making reverted back to what it was before the emergency. By 1877, the emergency had been lifted.[193] In this case, lifting the emergency meant making race a nonessential factor in interpreting the

Constitution, and thus explains why Woods was able to make race irrelevant when interpreting the Fourteenth Amendment. This differential role of race based on the context of whether there was an emergency explains why Woods had a different understanding of race than Waite or Miller. It also provided a way for the Court to be legally coherent while nevertheless making inconsistent decisions.

THE TRAGIC LEGACY OF THE RACIAL EMERGENCY

In a 1903 case involving racial discrimination in voter registration, Justice Holmes wrote in the majority opinion, "It seems to us impossible to grant the equitable relief which is asked . . . the court has little practical power to deal with the people of the state in a body."[194] The defeatist tone that Holmes took was indicative of the disappearance of the revolutionary potential that was Reconstruction. One of the greatest extensions of rights for blacks was done under the auspices of an emergency and, as such, made it that much harder to reactivate and thus left blacks susceptible to the vicissitudes of "normal" jurisprudence.

A key characteristic that often gets overlooked was that the Court did not eliminate completely the possibility for federal rights enforcement for blacks. Although the emergency was lifted, there was no reason why another emergency could not be reinstituted. The whole purpose of instituting an emergency was for the Court to be able to accommodate whatever Congress wanted to do. Pamela Brandwein has a somewhat similar view of the Reconstruction Court. Contrary to the standard argument that the Court revoked of the rights of blacks completely, Brandwein argued that "the intertextual study of Justice Bradley's language demonstrates that the *Civil Rights Cases* was not a definitive abandonment of blacks, and that the decision left open constitutional possibilities that scholars and jurists have presumed closed."[195] By resurrecting the "hierarchy of rights" concept, Brandwein showed succinctly how it was "possible to ridicule public accommodation claims while expressing commitment to the protection of black physical safety."[196] In the *Civil Rights Cases*, she went on to conclude that the Court was "limiting the application of state neglect concepts to rights a consensus regarded as fundamental."[197] In other words, the *Civil Rights Cases* delineated which rights of blacks could be curtailed formally and hence no longer considered an emergency. Those rights that are not fundamental in nature, such as the "right of the negro to see the ballet dance," could be outlawed formally and hence were no longer subject to emergency provisions. However, the right to "pillage and murder was more precious and beneficent privilege," and thus could not be sanctioned formally and hence was still subject to being an emergency.[198]

What Brandwein failed to mention, however, was that although the *Civil Rights Cases* did not represent "a definitive abandonment," it nonetheless did signal the difficulties it would have in returning to those rights that could not be outlawed formally but could be accommodated informally. The horrendous legacy of lynchings confirms this. During this period, the Supreme Court, for the most part, did not intervene.

CONCLUSION

In 1887, fourteen years after the *Slaughter-House* decision came out, Justice Miller gave an address to the Law Alumni of Michigan University during which he reflected back on his decision. Not only did he emphasize how the public sentiment following *Slaughter-House* "accepted it with great unanimity" and that "no attempt to overrule or disregard this elementary decision has been made," but also that "it may be considered now as settled that, with the *exception* [emphasis added] of the specific provisions in them for the protection of the personal rights of the citizens and people of the United States."[199] Miller's comments suggest that he did not consider *Slaughter-House* a sign of judicial activism, but rather a decision of judicial moderation. He also suggested that there were certain aspects that had yet to be reconciled. This claim for moderation and open-endedness is not quite aligned with traditional accounts of Miller, who either see him as a judicial activist or as someone who closed the door on Reconstruction.

This chapter refutes the claim that the Court's behavior during Reconstruction can be explained solely by the ideologies of the respective judges, and provides an immanent critique of the viewpoint that argues the Court was responding solely to the political changes going on during Reconstruction. Whether it was Woods's reversal in *Harris* or Bradley's reversal in *The Civil Rights Cases*, there was no direct correlation between the political ideologies of the judges and their subsequent decisions. The Court was trying to stay in line with the changing political winds at the time, but to presume the Court was a complete hostage to those winds would strip essential qualities such as stare decisis of any standing and thus call into question the very nature of jurisprudence. Rather than fall prey to the false legal–political dichotomy, the Court instead tried to accommodate all the pressures it was facing. The framework of racial emergency that Miller introduced, Waite systematized, and Woods discontinued was the most holistic approach in that it took into account the volatile political conditions of the time and the legal demands for coherency.

As mentioned earlier, the importance of race in Miller's decision in *Slaughter-House* is unclear, and by no means am I trying to elevate the impact of his comments on race as they relate to that particular decision. However tenuous the impact of race may or may not have been in Miller's decision, it was nevertheless something that Bradley elucidated and Waite drew on and subsequently elevated in *Cruikshank*.

It became the lynchpin by which Waite was able to maintain legal coherency while also addressing political expediency. It also explains how Woods in *Harris* could provide a discontinuous interpretation in a legally viable way. In other words, however relevant Miller's framework of racial emergency was in *Slaughter-House*, it nonetheless legally rounded the political square that the Court would face after *Slaughter-House*.

By establishing a racial emergency that could delegate responsibility to quell racial violence without necessarily relinquishing sovereign authority, the Court also helped facilitate the central state by creating a legal framework that marginalized the biggest impediment to state centralization. The development of national administrative capacities, or strengthening of the state in key areas, was predicated on the withdrawal from rights enforcement for blacks. These other aspects of state development would probably not have arisen had they been intertwined with a concomitant expansion in federal rights enforcement for blacks.[200] Taking it one step further, by instituting an emergency and then manipulating it to obscure its continuing authority, the Court can be said to have encouraged the racial lynchings that occurred in the South after Reconstruction. As the U.S. Commission on Civil Rights reported in 1965, "every assault or murder which goes unpunished reinforces the legacy of violence—the knowledge that it's dangerous for a Negro to depart from traditional ways."[201]

They have promised us law and abandoned us to anarchy.[1]

—FREDERICK DOUGLASS

How could liberalism take up a struggle against such an indefatigable foe?
The solution was, first, to localize terror, and second, to externalize it.[2]

—COREY ROBIN

4

Constitutional Anarchy: 1883–1966

INTRODUCTION

In 1922, NAACP Secretary James Weldon Johnson described the legal vacuum that resulted from the fallout from Reconstruction: "American citizens in southern states where lynching prevails found themselves in the anomalous position of being residents in states which refused to guarantee them trial by due process of law when accused of crime and citizens of a government which confessed its inability to do so."[3] It was not completely anomalous however. It was only for a select, discernible few. In the words of Oliver Cox, "it is a special form of mobbing—mobbing directed against a whole people."[4] In this case, it was "Negroes who are extralegal, extrademocratic objects."[5] In the previous chapter, I demonstrated how the Supreme Court instituted an emergency to activate federal rights enforcement for blacks; in this chapter I examine the interregnum period, which is marked by what political scientist Robert Dahl has termed an "active policy of non-enforcement."[6] Lynchers, during the late nineteenth century to the mid twentieth century, were able to operate fairly unencumbered by the law. After Reconstruction, the Court schematized the active policy of nonenforcement through what I term *constitutional anarchy*. Constitutional anarchy is a further elaboration of Dahl's initial concept that draws out in more detail exactly how this policy was established, maintained, and eventually dismantled. Drawing from Ernst Fraenkel's model of the dual state and Gerald Neuman's concept of anomalous zones, constitutional anarchy illuminates how the United States carved out legally bounded regions of lawlessness.[7] The operation of constitutional anarchy depended primarily on the federal government's active nonenforcement of the law and, secondarily, on local officials. It was as if the federal laws that pertained to lynchings were placed in a prolonged holding pattern. The South did not wrest power away from the federal government. Instead, stopping short of formal constitutional nullification, the federal government provided the South the autonomy to manage its own racial affairs. Constitutional anarchy is intended to reveal the federal government's providing for autonomy while nevertheless retaining authority.

This chapter focuses mainly on the theoretical construction and historical operation of constitutional anarchy, and it is divided into three parts. The first part examines the emergence of the word *lynchings* to describe racial violence following Reconstruction. The second part outlines the theoretical construct of constitutional anarchy. Last, the third part analyzes constitutional anarchy historically, at its height. Examining underappreciated Supreme Court cases such as *Moore v. Dempsey*[8] and *Logan v. U.S.*,[9] I shed light on how the Supreme Court's primary focus during this period was on containment, and maintaining a distinction between the higher jurisdictional state and the anomalous zones. In so doing, the Court was not only able to maintain at least the allure of "a steady, upright, and impartial administration of the laws,"[10] but also to retain jurisdiction over the jurisdiction of the anomalous zones. In other words, by instituting constitutional anarchy, the Court was able to demarcate the higher jurisdictional state and the anomalous zones, thus allowing the federal government to evade culpability while retaining authority.

THE RACIALIZED TEMPORALITY OF LYNCHING

The characterization of racial violence as lynchings represented the change in the modus operandi and modus vivendi of racial violence after Reconstruction. Lynchings represented the depoliticization of racial violence that occurred as a consequence of a partisan shift to bipartisanship, the federal government's strategic shift to focus on racial violence that pertained to voting, and the discursive shift toward protecting Southern women. The very act of depoliticizing racial violence was, in and of itself, a highly politicized act—one on which this book focuses.

Although there is evidence of lynchings occurring as far back as colonial America, the association of lynchings with racial violence in the South did not emerge until after Reconstruction. Historian Christopher Waldrep found "changes in language mark the difference between the Reconstruction era's revolutionary violence and that found in the Gilded Age"[11] and that "the word lynching appears only rarely in the extensive record of Reconstruction violence."[12] He goes on to reason that this was "because white societal support for the killings was not yet solid or beyond dispute."[13] Waldrep's point regarding the disagreement among whites about the use of violence is backed by historical testimonials that were made during the early period of Reconstruction that point to white Southerners' disinclination for violence. George H. Thomas, Major General of the U.S. Army, testified to Congress that "a great many of [Southerners] say that they failed in their attempt to gain their independence of the United States, and that they now wish to be quiet citizens of the country."[14] Joseph Stiles, a citizen from Virginia, confirmed this in his testimonial to Congress: "[Southerners] are anxious to see peace and quiet restored to the country."[15] Colonel Lewis Merrill observed, "in all my conversations with people, I have been met constantly with the palliative remark in regards to these [Klan] outrages—conceding that they are wrong and all that."[16] Congressional testimonials and military reports thus seem to suggest a strong proclivity against violence of any sort.

During these early stages of Reconstruction, racial violence was characterized in a very partisan manner. Historian Eric Foner described the Klan during this period "as a military force serving the interests of the Democratic party."[17] Historian Allen Trelease labeled them "a counter-revolutionary device to combat the Republican Party and Congressional Reconstruction policy."[18] And historian Richard Zuczek depicted the Klan more pointedly as an insurgent group that had engaged in guerilla warfare.[19] This highly partisan characterizations were also considered to be a matter of the utmost urgency because of the violation that it represented. Representative James Wilson of Iowa elaborates this point succinctly: "The absolute rights of individuals may be resolved into the right of personal security, the right of personal liberty, and the right to acquire and enjoy property. These rights have been justly considered, and frequently declared, by the people of this country, to be natural, inherent, and inalienable."[20] Pamela Brandwein noted that at this time, "Congressmen did not utilize a distinction between 'political' and 'racial' violence because they aimed to reach unpunished violence against blacks and white Republicans."[21] According to this view, racial violence fit under this rubric of right of personal security, which was natural, inherent, and inalienable.

Around 1875, the tenor surrounding racial violence started to change. Eric Foner observed that "violent bands in 1875 operated without disguise, as if to flaunt their lack of fear of legal reprisal."[22] Waldrep noted the same thing: "Gilded Age lynchers acted with community approval, rarely donning the masks and robes favored by the Klan. Rather than skulking in the dark, they killed their victims in broad daylight and posed for photographs."[23] Racial violence seemed to have become acceptable. It is at this point, according to Waldrep, when "the white population seized power and rallied itself into a racial bloc,"[24] that the depiction of racial violence started to become associated with lynching. Although there is disagreement about how united this "racial bloc" actually was, it was nonetheless the case that most white Southern-ers were passively compliant. Historian Gunnar Myrdal depicted the racial consen-sus in less glowing terms: "[F]ew whites of the middle and upper classes in the South have expressed themselves as in favor of lynch justice. But equally few have pretended that they would take any personal risks to hinder a lynching, and they make no effort to punish the lynchers."[25] Howard Odum described the consensus in some-what starker terms: "[T]the great body of people who are horrified by lynching . . . are afraid to protest."[26] However passive this compliance, it nonetheless seems to be the case that "more than the Reconstruction Klan, lynchers credibly claimed to act on behalf of all whites."[27]

As mentioned, when this consensus was achieved, the modus operandi and modus vivendi changed. Racial violence was characterized increasingly in apolitical terms that transcended partisanship, and was alluded to in ways that evoked popular sov-ereignty. What had been a partisan tool that operated to the benefit of the Democra-tic Party had somehow morphed into something that transcended partisanship en-tirely. There emerged a flourishing of accounts of racial violence as primarily, a result of psychological theories of aggression,[28] violation of social/racial norms,[29] and/or responses to economic downturns.[30]

The justifications for these acts changed as well. James Cutler concluded, "popular justification is the sine qua non of lynching. It is this fact that distinguishes lynching, on the one hand, from assassination and murder, and on the other hand, from insur-rection and open warfare."[31] In the United States, "The people consider themselves a law unto themselves. They make the laws; therefore they can unmake them."[32] An article in the *Duke Law Journal* summed it up the best: "[I]t is arguable that [the lynch mob] invades this province of the state and, acting in loco reipublicae, dis-places the state organs as political 'sovereign.'"[33] Referencing post-Reconstruction acts of racial violence as lynchings invokes this folk tradition of situating particular acts of violence as an act of the constituent power, thereby transcending ordinary politics and becoming immune from the vicissitudes of the political. What had been previously understood to be a highly partisan act done by a few for the sake of a par-ticular party and thus deserving of rebuke, turned into a sovereign act done by the People for the sake of the community and thus was seemingly immune to review.

Even staunch opponents of racial violence confirmed the change. In an 1894 letter titled "Why is the Negro lynched?," Frederick Douglass wrote how

> there were three distinct periods of persecutions of Negroes in the South, and three distinct sets of excuses for their persecution. They have come along pre-cisely in the order they were most needed. Each was made to fit its special place. First, you remember, as I have said, it was insurrection. When that wore out,

Negro supremacy became the excuse. When that was worn out, then came the charge of assault upon defence-less women . . . this new charge has come at the call of new conditions. . . . It is a crime that places him outside of the pale of the law.[34]

Douglass's tripartite schematization of racial violence suggests a degree of change and continuity. Each period connotes not only a different goal, but also a different relationship with the law and politics. The first period associated with insurrection was trying to overthrow the law and was thus prepolitical. The second period, which was characterized as Negro supremacy, was trying to dominate within the law and was thus working completely within the political. The third period, associated with defenseless women, was operating outside the pale of the law and hence was apolitical. To be "outside the pale of the law" carried an apolitical taint that is in direct contrast with the previous, more politicized iterations of the previous two periods of insurrection and Negro supremacy.

Waldrep's emphasis on consensus and Douglass's depiction of lynchings as apolitical are intimately interrelated. Reconstruction violence was understood to be highly political if only because it seemed to operate in a highly partisan fashion. Post-Reconstruction violence was characterized as apolitical—in part because it seemed to operate independently of any partisan advantage and because its modus vivendi changed from being a divisive, partisan act that stifled opposition to a unifying, social act that suppressed insubordination.

Although lynchings are often characterized in apolitical terms, it is important to note that this was a result of political choices.[35] The white consensus around racial violence did not coalesce instantaneously. It happened incrementally, and federal efforts to combat racial violence also contributed unintentionally to the depoliticization of racial violence. During the early stages of Reconstruction, the federal government engaged in a broad attack against racial violence.[36] As federal support for federal rights enforcement for blacks appeared to dissipate, as evidenced by the vacillating behavior of President Grant, Congress, and the Court, many noted a corresponding change of behavior among the Klan. The political wavering provided a signal to racist extremists that "they could take their victims without incrimination."[37] According to James McGovern, "[O]verall, it is estimated that only 0.8 percent of lynchings in the United States were followed by criminal conviction of the lyncher."[38]

As the political and legal will to protect blacks from violence began to waver, the remaining Republicans who still wanted to maintain some semblance of federal rights enforcement narrowed their attention only to those acts of racial violence that pertained to voting. From a political and legal point of view, this made sense. Political historian Pamela Brandwein notes how "protection of black voting rights was the most that regular Republicans like [Senator William E.] Chandler could achieve" and also that U.S. attorneys "preferred bringing cases they were more likely to win."[39] She goes on to conclude that this strategy "was not a definitive or wholesale abandonment of black rights . . . black voters remained significant players."[40] Although it was not a wholesale abandonment, it was a definitive partial abandonment of black rights, particularly those acts of violence that did not pertain to voting.

This instrumental shift signaled the abandonment of the fight against the more pervasive forms of racial violence and muddied the nature of racial violence. Although the choice to narrow efforts to voting was understandably instrumental and strategic, it nevertheless opened up the question of the status of racial violence that did not pertain to voting. If the only aspect of racial violence worthy of federal intervention was that associated with voting, then that would seem to suggest that racial violence that was not associated with voting was something altogether different. Although the right of personal security was considered inalienable, after the Compromise of 1877, racial violence seemed to have become disaggregated and displaced into the categories otherwise known as *social* and *political*. Unlike before, when the right to personal security seemed to be a natural, inherent, and inalienable right, it seemed that the right to personal security was inalienable only if it related to voting. In narrowing its efforts to voting- related acts of racial violence, the federal government ostensibly grafted racial violence that was not related to voting to the social realm that is oftentimes characterized as being apolitical. Pamela Brandwein elaborates on the difference between the social and political realm: "[T]he debate reveals both pragmatic and principled efforts to differentiate between a pre[-] or extrapolitical realm—that is, society—and one subject to legal regulation—that is, politics. While the former is ruled by nature or individual choice, the latter entailed state intervention, itself subject to the principles of federalism."[41] But as Ashraf Rushdy points out, the distinction between social and political obscures more than clarifies: "it is also worth considering the degree to which lynchings were motivated by political concerns – both the specific concerns with black accumulation of wealth or electoral power, or the general concern of the threats to white supremacy."[42] The false dichotomy that had been constructed between the political violence that is commonly associated with elections and the apolitical social violence that is commonly associated with lynchings might be incoherent conceptually, but it was nevertheless viable instrumentally for those who wanted to salvage some semblance of federal rights enforcement. However much unintended, this strategy contributed further to the mischaracterization of lynchings as apolitical.

Although there is an argument to be made that racial violence should not be differentiated regardless of whether it was related to voting, the federal government and subsequent analyses of violence nevertheless distinguished different acts of racial violence in a manner that overemphasized violent acts related to voting and underemphasized the more prevalent acts of violence not related directly to voting.[43] Tolnay and Beck chronicle the different reasons given for black lynchings and, of the eighty-one reasons given, only two were related to voting. They also document how lynchings related to voting were virtually nonexistent.[44] When the split between the political nature of electoral violence and the apolitical nature of lynchings was made, each followed a somewhat different timing and historical trajectory. The apolitical nature of lynchings was settled politically with the Compromise of 1877 and re-solved judicially in 1883 whereas the political nature of electoral violence was still being debated.[45] Although electoral violence did not constitute a significant amount of racial violence after Reconstruction, it nonetheless has gotten an inordinate amount of attention because it was one of the last vestiges of federal intervention.[46] Because the federal government divided these acts, it is important to distinguish be-tween the two because they have operated somewhat differently.[47] This book is not intended to be a correction of other accounts that examine the federal government's role in electoral violence, but rather as a supplement to those accounts that include other acts of racial violence that have not gotten sufficient attention.

By the beginning of the twentieth century, partial abandonment turned into wholesale denial. Racial violence tended to be unworthy of political debate both analytically and normatively. For example, when the Dyer antilynching bill reached the Senate, Senate Democrats not only filibustered, but they refused even to talk about any of the contents. Claudine Ferrell wrote that proponents for lynchings would "ignore legitimate arguments, analogies, and theories and to avoid substan-tive issues that worked against local rule and white supremacy."[48] It was not just Democrats. According to NAACP Director Walter White, "Republicans were apa-thetic to the point of cowardice."[49] Lynchings were beyond reproach. When the po-litical dust surrounding Reconstruction finally settled, the political strategy thus seemed to be to deprive racial violence of any political content.

The use of the term *lynchings* reflects the role reversal of the political that was front and center during Reconstruction. Racial violence was depoliticized, in part, because it no longer seemed to serve partisan interests, Republicans narrowed their attention only to those acts that were related to voting, and it operated under the guise of protecting Southern women, thereby relegating every other act of racial violence to the social realm. Although the shape, scope, and activity of racial vio-lence after Reconstruction is of a different nature than what occurred during Re-construction, to disavow post-Reconstruction violence of any political content is to mischaracterize what essentially was a political settlement. Characterizing racial vi-olence as "lynchings" connotes a political move made to depict post-Reconstruction racial violence in a manner that not only absolves political authorities of any responsibility, but also presumes lynchings operate completely outside the realm of the political.[50] To characterize post-Reconstruction violence as apolitical hence obscures the political consensus on the subject. Post-Reconstruction violence was highly political in that many political officials, across partisan lines, agreed to not intervene. Whether it was invoking claims regarding popular sovereignty or refusing to talk about it, political authorities often waged a strategy of misdirection and deflection.[51] Preventing the federal government from interfering with lynchings was an issue that carried bipartisan support. Stripping lynchings of political content was one of the reasons for its persistence, and was itself a political act. Unlike Reconstruction, during which racial violence was operating in part to sway political matters, lynchings operated in a manner that was circumscribed by the political. It went from an act that helped shape the political to an act that was being shaped by the political. To understand the political nature of lynchings, it is important to problematize lynchings as acts of racial violence that had become depoliticized, as opposed to something that was inherently apolitical. Racial violence morphed from a tactic of political change to an object of political containment. The political nature of racial violence shifts after Reconstruction; but, contrary to most analyses, not to the extent that it severed any relation to the political. It was politically depoliticized. This book shines a light on these more prevalent aspects of racial violence and problematizes its apolitical nature. Constitutional anarchy is meant to reassert the political nature of lynching.

OUTLINING CONSTITUTIONAL ANARCHY

With respect to lynchings, the Supreme Court created a framework that relieved itself of any culpability for what might happen under its sovereign domain while simultaneously reserving to itself sovereign authority. The federal government did not completely eliminate the possibility for federal intervention. Instead, it limited itself, albeit with the proviso that it could, if it chose to, intervene. Because it was self-imposed, the federal government could not only engage whenever it wanted, but it could also set where its jurisdiction stopped and started. Rather than cracking down on lynchers and/or the states that failed to deal with lynchers, the Supreme Court instead decided to create "zones" in which questionable activities such as lynchings could occur unhampered. These "anomalous zones" were, essentially, legally bounded regions of lawlessness that operated semi-autonomously under the overarching framework of a constitutional regime. These racialized spaces of exception served to insulate and unadulterate the norm from the vicissitudes that the lawlessness of the anomalous zone could and did engender. Without ever sanctioning or prohibiting lynchings, the Court narrowed its attention to issues of containment. Lynchings, for the most part, were situated within a constructed zone of permissiveness that was contingent, not on the sanctioning of political authorities per se, but on political authorities choosing to maintain an active policy of noninterference. As mentioned, the term I use to capture this framework is *constitutional anarchy*. Derived from Ernst Fraenkel's framework of the dual state, constitutional anarchy is a modified version of the dual state that allows for legally bounded regions of lawlessness.

German legal theorist Ernst Fraenkel formulated a theory of duality that can help illuminate the political nature of lynchings.[52] Although in many ways opposite to what happened in the United States, much can be gleaned by Fraenkel's formulation of a state that created a dualistic system via the active withdrawal from a certain range of activities. Although Fraenkel uses the dual state to qualify the totalitarian nature of Nazi Germany, an inverted model of the dual state can be used to qualify the liberal nature of the United States during the era of lynchings.

Fraenkel conceived of what he called the dual state to understand how capitalism could have functioned paradoxically in Nazi Germany:

> We must then resolve the paradox of a capitalistic order continuing within a system under which there is no possibility of rationally calculating social chances. Rational calculation is not consistent with the rule of arbitrary police power which is characteristic of the Third Reich.[53]

By illustrating how capitalism was accommodated within the Nazi regime, Fraenkel qualified the totalitarian nature of the Nazi regime.

In the case of Nazi Germany, Fraenkel differentiates between two jurisdictional states: the Prerogative State and the Normative State. They both operate within a single polity. He defines the Prerogative State as

> a government system which exercises unlimited arbitrariness and violence unchecked by any legal guarantees, and the Normative State refers to an administrative body endowed with elaborate powers for safeguarding the legal order as expressed in statutes, decisions of the courts, and activities of the administrative agencies.[54]

There is "constant friction between these two states since they are competitive and not complementary parts."[55] This "friction," although not necessarily resulting in the elimination of either state, does nevertheless negate the possibility of equilibrium between the two states.[56] This "friction" thus results in one of the states necessarily having what he calls "jurisdiction over the jurisdiction" of the other state. Having "jurisdiction over the jurisdiction" entails—at the very least—for Fraenkel "a guarantee of priority" that is predicated on the higher state "self-restraining" itself, thereby allowing the other state to function.[57] In the case of Nazi Germany, Fraenkel argues that the Prerogative State had jurisdiction over the jurisdiction of the Normative State.

Having jurisdiction over the jurisdiction reflects Fraenkel's attempt to imbue a certain degree of independence and autonomy to both jurisdictions while at the same time providing for a hierarchical ordering of the two. For the dual state to function properly, both states have to have a certain degree of independence and autonomy. Although one state has jurisdiction over the jurisdiction of the other state, it is not the case that one state manages the other completely. With respect to Nazi Germany, he commented:

> [L]egally the Prerogative State has unlimited jurisdiction. Actually, however, its jurisdiction is limited. . . . Although the Third Reich reserves for itself the power of regulating every aspect of social life, it deliberately limits its use of this power. . . . These self-imposed restraints of the Prerogative State are of cardinal importance for the understanding of the Dual State.[58]

Although this concept of self-imposed restraint raises the question of whether the Third Reich's jurisdiction was truly limited if it reserved for itself the power to remove its own restraint, the fact that the Third Reich did commit to restraining itself creates the existence of another body that could step in and fill the void that was being created.

For the lower jurisdictional state to be autonomous meant that it was bestowed the legal authority to make decisions regarding issues over which it had jurisdiction. To use Fraenkel's wording, "its discretion can be exercised only within the limits of its clearly defined jurisdiction."[59] But although its autonomy was presumed by its existence, its existence was nonetheless dependent on the higher jurisdiction. The hierarchical ordering of the two jurisdictional states meant there was no guarantee the lower jurisdictional state would continue to exist. Because the higher jurisdictional state had "jurisdiction over the jurisdiction" of the lower jurisdictional state, the very existence of the lower jurisdictional state was dependent on the self-restraint of the higher jurisdictional state.

Thus, the Prerogative State of the Third Reich bounded itself to make room for the Normative State. Rather than the Prerogative State trying to encapsulate the Normative State within itself, the Prerogative State provides for the autonomy of the Normative State by stopping itself short of total jurisdiction. The Prerogative State could extend itself if it wanted to, but it chose not to explicitly. It is the autonomous nature of the lower jurisdictional state that provided the crux of Fraenkel's argument against classifying the Nazi regime as a pure totalitarian regime. By demonstrating the qualitative nature of the Nazi regime via a legal analysis of the self-bounding of the Prerogative State, Fraenkel detailed how capitalism could and did exist within a totalitarian regime.

With respect to lynchings in the United States, it might appear, at first, to be the same kind of paradoxical coupling that occurred in Germany, but there are enough differences to suggest that the dual state operating in the United States was of a qualitatively different kind than the one that operated in Nazi Germany. The dual state in Nazi Germany was instituted to restore a qualified degree of normalcy during an exceptional time. In the case of Nazi Germany, normalcy meant capitalism. The dual state was instituted to install a previous way of operating within the new regime. It was a way of retaining a degree of continuity with the past without disrupting and/or challenging the integrity of the new regime. In the United States, the opposite occurred. There was nothing analogous to the Fuhrer's will being law in the United States. Even during the worst period of lynchings, the United States operated as a "normal" constitutional regime with checks and balances, separation of powers, federalism, an independent judiciary, and political parties that alternated power. The United States was never a totalitarian regime akin to that of Nazi Germany.

Also, unlike in Germany, where they instituted a dual state to restore a qualified degree of normalcy during an exceptional time, in the United States, the dual state was instituted to create a qualified degree of exceptionality. In the case of the American South, this exceptionality took the form of lynch mobs. The acts of violence perpetrated by lynch mobs in the United States were somewhat comparable with what the Nazis were doing in Germany.[60] However, although the practices of lynch mobs resembled the practices of the Third Reich in that they both "exercised unlimited violence" on their victims, it is important to note that lynch mobs had neither the organizational unity nor the monopoly of political power of the Third Reich.[61] Eric Foner, a preeminent historian of Reconstruction, states that the "acts of violence were generally committed by local groups on their own initiative."[62] Ku Klux Klan historian Allen Trelease notes that "the Ku Klux Klan was so decentralized that it is hardly proper to refer to it in the singular number."[63] Only the Third Reich had unlimited jurisdiction to do what it wanted. Lynch mobs in the American South did not have the same license and freedom as the Third Reich in Nazi Germany. Although lynch mobs seemingly had an "inalienable right to lynch," it was limited. They could not go after just anybody. There were certain restrictions or understandings regarding whom they could terrorize and whom they could not. As Alabama Provisional Governor Lewis Parsons stated in his testimony to Congress, it was restricted to "a certain description of offenders and a certain description of offenses."[64]

Unlike the Third Reich, which authored its own laws, the lynch mobs of the South were never given unlimited jurisdiction to terrorize whomever they wanted. Although they could not pick victims indiscriminately, lynchers wreaked havoc on those they could and did pick. Thus, although the Third Reich had both unlimited arbitrariness and unlimited jurisdiction, lynch mobs had unlimited arbitrariness but limited jurisdiction.

Although the differences between Germany and the United States are significant, these differences do not beckon a complete repudiation of the dual state. In Germany and the United States, the national state maintained a measure of its own integrity and autonomy, standing apart from society by splitting itself into two. Taken abstractly, the dual state is illuminating in four different ways: (1) it offers a way to conceptualize the coexistence of two different normative orders, hence going beyond the legal/illegal dichotomy; (2) it situates these orders in a hierarchy, hence going beyond the strong/weak dichotomy; (3) the self-restraint of the higher state provides a way to understand how the choice not to act can be regarded legally as an active will of the sovereign; and (4) the idea of friction or antagonism between the two legal orders illustrates how the state can strengthen itself by creating something it does not really like very much, at least for some time. But the empirical evidence with regard to lynchings necessitates a different kind of dual state than the one Fraenkel had posited.

In this Americanized version of the dual state that I call *constitutional anarchy*, it is the Supreme Court that chooses to limit the constitutional order short of total jurisdiction. To use Fraenkel's words, although the Nazi dual state represented "a rational core within an irrational shell," this Americanized model of a dual state that I propose represents "an irrational core within a rational shell."[65] This American type of dual state has the constitutional order as the higher jurisdictional state. The constitutional order is defined as a government system that exercises sovereign authority over a bounded area of land under the aegis of a written body of laws. Like Fraenkel's Prerogative State, the constitutional order has "jurisdiction over the jurisdiction" of the lower jurisdictional state, thereby entailing "a guarantee of priority" that is nevertheless predicated on the constitutional order "restraining" itself for the lower jurisdictional state to emerge.[66] The lower jurisdictional state of this American dual state was composed of anomalous zones that operated via the racialization of space. Figure 4.1 summarizes the qualities of constitutional anarchy.

The qualities of limited jurisdiction and lack of state-sponsored violence is why I characterize this American version of the dual state as constitutional anarchy. The constitutional part refers to the "higher" jurisdictional status of the constitutional order. I chose the word *constitutional* purposefully, instead of *legal*, because I want to highlight the behavior of the federal government. Although the federal government

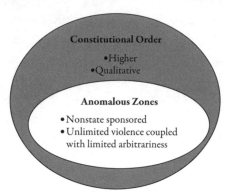

FIGURE 4.1 Diagram of constitutional anarchy

and the respective state governments played a role in the active enforcement and nonenforcement of the law with regard to lynchings, I have found the fluctuating nature of the federal government more relevant than the behavior of the respective state governments. It is the active withdrawal of the federal government that allowed for the respective state governments to be neglectful. With regard to lynching, the federal government had ultimate jurisdiction; it could and did choose to intervene and not to intervene.

The *anarchy* part refers to the decentralized, nonstate-sponsored nature of the violence that was occurring in the postbellum South. Anarchy is not meant to connote a complete absence of any order.[67] Contrary to the concept of chaos, I use the term *anarchy* as many political economists and international relation theorists have defined it:

> [A]narchy is defined as a system in which participants can seize and defend resources without regulation from above. Anarchy is not chaos but rather a spontaneous order that can constitute a stable system.[68]

If the violence is in any way construed to be state sponsored, the dividing line separating the two jurisdictions collapses and there is no dual state. But, just because violence was decentralized and nonstate sponsored, it would be a mistake to assume it was random. It had "a unity of purpose."[69] As *The Atlanta Constitution* urged in 1893: "It may be hard to draw the line, but it must be done somewhere. The stern justice administered by the people in their sovereign capacity must not be made too common."[70] The reason why this "line" was so important was because it was the key to constituting a stable system. This line connotes a degree of containment; it is what made the system anarchic and not chaotic.

Building on the work of legal theorist Gerald Neuman, I argue that the anarchy was contained via the formulation of anomalous zones. Legal theorist Gerald Neuman elaborated how a state can provide for a spatialized suspension of the law. In an article titled "Surveying Law and Borders: Anomalous Zones," Neuman defines an anomalous zone as "a geographical area in which certain legal rules, otherwise regarded as embodying fundamental policies of the larger legal system, are locally suspended."[71] These zones are marked by limited jurisdiction and nonstate-sponsored violence. Neuman demonstrates successfully how these anomalous zones are created:

> [T]he government resorts to geographically limited suspension of a policy it otherwise deems fundamental when it concludes that uniform implementation of the policy is impracticable or even impossible . . . creation of an anomalous zone is a containment strategy, an attempt to isolate the necessary suspension of a fundamental norm.[72]

He cites the ambiguous legacy of prostitution along with the disenfranchisement of residents of the District of Columbia as examples of anomalous zones:

> In Storyville and other red light districts, the suspended rule [regarding prostitution] governed the behavior of private individuals; in the District of Columbia, residents suffered the suspension of a fundamental norm of public law. In both cases, government professed allegiance to the suspended rule, yet justified its exceptional suspension in a limited area.[73]

With regard to prostitution, he notes that although "the United States has criminalized prostitution . . . [it] also has a long history of informally tolerated vice zones in which brothels, while technically illegal, have been permitted to flourish."[74] Neuman demonstrates effectively how a legal system can institute a dual state in which the rule of law limits itself actively, thereby leaving open pockets of spaces, otherwise known as *anomalous zones*, which are not subjected to the rule of law but nevertheless are confined by it.

In the American version of the dual state, the lower jurisdictional state of this American dual state was composed of anomalous zones that operated via the racialization of space. Nestled as they were within the political–legal rubric of constitutional anarchy, in which the constitutional order maintained the "higher" jurisdiction, these anomalous zones were demarcated racially and spatially. Within particular localities, race became the marker that contoured the "borders" in which an anomalous zone could emerge. Race provided a convenient discursive framework to discern demographic boundaries and served to insulate and "unadulterate" the "civil" order from the vicissitudes that lawlessness could engender. In other words, race/racism was a nontemporal way of distinguishing the exception from the norm, buttressing sovereignty in that it marked the parameters of lawlessness preordained by the sovereign to be exceptional.

This unconventional approach of anomalous zones to delineate different arenas of jurisdiction resembles what has occurred in other countries. In his examination of British rule in India, anthropologist Partha Chatterjee notes how British authorities apportioned "the space of governmental action into what may be called a domain of the 'civil' and a domain of the 'other.'"[75] In British India,

> there were real distinctions between a domain of the "civil," mainly located in the cities and consisting of Europeans and educated and propertied Indians, and a domain of the "country" (mufassal), populated by rural landlords, peasants and labourers. . . . Civil liberties were meant to apply only to the former domain and not to the latter. The distinction between the two domains was signified by various criteria, depending on the context. It could be geographical—the difference between town and country. Sometimes, the difference could be racial—a European living the country could not be denied his or her civic rights.[76]

This racial and geographic distinction between the "civil" and the "other" was instituted primarily to insulate and unadulterate the domain of the "civil":

> There was a strong tendency to trace the effective source of terrorism to some element outside the domain of the "civil." This could be an element of a noncivic "other" culture that had not been tamed and domesticated by the "civil." If the effective source of terrorism could be identified as lying outside the domain of the "civil," one could draw the comforting conclusion that the civic was safe from threats from within. . . .[T]he locus of these emergency restrictions should also be, as far as possible, specific; a general suspension of all civil liberties would jeopardize the very existence of the civic.[77]

Partha Chatterjee thus points to how the active withdrawal of the state can occur racially and geographically.

Mahmood Mamdani also postulated a set of laws that were differentiated across identity and space. In what he termed "decentralized despotism," Mamdani describes the African colonial experience as Janus-faced, bifurcated. It contained a duality: two forms of power under a single hegemonic authority.... Direct rule was the form of urban civil power.... Indirect rule, however, signified a rural tribal authority.... Urban power spoke the language of civil society and civil rights, rural power of community and culture.[78]

This indirect rule relied on customary law to regulate nonmarket relations.[79] Customary law was defined, according to Mamdani, "in the plural, as the law of the tribe, and not in the singular, as a law for all natives. Thus, there was not one customary law for all natives, but roughly as many sets of customary laws as there were said to be tribes."[80] He was quick to note, however, that this framework of customary law was buttressed by the state: decentralized despotism "encapsulated the individual in a set of relations defined and enforced by the state as communal and customary."[81] This is why Mamdani refers to it as being "autonomous but not independent."[82] Thus, although chiefs administered customary law primarily, the state buttressed and sanctioned their authority. Because the state ruled indirectly through the chieftains, it was able to "barricade the 'savages' from the world of the 'civilized.'"[83] This bifurcation of law rendered members of the subject population "containerized."[84] People became subject to the whim of their corresponding chieftain: "[C]ustomary law was not about guaranteeing rights; it was about enforcing custom. Its power was not to limit power, but to enable it."[85]

The next section reassesses the Supreme Court's handling of racial violence using this framework of constitutional anarchy. Contrary to the standard account, which suggests the Court gave a "green light to terror," I argue that the Supreme Court during Reconstruction gave a yellow light to terror by sanctioning lynching negatively. In providing a yellow light to terror, the federal government suspended its responsibility without necessarily relinquishing authority.

OPERATIONALIZING CONSTITUTIONAL ANARCHY

The Compromise of 1877, which included pulling out military troops from the former Confederate states, signaled an end to federal efforts against the aspect of racism that Justice Bradley referred to as "the war of race."[86] Although other aspects of racism that sprung "from the ordinary felonious or criminal intent"[87] had yet to be resolved, President Grant made it clear as early as 1875 that "the whole public are tired out with these autumnal outbreaks in the South, and the great majority are ready to condemn any interference on the part of the [federal] Government."[88] Henceforth, racial violence commonly known as lynchings became depoliticized by appearing to operate outside political channels, where it was governed not by collective political decisions but by the dynamics determined primarily by lynch mobs against their victims. This is in contradistinction to other aspects of race relations, such as segregation, which was very much politicized and operated squarely within political channels. The depolitization of racial violence was in part a consequence of the Supreme Court's incomplete handling of the racial emergency during Reconstruction that left the legacy of the emergency unhinged. Although Justice Miller in *Slaughterhouse* and Justice Bradley in his circuit court decision in *Cruikshank* distinguished "the war of race" from all other aspects of racial discrimination to justify federal intervention, this dualism becomes unhinged from its original intention and was reappropriated to justify federal inaction. This section reexamines the Supreme Court decisions concerning lynchings during this period under the framework of constitutional anarchy.

The Supreme Court's Containment Policy

Politicizing lynchings in this manner runs contrary to conventional accounts that blame the Supreme Court during Reconstruction for having halted the possibility of federal rights enforcement for racial violence. Historians such as Eric Foner concluded that the Supreme Court "render[ed] national prosecution of crimes committed against blacks virtually impossible, and gave a green light to acts of terror where local officials either could not or would not enforce the law."[89] Critics have concluded that *The Slaughterhouse Cases* "rendered the attributes of national citizenship all but meaningless to blacks,"[90] thereby inaugurating a "judicial coup d'Etat"[91] against Reconstruction. Legal scholar Leonard Levy provides the standard interpretation of *U.S. v. Cruikshank*: "Cruikshank paralyzed the federal government's attempt to protect citizens by punishing violators of their civil rights and, in effect, shaped the Constitution to the advantage of the Ku Klux Klan."[92]

This claim for a Court-induced paralysis has been subsequently legitimated and perpetrated mainly through the state action doctrine. State action doctrine is often understood as locating all private action as beyond the scope of the federal government. As stated in the *Civil Rights Cases*, "individual invasion of individual rights is not the subject-matter of the [Fourteenth] Amendment."[93] Unless there was a provision in state law that discriminated explicitly against blacks, it would seem to be the case that the federal government relinquished and/or delegated complete authority to the states to combat racial violence.

There has, however, been a significant upsurge of accounts by legal scholars that have challenged subtly this interpretation of state action and the Supreme Court's role during Reconstruction. Robert Kaczorowski exhumed the original intent of federal rights enforcement and found that it was actually expansive in nature.[94] Pamela Brandwein revisited judicial interpretations of state action and discovered they included a broader notion of "state neglect."[95] Critiquing the narrow confines of the conventional understanding of state action, these revisionist accounts not only situate the Court as being more reactionary during Reconstruction, but—more important—salvage a semblance of national sovereignty for the federal government. This salvaging is critical because, had the narrow conception of state action been correct, then some new law should have been needed to reinstall the legal capacity for the federal government to intervene. But, the Supreme Court was able to defend federal rights enforcement without additional legislation. It simply "reinterpreted old statutes."[96] In 1966, the Supreme Court ruled in *United States v. Price* and *United States v. Guest* that Section 5 of the Fourteenth Amendment empowered Congress to enact laws punishing conspiracies with or without state action.[97] Writing in 1966, Arthur Kinoy pointed out:

> The executive branch of the Government still has at its disposal a panoply of existing Reconstruction statutes which could have been, and still can be, invoked to provide for federal protection against violence inflicted upon citizens, black and white, engaged in activities designed to achieve political and economic freedom for the race of black men. New legislation is always helpful, but this is simply not the crux of the problem.[98]

The fact that federal rights enforcement was resurrected without Congress passing any new legislation, the Court not having overturned any law, and/or the president not proclaiming any executive decree suggests that the federal government retained its authority to engage in federal rights enforcement. Instead, the Court suspended this authority and provided space for informal actors to engage in nefarious activities.

The Court's inconsistency in these matters had less to do with legal maneuverings than with the fluctuating political support for federal rights enforcement. When the federal government wanted to combat racial violence, it simply resurrected old laws that were always there but rarely used. Although the legal principle of state action was subordinate to the political calculus of engaging in racial violence, when political support for engagement was lacking, the state action doctrine was conveniently raised as a rhetorical ploy used by political actors to obfuscate their responsibility and accountability.[99] Although revisionist accounts critique the narrow character of the conventional depiction of state action accurately, no one has yet provided a schema by which to frame the maintenance of federal sovereignty in the face of inaction, and this lack has contributed to the mischaracterization of political inaction as primarily an issue of legality. Constitutional anarchy is meant to frame the federal government's fluctuating disengagement with the rights enforcement of blacks in such a way that subordinates accurately the legal complexities of such enforcement to the more pertinent question of political will formation.

Although many of the cases heard during Reconstruction rule in favor of a narrow conception of federal rights enforcement, each did so in a way that did not necessarily preclude the possibility of future intervention. The decisions were made in a similar manner to that described by legal historian Charles Mangum in which the Court disposed of disenfranchisement challenges "on some technical or subsidiary point, leaving the merits of the real issue untouched."[100] Couple these cases of acquittal with the later cases that resulted in the prosecution of lynchers, and it would seem to be the case that the Court could have ruled in favor of upholding the prosecution of lynchers, but at times chose not to.

As mentioned in the previous chapter, Chief Justice Waite's decision in *Cruikshank* illuminated the ways in which he was able to make very definitive statements regarding constitutional interpretation while nonetheless subtly leaving open the possibility of federal action if there was racial intent. In *U.S. v. Harris*, although the Court formalized the informality of lynching, it did so in a very narrow fashion.[101] In the majority decision, Supreme Court Justice Woods simply declared Section 2 of the Ku Klux Klan Act of 1871 unconstitutional, and hence federal protection from violence based on this particular section was not warranted. Is federal protection from violence always unwarranted? Is there another law that can justify federal protection? Does *Harris* invalidate all previous federal prosecutions of violence? Although *Harris* appeared to signal an end to federal rights enforcement for blacks, *Harris* nonetheless left these questions unanswered. Woods's decision should not be read as invalidating all federal efforts to ensure the rights of blacks to be protected against racial violence; it only invalidated federal efforts under the rubric of one particular statute, which by no means exhausted the gamut of what the federal government could do.

Couple these cases with *Plessy v. Ferguson* and we begin to see the kind of spatialized logic under which the Court was operating.[102] In *Plessy*, the Court allowed local communities to determine the reasonableness of actions. *Plessy* was decided in 1896 and involved the constitutionality of a Louisiana statute requiring railroads to provide separate and equal accommodations for black and white passengers.[103] The Court upheld the constitutionality of segregation in part because it was deemed in congruence with the customs and traditions of the people:

> In determining the question of reasonableness it [the state legislature of Louisiana] is at liberty to act with reference to the established usages, customs and

traditions of the people, and with a view to the promotion of their comfort, and the preservation of the public peace and good order.[104]

By situating reasonableness in this fashion, the Court does not mandate or sanction segregation per se. Rather, it is more accurate to say if segregation so happens to be part of "the customs and traditions of the people," then the Court will allow it. In so doing, the Court thus provided constitutional cover for localized acts of segregation. Although contemporary analysts have derided the *Plessy* decision as backward and racist, the decision at the time was understood as "embodying conventional wisdom" and that it so closely "mirrored the spirit of the age . . . that the country hardly noticed."[105]

The *Plessy* case provided what legal theorist Jeremy Waldron referred to as a legal "archetype" for selective law enforcement and local autonomy.[106] Jeremy Waldron defines an archetype as "a particular provision in a system of norms which has a significance beyond its immediate normative content . . . operates in a way that expresses or epitomizes the spirit of a whole structured area of doctrine."[107] Although Jeremy Waldron argues that the fairly narrow proposition of *Brown v. Board of Education* would later provide the "archetype" for a more broad dismantling of segregation and discrimination, I would use a similar argument to suggest that *Plessy* was the archetype through which a degree of racialized localism could flourish.[108]

Plessy was archetypal not because it sanctioned segregation per se; rather, *Plessy* was archetypal for outlining a broad mandate for racialized localism with segregation as one instantiation. Lynching was another. By leaving questions of reasonableness to "the customs and traditions of the people," the Supreme Court opened itself up to the various interpretations of what customs and traditions are. By being so vague, even if the Court might have had in mind the legally constituted state authorities exercising their police powers, the Court nonetheless left itself open to a more populist, mob interpretation of the people. Perhaps the article in the Spring 1966 edition of the *Duke Law Journal* summed it up best: "it is arguable that [the lynch mob] invades this province of the state and, acting in loco reipublicae, displaces the state organs as political 'sovereign.'"[109] Rather than creating clear legal principles that avoided any semblance of sanctioning mob rule in the South, the Court in *Plessy* seemed to be more interested in securing its retreat. Intended or not, the ambiguous and vague formulation made in *Plessy* regarding the "established usages, customs and traditions of the people" gave tacit legal sanction to whoever could act plausibly in the people's name.

Although *Plessy* served as an archetype for both lynching and segregation, it is nonetheless important to distinguish lynching from segregation. Like segregationists, lynchers were seemingly "at liberty to act with reference to the established usages, customs and traditions of the people, and with a view to the promotion of their comfort, and the preservation of the public peace and good order."[110] But unlike segregation, lynchings consisted of acts that were not formally sanctioned and/or administered by local officials. That is to say, segregation had been voted on, passed as law, and enforced legally. There was no formal "lynch law" that outlined the crimes, trial mechanisms, and means of punishment. However anarchic Jim Crow was, it was not as anarchic as lynching. It is one thing to mandate different schools for blacks; it is altogether something else to sanction the murder of blacks. Segregation at least justified itself as consistent with equality before the law—separate but equal. That is why, in part, it could be sanctioned positively as consistent with constitutional law. Lynching simply could not make that claim. There was no law and/ or Supreme Court case that positively sanctioned lynching. As Judge Emmons noted, the "right of the negro to see the ballet dance" could be outlawed formally whereas the right to "pillage and murder was more precious and beneficent privilege" and thus could not.[111] Although segregation and lynchings both operated under the broader rubric of racialized localism as established in the archetypical case of *Plessy*, it is nonetheless important not to lump one within the other.

A further feature that distinguishes lynching from segregation is that lynchings tended to be spontaneous acts that were either legitimated retroactively and/or covered up. Although segregationists were clearly operating under a legal order that sanctioned segregation, lynchers maintained a more tenuous relationship with the law. This is, in part, why those who describe lynchings use the term "extralegal."[112] The term connotes a degree of ambiguity for how to situate lynchings vis-à-vis the law. It is not quite legal; it is not quite illegal.

This then raises the question of how to situate lynchings legally. As mentioned in the previous chapter, *U.S. v. Harris* negatively sanctioned lynching.[113] In terms of constitutional anarchy, the federal government qualified its sovereign authority. Nonenforcement created a legal void. The Court did not state explicitly what would fill in the void left after *Harris*, but instead simply created an opening.

Legal theorist Gerald Neuman postulates three different alternatives to how the federal government could have created an opening:

> Policymakers may attempt to channel noncompliance into legally regulated exceptions. These exceptions may apply to a specific type of activity, to persons obtaining permission through an individualized licensing scheme, or to activity taking place within certain limited enclaves.[114]

In terms of lynching, these alternatives can be translated as the following:

1. Did the Supreme Court categorize lynching as some sort of legally regulated exception?
2. Did the Supreme Court create a licensing scheme for lynchers?
3. Did the Supreme Court make an exception for lynching spatially?

We can reject the second option outright. There was no individual licensing scheme for lynching. If it had existed, it would have amounted to a positive sanctioning of lynching.

Although an explicit licensing scheme did not occur, a slight variation might have. It could be argued that the federal government somehow delegated authority to lynch mobs. Although the Court in *Harris* did not transfer jurisdictional authority to lynch mobs explicitly, it did signal to lynch mobs that their terrorist acts against blacks would not be prosecuted by federal authorities. Perhaps the signal for the active nonenforcement of the law should be understood as an implicit license for lynch mobs to wreak their havoc.

This claim raises the question of how the federal government could delegate authority to a group that was neither permanent nor official. Lynch mobs were spontaneous formations, composed mostly of white men from local vicinities who tended to emerge in reaction to an allegation of a crime and/or transgression of a social norm. Most lynch mobs tended not to be permanent organizations with explicitly formal responsibilities. They would form in response to an event and dissipate after closure, which usually came in the form of a lynching.[115] How could the federal government delegate authority to an entity that was not always there?[116]

In addition, the Supreme Court did rule, however seldom, against lynch mobs. In *Moore v. Dempsey*, the Court reversed the convictions of six blacks on the ground that their trial was mob dominated. The Supreme Court regarded mob-dominated trials as a significant obstruction of justice. In the majority opinion, Supreme Court Justice Holmes stated that "if in fact a trial is dominated by a mob so that there is an actual interference with the course of justice, there is a departure from due process of law."[117] Holmes also made it a point to indicate that this departure represented a significant transgression of what the people wanted, thereby situating *Moore* under the rubric of *Plessy*:

> The averments as to the prejudice by which the trial was environed have some corroboration in appeals to the Governor, about a year later, earnestly urging him not to interfere with the execution of the petitioners. One came from five members of the Committee of Seven, and stated in addition to what has been quoted heretofore that "all our citizens are of the opinion that the law should take its course."[118]

Moore seems to represent an instance when lynch mobs overreached. From *Moore*, we learn that the Supreme Court did not tolerate certain behavior from mobs.

Logan v. U.S. is another instance of the Court ruling against lynch mobs.[119] The situation involved six black men under federal custody who were eventually taken by a mob and lynched. The Supreme Court agreed with the decision made in the district court of Texas that

> when a citizen of the United States is committed to the custody of a United States marshal by process issuing from one of the courts of the United States, to be held, in default of bail, to await his trial on a criminal charge within the exclusive jurisdiction of the national courts, such citizen has a right, under the constitution and laws of the United States; to a speedy and public trial by an impartial jury, and, until tried or discharged by due process of law, has the right, under said constitution and laws, to be treated with humanity, and *to be protected against all unlawful violence* [emphasis added].[120]

The Supreme Court takes the district court decision one step further. In the majority opinion, Justice Gray quotes a passage of Justice Miller from a previous case:

> It is argued that the preservation of peace and good order in society is not within the powers confided to the government of the United States, but belongs exclusively to the states. Here again we are met with the theory that the government of the United States does not rest upon soil and territory of the country. We think that this theory is founded on an entire misconception of the nature and powers of that government. We hold it to be an incontrovertible principle that the government of the United States may, by means of physical force, exercised through its official agents, execute on every foot of command obedience to its laws, and hence the power to keep the peace to that extent.[121]

Although this ruling states clearly that people under federal custody are "to be secure in their persons from bodily harm and injury and assaults and cruelties until they have been discharged by due process of the laws of the United States," it begs the questions of what happens *after* they were discharged.[122] Is it only when black people are in the custody of federal marshals that they can be "protected against all unlawful violence?" How free are black men if they are safer in a federal jail than in their own homes? Regardless of the counterintuitive repercussions, *Logan* did impose a limit with regard to who can and cannot be lynched. With *Logan*, we learn that a black person in federal custody was outside the anomalous zone and hence beyond the reach of mobs.

Highlighting these cases is in no way meant to exaggerate the federal government's role in combating racial violence. It is simply meant to suggest that the legal capacity to deal with racial violence was never eliminated. Instances of federal intervention were considered at the time as "isolated and temporary departures from a general policy of leaving the problem of racist terrorism to the states."[123] The majority of lynchings failed to elicit any formal investigation.[124] In the few instances in which there were formal investigations, the conclusion was often death at the hands of persons unknown.[125]

In light of these few rulings, it seems clear that the Supreme Court never positively sanctioned lynch mobs. In fact, there is reason to believe the Court actually regarded mobs with disdain. In *U.S. v. Shipp*, the Court found a sheriff and one of his deputies guilty of contempt for aiding and abetting a lynch mob.[126] Chief Justice Fuller stated in the majority decision: "[I]t is apparent that a dangerous portion of the community was seized with the awful thirst for blood which only killing can quench, and that considerations of law and order were swept away in the overwhelming flood."[127] He concluded that "this lamentable riot was the direct result of opposition to the administration of the law by this Court."[128] The Court clearly wanted to distance itself. Any positive sanctioning of lynch mobs would have brought the two entities closer and thus would have marred the "steady, upright, and impartial" nature of the Court that is essential if it is to administer the law. Any sort of licensing scheme, explicit or implicit, seems thus rather dubious.

When conceptualizing the legal status of lynching, we are then left with the first and last options—legally regulated exception or spatialized exception. Consider the first option: the Supreme Court somehow categorized lynching as some sort of legally regulated exception. If the Supreme Court, in fact, chose the first option, the Court would have to have been more explicit about the definition of lynching. But, the Court never was. The *Corpus Juris*, the authoritative 20th century American legal encyclopedia, states:

> Lynching has no technical legal meaning. It is merely a descriptive phrase used to signify the lawless acts of persons who violate established law at the time they commit the acts. . . . The offense of lynching is unknown to the common law.[129]

More important, as we saw in *Logan*, the Supreme Court in fact did not allow all lynchings to occur. Thus, the claim that the Supreme Court somehow categorized lynching as a legally regulated exception is historically inaccurate. Also, there were cases when lynchings were prevented, redirected, and/or prosecuted. Historical analysis suggests that lynchings were not allowed across the board; in fact, there was much local variation.[130]

This then leaves the third option—namely, the Supreme Court somehow "exceptionalized" lynching spatially. The difference between the first and third option is the element of space. Although the first option involves more of an open-ended endorsement of a specific type of activity, this last option is less about the specificities of the act and more about contextualizing the parameters within which activities such as lynchings occurred. This last option is conducive to the Supreme Court's broad mandate for racialized localism—namely, of accommodating perceived local preferences from the top down. By no means was the Supreme Court trying to establish a universal procedure for lynching. The Supreme Court did not obstruct local communities and/or states that wanted to prosecute lynchers. Neither did the Court, for the most part, obstruct those that did not want to prosecute lynchers. Rather, the Court qualified the federal government's responsibility while nonetheless retaining its sovereign authority.

Although *Harris* signaled the suspension of federal rights enforcement, *Plessy* broadly outlined the procedure that would operate in its wake. Under the rubric of racialized localism as set forth in *Plessy*, the Court during this period relegated, for the most part, the "reasonableness" of lynching to the opinions of a vaguely defined notion of "the people." Under this logic, lynchings were not legitimate per se, but they could be made to be legitimate if done in accordance with the customs and traditions of the people. James Cutler makes this point: "If the lawless violence was the work of the 'many,' if it was committed by a representative number of the citizens while in a state of frenzy and excitement, it must be considered beyond the reach of human law."[131] Although this legitimizing process might appear to some as clear, consistent, and coherent, it was, in fact, rather muddy, if only because there were a plurality of customs and traditions just within the South alone, not to mention the rest of the country. This pluralistic account of customs and traditions is consistent with the variations of "lynch law" that spanned across different regions, states, cities, and localities. Lynch law operated differently in the black belt of the South than in the border states; it was different in the rural areas of Mississippi than in the more urban areas.[132] Although the same can be said about segregation, lynching was even more reliant in pluralistic customs and traditions than segregation, because lynching operated more informally and spontaneously.

I have appropriated legal theorist Gerald Neuman's conception of anomalous zones to take into account the informal administration of lynching and the federal government's allowance for local variation. Neuman points out how "governments occasionally suspend fundamental norms within a territorially limited enclave in response to perceived necessity."¹³³ Perceived necessity includes regions where "uniform implementation of the policy is impracticable or even impossible."¹³⁴ Suspension of this kind can take the form of an anomalous zone, which refers to "a geographical area in which certain legal rules, otherwise regarded as embodying fundamental policies of the larger legal system, are locally suspended."¹³⁵ In an attempt "to accommodate perceived local preferences from the top down,"¹³⁶ anomalous zones are "sites where the law expressly authorized insuperable barriers to its own enforcement."¹³⁷

Anomalous zones are those "certain limited enclaves" that are allowed to operate under their own distinctive customs and traditions, and they affirm NAACP Secretary James Weldon Johnson's depiction of Southern blacks as being in an "anomalous position."¹³⁸ These zones are not completely self-referential. It is only for a certain range of activities that these enclaves are to be regulated from within and not from above. Because they operate under their own inner logic for certain activities, it can thus be said to be self-referential in part, which makes them lawless to a certain extent. Historian Allen Trelease alluded to the peculiar situation of anomalous zones in the arena of lynching: "in all other respects the laws operated and the courts functioned as usual, but in Ku Klux cases the judicial process broke down completely."¹³⁹ Although these zones were selectively lawless, the Supreme Court made sure these selective zones of lawlessness were nevertheless legally bound. In other words, these zones were legally bounded regions of lawlessness. Without ever dictating or judging the content of this self-referential logic, the Court nonetheless provided the space for this partly self-referential process to occur. During this period in the South, there were several concurrently existing anomalous zones operating under different variations of a "lynch law" that was predicated mainly on whatever customs and traditions prevailed in any given "enclave." This term *enclave* can take on several connotations, but the exact definition of an enclave is not as crucial as understanding the Court's permission for something like an enclave to be the determining factor of whether a lynching is deemed "reasonable." By delegating judgment to the people without ever defining who the people were, the Court thus enabled racist local customs and practices to decide what qualified as murder versus what fell into the category of a lynching. As Walter Royal Jones Jr., a Unitarian clergyman stated during the trial of Collie Leroy Wilkins, "[M]urder is not murder except in the community that regards it as so."¹⁴⁰

Revisiting the Supreme Court through the Lens of Constitutional Anarchy

However loose the Supreme Court may have been with definitions, it was anything but when it came to insulating the federal government from the vicissitudes of

Southern violence. To insulate the federal government, it was essential to maintain strict boundaries. Although the anomalous zones operated under the overarching auspices of the federal law, they functioned autonomously, hence the phrase *jurisdiction over the jurisdiction*. As stated in the second section of this chapter, having jurisdiction over the jurisdiction entailed a guarantee of priority for the lower jurisdictional state that is predicated on the higher state self-restraining itself, thereby providing the lower jurisdictional state a qualified degree of autonomy. By having anomalous zones operate autonomously, the federal government ensured it was not directly responsible for what occurred within these zones.

Anytime these activities impinged on and/or related back directly to its own sovereign authority, the federal government intervened. The Court engaged only in cases that implicated the federal government directly. The Court seemed primarily interested in minimizing the direct collusion of law enforcement officials with lynch mobs and not with administering the letter of the law. The Court's reluctance to engage in federal rights enforcement for blacks is clearly evidenced in *Giles v. Harris*. In this 1903 case involving racial discrimination, Justice Holmes wrote in the majority opinion, "It seems to us impossible to grant the equitable relief which is asked ... the court has little practical power to deal with the people of the state in a body."[141] The defeatist tone that Holmes took was indicative of the disappearance of the revolutionary potential that was Reconstruction, and it illuminates that—however sympathetic different Supreme Court Justices may have been in combating racism—there were "practical" impediments that restrained the Court from acting on such concerns. These impediments are perhaps best summed up by the chairman of the Kansas Republican state committee after the election of Samuel Hayes to the presidency: "I think the policy of the new administration will be to conciliate the white men of the South, Carpetbaggers to the rear, and niggers take care of yourselves."[142] During this time, when white supremacy was firmly embedded, the Court's narrow focus on containment reflected its efforts at trying to keep the rule of law from getting tainted by the lawlessness of lynching.

In each case of federal intervention during this period, Southerners were either challenging national supremacy directly and/or trying to implicate the federal government further in the racial happenings of the South. Each time the federal government intervened, the intervention was regarded as an isolated and temporary departure. In that federal intervention at that time was to be considered an exception to the norm, these instances of federal intervention did not suggest any alteration of the normal operating procedure. For the most part, the racial agreement was intact; it was only when Southerners tried to insinuate federal complicity further on Southern race relations that the federal government intervened. By maintaining strict boundaries with regard to where the jurisdiction of the anomalous zones stopped and started, the federal government could relieve itself of culpability while retaining sovereign authority.

The Supreme Court rulings in *Moore* and *Logan* operated under this pretense. As mentioned earlier, in *Moore* the Court did not find lynch mobs as inherently troubling. It was only when lynch mobs started to interfere directly with trials did the Court find their conduct worthy of prosecution. Following this line of reasoning, it could be presumed that as long as lynch mobs do not directly interfere with jury trials, they are not necessarily interfering with justice or representing a departure from the law. As for *Logan*, the fact that the lynch mob lynched somebody in federal custody implicated the federal government directly. If the Supreme Court did nothing, then the federal government could be considered wholly complicit with Southern lynchings. The fact that the Supreme Court chose to intervene in these cases and not the thousands of other lynchings that had occurred in the South at the time suggests that the Supreme Court was not as interested in combating lynchings as it was concerned with insulating the federal government from the racial violence occurring in the South at the time.

Each intervention by the federal judiciary during this period was not only further evidence that the federal government could intervene when it chose to, thereby evincing proof of national supremacy, but also it indicated further that the federal government was keen on maintaining a distinction between how Southerners managed racial affairs and the federal government's responsibility. In terms of constitutional anarchy, the federal government during this period was intent on maintaining a strict boundary of where the jurisdiction of Southern anomalous zones stopped and started. When activities of the anomalous zones began to spill over into the higher jurisdictional state, the boundaries were blurred and hence those activities began to implicate the federal government directly. By blurring the lines, Southerners were trying to insinuate further the complicity of the federal government with the racial violence erupting in the South. When activities were contained strictly within the anomalous zones, the federal government could claim no direct responsibility, and hence would not be wholly implicated in what occurred within these anomalous zones. By blurring the line, Southerners forced the hand of the federal government, and the federal government acted reluctantly. Although the federal government had been pursuing an active policy of nonenforcement, white Southerners compelled the federal government to pursue an active policy of enforcement.

It would thus seem to be the case that the Court signaled, through cases such as *Cruikshank* and *Harris*, its disinclination to prosecute lynchings without necessarily relinquishing its ability to prosecute lynchings. Unlike most analysts of the period who have concluded the federal government gave a "green light" to more extreme acts of racism, it is more accurate in light of the *Price* and *Guest* to say the Court gave a yellow light to racialized terror.[143] In other words, the Court merely suspended its authority. The metaphor of a "green light" is meant to suggest a repudiation of sovereignty and even encouragement that the South embarks on racial acts of terror. The Court's behavior, however, is better understood as a kind of "yellow light," or a decision to suspend temporarily and qualify national jurisdiction without revoking this authority in principle or intention. Lynching thus seemed to be less a matter of legal incapacity and more a matter of active nonenforcement of the law. The active policy of nonenforcement was more of a political agreement mired in comity than a legal principle of incapacity. In other words, the federal government's inaction regarding racial violence was less an institutional matter of resources or legal capacity and more of a sovereign decision not to act.

Here is where my concept of constitutional anarchy helps illuminate matters. Constitutional anarchy provides a way of understanding how an active policy of nonenforcement can operate and function. After Reconstruction, when the federal government provided white Southerners the autonomy to manage racial affairs in the South, the Supreme Court responded accordingly through cases such as *Cruikshank, Harris*, and the *Civil Rights Cases* that it was going to rule negatively on issues relating to federal rights enforcement for blacks in the South. In so doing, the Court did not repudiate and/or strip the federal government of its authority to engage in federal rights enforcement. In other words, although the Court clearly signaled that it was not going to uphold claims of rights violations of blacks in the South, it did so without ever making a substantive decision. Parts of the law were, in effect, placed into suspended animation and it was only when President Lyndon Johnson was willing to lead the federal government back to the arena of rights enforcement did the Court resuscitate these laws.

It is time for South Carolina to rejoin the Union.[1]

—U.S. DISTRICT COURT JUDGE J. WATIES WARING

5

Bringing Constitutional Anarchy to an End

ᴏ᪲ ───

INTRODUCTION

In this chapter I examine the end of constitutional anarchy. In 1966, the federal government returned to combatting lynchings. In many regards, the Court's switch to upholding the prosecution of lynchers is eerily reminiscent to the Court's previous switch to allow for lynchings. As was the case after Reconstruction, the Court's reactivation of federal rights enforcement followed only when there were clear indications of support by the executive and legislative branches for federal rights enforcement. In other words, the Court was in the rearguard in providing for lynchings and again found itself last in line when it came to stopping lynchings. By the time the Court reactivated federal rights enforcement with regard to lynchings, the president had already demonstrated his willingness to enforce the right of personal security for blacks in the South. Although the Court had overturned much of the Reconstruction legislation that pertained to lynchings, the Court never relinquished the legal capacity and/or authority to address lynchings. This argument for the partial suspension of the law—instead of the complete repudiation of the law—is, in fact, corroborated by how the Supreme Court returned to dealing with lynchings after approximately eighty years of, primarily, trying to avoid the topic. Rather than Congress instituting a new law, the executive ordering an executive decree, or the Court overturning a previous ruling, the Court instead simply seemed to change its mind or, as legal historian Michal Belknap more eloquently states, "reinterpreted old statutes."[2]

Had the Court completely repudiated past efforts to combat lynchings, this return to old law should not have been possible. The fact that the Court could return to old law confirms my claim that the Court did not overturn the federal government's legal authority to combat lynchings, but suspended the law until the other branches were ready and willing to enforce it again. When the other branches signaled their willingness to combat lynchings, the Court followed suit and ended constitutional anarchy. Although constitutional anarchy might appear complex, the ending was anything but. It simply involved the reactivation of old law. In a series of complex wrangling, the Court contoured the law to match the fluctuating political will.

The federal government gradually came around after years of mounting criticism and pressure brought on by opponents of lynchings. This occurred in two stages. The first stage was a long, drawn-out period during which the federal government engaged reluctantly in minimal amounts of federal rights enforcement. The second period was a short, intense period when the federal government, under the leadership of President Lyndon B. Johnson (LBJ), was engaged proactively. The layout of this chapter reflects these stages. The first section, "The Prelude to the End," outlines the growing opposition toward lynchings and the federal government's piecemeal reappraisal of federal intervention. The second section, "Rupture," outlines the federal government under LBJ. It was during LBJ's administration that the federal government returned fully to federal rights enforcement. I then conclude with remarks regarding the political ramifications of LBJ's decisions.

PRELUDE TO THE END

Although I have focused primarily on the behavior of the federal government in general and the Supreme Court in particular, by no means should this be taken as an attempt to minimize the role of societal actors in the rise and decline of lynchings. As legal historian Michael Klarman adeptly notes, "[W]hite supremacy depended less on law than on entrenched social mores."[3] Although the federal government's active non-enforcement of the law provided the background condition for lynchings to occur, the eventual decline in the number of lynchings during the early twentieth century was, in part, a result of the tireless efforts of concerned individuals and groups.

Many activists, including Ida B. Wells, devoted their lives to exposing the sordid details of lynchings. Wells went on speaking tours, published editorials, made pamphlets, organized community services, and participated in women's and civil rights groups in the hopes that public sentiment toward lynchings would change if people were just better informed. She was pivotal in making lynchings real to many Americans by providing names, dates, and graphic details to specific lynchings. She was also able to debunk many of the racist stereotypes of blacks that justified many of the lynchings in the South, as well as challenge the prevailing wisdom at the time that lynchings were simply isolated events and not part of a larger pattern of lawlessness. At a time when Southern newspapers were downplaying the gruesome nature of lynchings and Northern newspapers were downplaying the persistent nature of lynchings, Wells's contributions were invaluable for their constant reminder of the intolerability of what had become tolerable.[4]

Organizations such as the Association of Southern Women for the Prevention of Lynching (ASWPL) and the NAACP were also crucial in curbing the practice. The ASWPL focused on three distinct elements in southern communities: the general public, local law enforcement, and potential lynchers. The ASWPL initiated an extensive educational campaign that consisted of placing advertisements in local newspapers and church magazines, sending out press releases and letters to the editor, creating and distributing innumerable pamphlets, and sponsoring plays that had an antilynching theme. It also collected more than 40,000 signatures from Southern women who declared their opposition to lynching. The ASWPL collected the signatures of more than 12,000 peace officers who stated their opposition to lynching. If there was rumor a lynching might occur, a delegation of local members would either go visit the local sheriff or call him and urge him to do his duty. Then, members' respective husbands, friends, and the husbands' friends would receive calls. If the sheriff failed to act, he would be denounced in the local newspaper and/or denied campaign funds for his upcoming reelection. With regard to potential lynchers, members of the ASWPL would call on their husbands to intimidate would-be lynchers economically. Not only were these tactics effective in curbing the number of lynchings, but also the very fact that this group, which was composed mainly of white women of the South, was calling for the end of lynching was significant in and of itself if only because many lynchings had been rationalized as necessary to retain and protect the sanctity and purity of white women.[5]

While the ASWPL focused on using informal social networks to curb lynchings, the NAACP focused its efforts on pressuring political officials. And although the NAACP campaign against lynching included on-site investigations, fund-raising, protest meetings, news releases and published research on the subject, the organization focused much of its attention on the federal government—in particular, (1) securing the passage of antilynching legislation through Congress, (2) pressuring the Department of Justice to prosecute lynchers, (3) pressuring the president to quell racial violence in the South, and (4) in the words of FBI Director J. Edgar Hoover, "forcing various issues involving the Negro before the [federal] Courts."[6] Activities included investigations, disclosures, conferences, publicity, lobbying, litigation, and negotiations with influential persons in the government, including Eleanor Roosevelt, Attorney General Francis Biddle, and Congressman Leonidas Dyer. The efforts of the NAACP was crucial in fashioning lynching as a tragedy that besmirched not just the South, but also the country as a whole, which thus required a national response.

Southern blacks were also instrumental in reducing the number of lynchings. In many instances, they asserted the economic disadvantages to lynching. In some instances, they would boycott businesses whose employees participated in lynch mobs.[7] Also, the exodus of blacks that would typically occur after a lynching created a labor shortage to the extent that, in some instances, concerned white citizens would issue a public statement calling for a halt on attacks against blacks.[8] Another subtle tactic used by blacks was to appeal to the economic self-interest of white planters to intercede on their behalf. Lynching meant there was one less person that could be exploited economically.[9] In addition to myriad economic tactics, Southern blacks also confronted lynchings directly. Whether in the form of spontaneous collective actions,[10] organized groups of self-defense,[11] and/or individual acts of defiance,[12] Southern blacks prevented a number of lynchings from occurring.

In addition to individuals and groups pushing for the end of lynchings, there were also historical forces at work that led to the decline of lynching. Urbanization and industrialization in the South contributed to an atmosphere that was not conducive to lynching. With urbanization and industrialization came improvements in transportation, communication, and education. These improvements interwove communities that were once considered isolated into a broader cosmopolitan network, thereby problematizing the localized nature of lynchings and rendering them increasingly anachronistic. These improvements also made it harder for proponents of lynchings to disavow and/or dispute newspaper reports.

Both world wars also proved to be instrumental in shaming America into confronting its racist legacies and emboldening the disenfranchised. The hypocrisy of American foreign policy and American domestic policy came to a head during this time. As democracy became the watchword for American foreign policy, it subsequently began to illuminate the racist deficiencies in American domestic policy. Michael Klarman states:

> [T]he purpose of World War I was "to make the world safe for democracy" and that of World War II to defeat fascism. The democratic ideology of such conflicts forced Americans to confront, and sometimes to reform, their own contradictory practices, such as racial subordination.... The commitment of Nazis to Aryan supremacy helped give racism a bad name in the United States.[13]

The NAACP also made a connection between what we were fighting for abroad and what was occurring at home: "[O]ur government, raising its hands in horror over persecution on the other side of the world, might take a moment to glance at its own back yard [*sic*], where it would see Hitlerism . . . directed against citizens who happen not be white."[14] In his book on the history of suffrage in the United States, Alexander Keyssar notes the general pattern of extending the franchise after wars.[15]

The migration of blacks from the South to the North also proved to be deleterious for maintaining the stranglehold whites had over the South. Black migration spurred a labor shortage in the South and made black voters more influential in presidential elections in several pivotal states, which proved critical in the 1948 election. According to historian Harvard Sitkoff,

> many political analysts credited the Negro vote with being the decisive factor [in the 1948 presidential election]. Dewey would have won if Truman had not polled a higher percentage of the Negro vote than Roosevelt had done in any of his four presidential victories. Truman's plurality of Negro votes in California, Illinois, and Ohio proved the margin of victory.[16]

The increasing electoral importance of blacks who lived outside the South contributed to loosening the grip that white Southerners had in national policymaking.

Although the work of social actors and historical factors all seem to point to the demise of lynching, it did not translate directly into federal action. As opposition to lynching grew, the federal government faced mounting pressure to get involved. For Congress, this pressure translated primarily into new antilynching legislation. Although 257 antilynching bills were introduced in Congress from 1882 to 1951, none of these bills ever reached the Senate floor for a vote and hence did not become law. As mentioned in Chapter 3, the multiple veto points of Southern intransigence coupled with Northern passivity help explain why it was so hard to reactivate federal rights enforcement in the United States. Support for antilynching legislation was not deep or wide enough to warrant a frontal assault on Southern Democrats. In the end, antilynching legislation was simply not a high enough priority to sacrifice other aspects of the legislative agenda. The transaction costs were too high for many members of Congress to overcome and, with federal inaction being couched in legalistic terms, it made it easy for Congress to evoke their fealty to judicial rulings as a way to engage in blame avoidance. Political leadership on the issue would have to come from elsewhere.

Presidents were keenly aware of the political pressure directed at them to do something about the racial violence plaguing the South, but throughout this period they were very slow to react as a result, primarily, of the conflicting interests facing them at the time. Before Franklin Roosevelt's administration, presidents did very little to address lynchings in the South. Benjamin Harrison was the first president to advocate a new federal law against lynching, but he stressed the limitations of federal power in interracial matters and emphasized, instead, the importance of sectional harmonies.[17] Taft would go no further than to deplore mobbing, to hope that killers would be punished, and to recite the need for better law enforcement in general.[18] Although William McKinley served in the Civil War, championed civil rights in Congress, and dispatched troops to block lynchings while serving as governor of Ohio, as president, he did nothing.[19] Woodrow Wilson asked the states to curb lynchings, but he did not commit any federal resources or ask Congress to outlaw mob law.[20]

During Roosevelt's administration, things began to change slowly. In 1934, Roosevelt denounced lynching as one of the nation's major crimes.[21] In 1937, Roosevelt arranged to have Justice Department attorneys help the NAACP legal staff prepare a new bill that could be approved as constitutional.[22] In 1942, Roosevelt directed the Department of Justice informally "to make an automatic investigation in all cases of Negro deaths where the suspicion of lynching is present."[23] But, Roosevelt's ambivalence regarding new antilynching legislation suggests that he was only willing to go so far. In 1935, when the Wagner–Costigan antilynching bill was being filibustered by the Senate, Roosevelt told NAACP Secretary Walter White, "The Southerners by reason of the seniority rule in Congress are chairmen or occupy strategic places on most of the Senate and House committees. If I come out for the antilynching bill now, they will block every bill I ask Congress to pass to keep America from collapsing."[24] Roosevelt only went as far as the Southern Democrats would permit.

President Truman faced similar obstacles during his administration. Truman publicly supported the Fair Employment Practices Committee in 1945, urged for the abolition of the poll tax, endorsed wide-ranging civil rights legislation, and issued an executive order to desegregate the military and federal civil service. He was also horrified by the lynchings of black men who were still wearing their military uniforms. After being briefed on such violence, President Truman convened, in 1947, a special committee on civil rights, aptly named the National Emergency Committee against Mob Violence, which came out with a report that called specifically for the need to protect the rights of citizenship and personal security.[25] However, after Southern donors canceled an estimated half million dollars in contributions to the Democratic National Committee, and talk of a Southern revolt began to gain steam, Truman, according to historian Harvard Sitkoff,

> quietly backtracked. . . . Truman attempted to defuse the civil rights issue by remaining silent. . . . To underscore his removal from the civil rights issue, the President made seventy-three speeches on his "nonpolitical" tour of eighteen states in June, 1948, mentioning civil rights just once.[26]

But unlike Roosevelt, there was some thawing out of the electoral rigidity established and perpetuated by Southern Democrats. During the Democratic Convention in July 1948, although the president had revised his original position on civil rights and was now calling for a compromise, a civil rights revolt engineered by a small group of urban liberals and blacks were able to defeat the South and the Truman loyalists by 651 1/2 to 582 1/2, thereby pledging the Democratic Party to support the president's stated civil rights program.[27] Approximately four months later, Truman became the first American president to speak in Harlem. For the first time since Reconstruction, civil rights occupied a central place on the political stage.

Although by no means a civil rights enthusiast, Eisenhower nevertheless took this forward momentum for federal rights enforcement one step further. In 1956, President Eisenhower federalized the Arkansas National Guard and ordered elements of the 101st Airborne Division into Little Rock, Arkansas, after Governor Orval Faubus's refusal to put down violence that was expected to occur when plans for the integration of Central High School was being implemented. This integration was the result of a decision in the U.S. district court for the eastern district of Arkansas, which meant that it was under federal court supervision. Eisenhower viewed Faubus's intransigence as a challenge to national supremacy. In a letter to Georgia Senator Richard Russell, Eisenhower stated:

[W]hen a State, by seeking to frustrate the orders of a Federal Court, encourages mobs of extremists to flout the orders of a Federal Court, and when a State refuses to utilize its police powers to protect against mobs persons who are peaceably exercising their rights under the Constitution as defined in such court orders, the oath of office of the President requires that he take action to give that protection.[28]

According to legal historian Michal Belknap,

Confronted with violent resistance to the Brown decision, the administration had failed to assume any responsibility for the problem until the open defiance of Governor Faubus made a mockery of its reliance on the states, confronted the nation with a genuine constitutional crisis, and virtually compelled the president to use military force to restore order. Faced with an epidemic of racist bombings, the Eisenhower administration moved reluctantly toward an expansion of federal authority which even many white southerners regarded as essential.[29]

In other words, Eisenhower did not want to intervene; he was compelled to act. Inaction could have resulted in nullification.

Kennedy continued Eisenhower's policy of reluctant expansion of federal authority. In 1961, President Kennedy made an official finding that law and order had broken down in Montgomery, Alabama, and he ordered the attorney general to take whatever steps necessary to restore it. Like the Little Rock incident, this Montgomery incident involved a federal court decision. In this case, the issue was the segregation of interstate buses. Federal marshals were sent to Monroe, North Carolina, and Department of Justice leaders sought an injunction and even prosecuted nine Anniston residents on charges of willfully burning an interstate bus. In 1962, President Kennedy federalized the Mississippi National Guard and the Alabama National Guard to maintain peace and order while schools were implementing the Supreme Court decision for desegregation. With regard to these instances of federal intervention, Attorney General Burke Marshall stated that federal incursions were "a temporary and localized alteration of the federal system."[30] According to Belknap, "the Kennedy administration manifested a similar reluctance to see the national government assume responsibility for protecting the victims of violent resistance to racial change. Only when no other option remained would the federal cavalry ride South to the rescue."[31] In other words, these instances of federal incursion were not indications of any change in the autonomy normally provided to Southerners regarding racial matters. Federal intervention was meant to be understood as the exception to the norm.

Presidential reluctance to engage in federal rights enforcement for blacks gradually waned over time. It was as if each president, starting from Roosevelt, expanded the federal government's efforts to curb racial violence in the South slowly and incrementally. But at that time, no president was willing to take the lead on federal rights enforcement. Although Eisenhower and Kennedy had sent in federal troops, it was out of desperation. Although there seemed to be a growing weariness with the racial status quo, the legislative and executive branches of government were clearly apprehensive in doing something drastic.

The federal judiciary was very careful in staying within the parameters set by the other branches during this period. The federal government would intervene only in cases of "crises" that implicated the federal government directly. That said, the federal courts during this period focused most of their attention on minimizing the direct collusion of law enforcement officials with lynch mobs.

On May 21, 1940, the Department of Justice postulated that it was possible to prosecute violent perpetrators with already existing legislation. There were two laws in the books that could be used: Sections 241 and 242 of Title 18 of the U.S. Code. Section 241 was taken verbatim from the Enforcement Act of 1870—the same one that Amos Akerman used to prosecute the Klan—and Section 242 was taken from the Civil Rights Act of 1866. A circular issued to U.S. attorneys in May 21, 1940, stated that Section 241 was available for prosecution of private persons who conspired to violate a limited class of civil rights. This limited class of civil rights explicitly included a "federal right not to be lynched." The memorandum went on to say:

> There appears to be no case foreclosing this interpretation. . . . Nevertheless, since such prosecution *may arouse antagonism* [emphasis added] on States' rights grounds, for jury reasons and perhaps also as a matter of constitutional law it should not be resorted to except in cases of flagrant and persistent breakdown of local law enforcement either in general or with respect to a particular type of cases.[32]

In other words, according to the Department of Justice, it was not a question of legal capacity or authority that prevented the federal government from curbing racial violence; rather, it was that federal intervention "may arouse antagonisms," antagonisms so firmly embedded politically that federal non-intervention had attained such a degree of consistency, stability, and rigidity that it had achieved a lawlike status. Grafting the political onto the legal in this manner made reactivating the law appear to be usurping the law. In so doing, it entrenched the active policy of non-enforcement that much more. Unlike other political policies that can change with simple majorities, the legalese of federal inaction made reactivating federal rights enforcement an act of extraordinary will. It necessitated a crisis of sorts, one not seen since Reconstruction.

To avoid stirring up antagonisms, the Justice Department initially focused primarily on what it thought was the least controversial aspect of lynchings, which was law enforcement officials who had participated directly in a lynching. The major hurdle in securing a conviction was figuring out what constituted "state action." Did state action simply consist of behavior legislated explicitly and sanctioned by the state? Did it include the actions of people employed by the state? Did it include inaction taken by the state and/or officials working for the state?[33] Although most, if not all, understood state action to include the first option, there was disagreement with regard to the second, and even more widespread disagreement about the last question. Thus, based on prevailing sentiment, many presumed it would be easier to secure a conviction against law enforcement officials who participated in a lynching than non-public officials who participated in a lynching. This strategy of going after law enforcement officials had mixed results in the beginning but would eventually prevail.

During the 1940s, the Justice Department clearly followed a conscious strategy to obtain judicial sanction for its interpretation of civil rights statutes.[34] In *United States v. Sutherland*, the Department of Justice went after a police officer who was accused of using brutal methods to exact a confession from a black prisoner.[35] One of the rights the Department of Justice sought to protect in this case was the right not be deprived of life and liberty without due process of law.[36] In *United States v. Holder*, the Justice Department indicted a jailer who took a black farmer out of jail and lynched him.[37] Although neither case led to a conviction, the judge in each respective case upheld the claim that the law enforcement official "acted under the color of law." This interpretation would be crucial for later cases if only because acting under the color of law presumes state action.

Although *Sutherland* and *Holder* might be considered mild setbacks, other cases proved otherwise. In *United States v. Classic*, the Supreme Court affirmed the Justice Department's claim that applies to the actions of law enforcement officials.[38] This case involved five election officials from Louisiana who were indicted for altering cast ballots by qualified voters and for falsely certifying the number of votes cast in the primary election. They were charged with conspiring to deprive citizens of their constitutional rights as voters to have their ballots counted as cast in a congressional primary, and conspiring to deprive candidates for federal office of their right to have ballots cast in their favor counted honestly. Although this case might at first appear tangential to lynchings, it is important because it outlined the extent of the federal government's reach. In the majority decision, Chief Justice Stone states:

> Misuse of power, possessed by virtue of state law and made possible only because the wrongdoer is clothed with the authority of state law, is action taken under color of state law.[39]

By clothing the actions of state officers as such, Stone affirmed the use of Section 242 as a weapon for prosecuting official deprivations of civil rights.[40]

In 1943, this interpretation of Section 242 was applied to a lynching. In June 1943, a black man was hunted down and shot to death by a mob of Indiana farmers led by a sheriff and his deputies. In *United States v. Trierweiler*, the officers were indicted under Section 242. This lower federal court case ended in nolo contendere (no contest) pleas from the nine defendants and, in 1946, they were fined $200 and costs. This "technically successful prosecution" confirmed the federal government's authority to act against local officials who participated directly in a lynch mob.[41]

In 1945, the Supreme Court, in *Screws v. United States*, upheld the conviction of a Georgia sheriff and his two accomplices who had beat up a handcuffed Robert Hall, a black citizen of the United States and of Georgia, with their fists and a solid-bar blackjack until he was unconscious and then dragged him to jail where he was left for dead.[42] Many at the time, including Robert Carr, who served as the executive secretary of President Truman's Committee on Civil Rights, hailed this ruling as "profoundly important to the cause of civil liberty."[43] Unfortunately, this case ended up, perversely, hindering later prosecutions because it hinged the constitutionality of Section 242 on a requirement of "willfulness." Willfulness is interpreted as "a specific intent to deprive a person of a federal right made definite by decision or other rule of law" or "made specific either by the express terms of the Constitution or laws of the United States or by decisions interpreting them."[44] This requirement of willfulness proved to be a major obstacle. Legal historian Eugene Gressmen notes how:

> It is difficult to convince a jury that the defendant police officer knew of a spe-
> cific federal right as spelled out by a badly-split Supreme Court decision and
> willfully intended to deprive his victim of that right. That difficulty was dem-
> onstrated by the acquittal that the retrial in the *Screws* case produced.[45]

So although *Screws* might at first appear to be a landmark decision that could have possibly paved the way for future prosecutions, it actually ended up hindering later cases because of the stringent standards it placed on Section 242. It was only in 1966, with *U.S. v. Guest* and *U.S. v. Price*, did the Supreme Court circumvent the stringent demands of *Screws*.[46] Before *Guest* and *Price*, it seemed clear that the Court wanted to distance itself from the vicissitudes of lynchings without necessarily being responsible for handling all lynchings. Any positive sanctioning of lynch mobs would have brought the Court closer to lynch mobs and thus would have unduly marred the "steady, upright, and impartial" nature of the Court that is essential if it is to administer the law.

Although Section 242 was used to indict law enforcement officials who partici-pated in lynchings directly, it was thought by some that Section 241 could be used to indict private persons. The Justice Department tested this hypothesis in the Cleo Wright lynching.[47] Unfortunately, the jury refused to indict. Legal historian John Elliff concluded that the jury's refusal to indict had nothing to do with the lack of evidence, but "rather disagreement with the Government's legal theory" that Sec-tion 241 covered lynchings primarily done by private persons.[48]

After the Cleo Wright case, the Justice Department followed developments but made no formal federal investigations of lynchings that involved primarily private persons. In the murder of Lamar Smith in Mississippi, the Department of Justice followed local developments closely, but no formal investigation was conducted.[49] Public outcry over federal non-intervention reached a fever pitch with the lynching of Emmett Till. In 1955, Emmett Till was killed for having whistled at a white woman. The case made national headlines. Although the Justice Department fol-lowed the case, no formal investigation was made for the reason that no violation of any federal statute was thought to be involved.[50] To be clear, the legal decision not to prosecute the lynchers of Lamar Smith and Emmett Till was made by the Justice Department, not the courts. This is important because by no means should the Justice Department's interpretation of Section 241 be taken as the official legal interpretation of the courts. By preventing these instances from even reaching the federal courts, the Justice Department effectively shielded the federal judiciary from having to make any substantive decision. Rather than forcing the courts to make a decision at a time when conditions were not favorable for conviction, the Justice Department waited until conditions were favorable. It was only when conditions turned favorable that the Justice Department pushed the courts into making a decision.

During this period, the racist status quo started to crack. Pressure brought on by individuals and groups seemed to be working, but all three branches of government were slow to respond. Congress showed signs of support, but was in no way able to lead. The president got involved reluctantly, but was adamant that each intervention be seen as temporary and isolated, and should thus not be seen as transforming normal federal–state relations. The federal courts were getting involved, but were clearly only willing to deal with one particular aspect of lynchings. The federal government was not yet ready to return to the kind of vigorous federal rights enforcement seen during the early period of Reconstruction.

RUPTURE

Leading up to the 1960s there was growing dissatisfaction with what was going on in the South. This dissatisfaction manifested itself in the form of lobbying Congress for an antilynching bill, urging the president to intervene, pressuring the Justice Department to prosecute lynchers, lobbying, holding rallies, conducting letter-writing campaigns, and so on. For the most part, those who wanted change operated peacefully, making sure to avoid confrontation. This, however, changed drastically during the 1960s. At that time, activist groups became aware of their collective ability to provoke a crisis and they changed tactics from peaceful persuasion to nonviolent provocation.[51] From sit-ins to freedom rides to marching into anticipated danger, civil right activists placed their body in harm's way in the hope of forcing the hand of the federal government. Although civil rights activists such as Bob Moses had, at first, concentrated efforts at trying to get Southern blacks to solve their problems alone, "the constant harassments faced by the civil rights workers" convinced him in the 1960s that "federal protection was necessary to achieve significant breakthrough."[52] With that in mind, civil rights activists began to devise various strategies that would expose the viciousness and barbarity of Southern racism, thereby garnering nationwide media attention, which would then, hopefully, spur the federal government to intervene. Legal historian Michal Belknap was drastic in his assessment: "[T]hey [civil rights activists] were shrewd enough to realize that, in order to capture the country's attention and force Washington to act, someone would have to die."[53]

This strategy of inciting brutal repression came to a head in Birmingham, Alabama. After a somewhat failed attempt at securing civil rights in Albany, Georgia, civil rights organizers in 1963 focused on one of the most segregated cities in the country, in part because they were searching for a city with a police chief who was prone to use violence. As Wyatt Walker, a lieutenant for Martin Luther King, stated: "We knew that when we came to Birmingham that if [police commissioner] Bull Connor was still in control, he would do something to benefit our movement. We didn't want to march after Bull was gone."[54] The strategy seemed to work. Television and newspaper coverage featured images of police dogs attacking unresisting demonstrators, some of whom were children. Newspaper editorials called it "a national disgrace." Congressmen condemned the "shocking episodes of police brutality." Even President Kennedy weighed in, stating that one of the photographs made him "sick."[55] Historians generally agree that Birmingham was the turning point.[56]

As the civil rights movement's strategy of nonviolent provocation was reaching its nadir, John F. Kennedy was assassinated and Vice President Lyndon B. Johnson was sworn in as president on November 22, 1963. As former Senate majority leader from Texas, Lyndon B. Johnson, according to historian Mark Stern, "scrupulously observed southern legislative norms when it came to race relations."[57] LBJ even said he "was not going to stick his neck out to do anything for Negroes and get defeated."[58] Under the tutelage of U.S. Senator Richard Russell from Georgia, who was known at the time as the leader of the South in the Senate, LBJ was being groomed to be the Southern reconciliation president.[59] His southern pedigree seemed so firmly established that insiders in the Kennedy administration such as Robert Kennedy declared: "Can you think of anything more deplorable than [LBJ] trying to run the United States? That's why he can't ever be President."[60] But, like the previous Johnson who was president after an assassination, LBJ wound up surprising both his critics and his supporters.

Although his congressional voting record on race was in complete accordance with the rest of the Southern Democrats, he nonetheless did intimate a degree of dissimilarity. In his debut on the floor of the Senate in 1949, he stated that "racial prejudice is dangerous because it is a disease of the majority endangering minority groups."[61] As vice president he went even further. In an article in the *Washington Post,* LBJ is quoted as saying:

> [T]he President has to go in there [into the South] without cussing at anybody
> or fussing at anybody . . . and be the leader of the nation and make a moral

commitment to them [the Negroes]. . . . You see, this fellow Baldwin, he says, 'I don't want to marry your daughter, I want to get you off my back,' and that's what these Negroes want. They want that moral commitment. The president should stick to the moral issue and he should do it without equivocation. . . . I know the risks are great and it might cost us the South, but those sorts of states may be lost anyway.[62]

Although previous twentieth-century Democratic presidents were wary of intervening in the South for fear of the electoral and political blowback that would inevitably occur among Southern Democrats, LBJ—when he became president in November 22, 1963—was willing to see past that.

Between overcoming the longest Senate filibuster in history—fifty-seven days— to pass the 1964 Civil Rights Act and the explicit acknowledgment that federal troops would be used if and when violent outbreak ensued, the federal government, led by President Lyndon B. Johnson, turned a new page in which the federal government signaled, once again, its proactive choice to quell racial violence in the South. In his first televised address as President, LBJ stated "We have talked long enough in the country about equal rights. We have talked one hundred years or more. It is now time to write the next chapter—and to write it in the books of law."[63] He even warned his former mentor, Senator Richard Russell: "Dick, you've got to get out of my way. I'm going to run over you. I don't intend to cavil or compromise. I don't want to hurt you, but don't stand in my way."[64] This stern commitment from the president was crucial in overcoming the normal senatorial pressures for concession and compromise.

In addition to passing strong civil rights legislation, President Johnson also was proactive with regard to federal rights enforcement. After the violent events that occurred in Selma, Alabama, in March 1964, LBJ told Alabama Governor George Wallace that "he would not hesitate one moment to send in federal troops."[65] LBJ followed up this strong wording in his speech to Congress: "[T]he time for waiting is gone. . . . Their cause must be our cause too. It is not just Negroes, but it is all of us, who must overcome the crippling legacy of bigotry and injustice. And we shall overcome."[66] Clearly, a new page had been turned and the federal government, led by LBJ, could not have given a more obvious signal that it was intent on using whatever means necessary to quell racial violence in the South.

It was only after LBJ's pronouncement "to write it in the books of law" did the Supreme Court, in effect, return to the law.[67] Up until LBJ's administration, there had been mounting criticism levied on the federal judiciary's lack of involvement on issues pertaining to racial violence in the South. This mounting pressure, alongside the transformations led by LBJ, catalyzed a change. There was historical precedent, dating back to the end of Reconstruction, for the federal government not to get involved in racial violence in the South. Although there had been instances of federal intervention since Reconstruction, these instances were considered at the time as "isolated and temporary departures from a general policy of leaving the problem of racist terrorism to the states."[68] For the Court to reverse such a historical precedent, one would think a new law passed by Congress, an executive order by the President, and/or an overtunig of law by the court would be necessary. But with regard to lynchings, the Supreme Court took none of these approaches. In *U.S. v. Price* and *U.S. v. Guest*, the Court simply seemed to change its mind or, as legal historian Michal Belknap states so eloquently, "reinterpret old statutes."[69]

These cases reflect not only the continuing capacity of the federal government to intervene in quelling racial violence, but also confirm this capacity tended to be reserved for emergency conditions. The quotidian nature of racial violence was clearly anything but exceptional. What was exceptional, however, was when that racial violence transcended its own banality and was elevated to the level of crisis. Attorney General Amos Akerman understood this. Akerman considered the actions of the Klan to have "amounted to war, and cannot be effectually crushed on any other theory."[70] Akerman believed that "unless the people become used to the exercise of these powers now, while the national spirit is still warm with the glow of the late war . . . the 'state rights' spirit may grow troublesome again."[71] So did the civil rights activists of the 1960s. Historian Clayborne Carson states that one of the significant legacies of the freedom rides was its ability to "provoke a crisis that would attract international publicity and compel federal intervention," and instilled in the participants "a moralistic sense of personal commitment that made them intolerant of political expediency."[72] Legal historian Michael Klarman also noted that

> to transform northern opinion, then, southern civil rights leaders concluded
> that they had to provoke violence against themselves, especially in settings that
> were likely to attract national media attention. Direct-action protest would
> probably incite brutal repression, and if the conflict lasted long enough, the
> national media would pay attention and so would the nation.[73]

Whether it was taking advantage of the crisis that had befallen the nation, as was the case after the Civil War, or whether it was creating a crisis the nation needed to confront, as was the case with the civil rights movement, each surmised the importance of a crisis to impress upon the president as sovereign authority that the exception of federal protection for blacks was needed.

It was the crisis setting spurred by the civil rights movement that allowed the Supreme Court to "push the reset button."[74] During the 1960s, the Supreme Court, without any new laws having been passed, finally reversed course and ruled in favor of prosecuting private citizens who deprived other private citizens of the rights afforded to them by the Fourteenth Amendment.[75] During this tumultuous period, justices voiced concerns about "issuing unenforceable orders" and how they might "bring the court into contempt and the judicial process into discredit."[76] They were also nevertheless cognizant, according to legal historian Michael Klarman, that there was a "conversion of an emerging national consensus into a constitutional command."[77] When the Johnson administration affirmed that when the "law of the land" was violated, "appropriate action" would follow and forced Archibald Cox to step down as solicitor general and replaced him with Thurgood Marshall to argue the government's case in *Price* and *Guest*, it sent a clear signal that the White House wanted to reactivate federal rights enforcement.[78] In what legal scholar Burt Neuborne has termed "a judicial version of Reconstruction," he characterized the dramatic reversal of the Warren Court as understandable only as operating within "an implied emergency" wherein the Court's decisions "reflect pragmatic responses to the moral crises over race relations that gripped the nation in the aftermath of WW II."[79] In a memorandum to his colleagues regarding the *Guest* case, Justice Brennan made note of the "urgent needs of the times,"[80] and it was this contextual situation that allowed the Court to render a decision that even sympathetic analysts have considered "nothing short of revolutionary."[81] In other words, it took another crisis—namely, the moral crisis that emerged because of the civil rights movement—for the Court to reengage in federal rights enforcement for racial violence.

CONCLUSION

In his book *The Divided Welfare State*, Jacob Hacker describes the social welfare policies in a manner that is also an apt depiction of the federal response to lynchings: "The choices and failures that created this distinctly unsatisfactory system grew out of embedded features of American politics and out of strategic choices at critical junctures."[82] With regard to lynching, these strategic choices were, essentially, political choices that later morphed into jurisprudential misconceptions mired in legalese. Although typically understood as primarily a matter of state rights, federal inaction concerning lynching was mostly a result of three factors: (1) the resilience of Southern racism, (2) the unwillingness of political authorities to suffer the transaction costs that would occur as a result of standing up against lynchings and (3) tactics of blame avoidance that included the depoliticizing tendency to isolate the issue of federal rights enforcement as solely a legalistic issue espoused by an activist judiciary.

LBJ expressed concerns that his efforts might spell the demise of the Democratic Party for years to come.[83] The exodus of Southern Democrats as epitomized by the Dixiecrat Revolt is evidence that his concerns were warranted.[84] The transaction costs of overcoming Southern intransigence and Northern passivity were indeed dire, but the key point here was that it did not include the usurpation of the law. The actions of LBJ had judicial precedent. For all the legalistic talk of state rights, federalism, and judicial activism, when LBJ signaled that "the time for waiting is gone," the judiciary was anything but a deterrent.

The judiciary's behavior in regards to lynching is reminiscent of Justice Jackson's commentary regarding the zone of twilight. In the Steel Seizure Cases, Jackson created a tripartite scheme of evaluating presidential action.[85] Although the first category involved a clear agreement between Congress and the president, and the third category consists of a clear violation between Congress and the president, Jackson describes the murky second category as such:

> [T]here is a zone of twilight in which he and Congress may have concurrent authority, or in which its distribution is uncertain. Therefore, congressional inertia, indifference or quiescence may sometimes, at least, as a practical matter, enable, if not invite, measures on independent presidential responsibility. In this area, any actual test of power is likely to depend on the imperatives of events and contemporary imponderables, rather than on abstract theories of law.[86]

Unlike the other two categories, in which it seems clear what the Court should do, Jackson paints a reluctant court in matters occurring within this zone of twilight. There are matters that are best left to the executive and legislative branches, and that are not really judicial in scope. The tenuous nature of this zone of twilight suggests that, rather than coming out strong one way or another, the Court is well served to bide its time.

One way to bide time is for the Supreme Court not to take on cases. Another way for it to bide time was to take advantage of the flexibility inherent in "abstract theories of law" that can accommodate temporarily "actual tests of power" while nonetheless allowing for the contingency of "contemporary imponderables." This second tactic risks "instrumentalizing" the law to a certain degree, but does not sacrifice the scope of the law as the first tactic does.

With regard to lynching, one can see both tactics being used. During the twilight zone otherwise known as Reconstruction, the Court instituted a racialized emergency to accommodate the imponderable task of providing federal protection for Southern blacks against racial violence. The Court subsequently backtracked when both Congress and the president signaled they were "tired of these monstrosities." When both the legislative and executive branches suffered from "inertia, indifference, or quiescence," the Court—for the most part—did not take on cases, except those that impinged directly on national sovereignty. Subsequently, the Court stopped taking on cases, limiting its involvement to matters that involved the federal government directly, and only then to revert back to its original stance after LBJ decided to reengage in federal rights enforcement.

I remember when I shared your never-say-die enthusiasm.
But now I am no longer certain that such earnest commitment
is a help to our people in the absence of a still-to-be-discovered
new approach to our age-old problem. In fact, I fear that your
efforts to effect change through unthinking trust in the law
and the courts place you not on the side of black people,
but rather in their way.[1]

—DERRICK BELL

Conclusion

⌒

INTRODUCTION

In 2005, the Senate published a resolution that apologized for lynching. It stated that "protection against lynching was the minimum and most basic of federal responsibilities." It goes on to note "the Senate considered but failed to enact anti-lynching legislation."[2] These two statements seem incongruous. If protection against lynchings was the minimum and most basic of federal responsibilities, why was it necessary for the Senate to enact additional legislation? Shouldn't something as "basic" as protection against lynching have already been provided for? Statutory authorization presumes an expansion of federal responsibility that had not previously existed, which it should not have needed considering it was "the minimum and most basic of federal responsibilities." Protection against lynchings had in fact been provided for. It just was not acted on.

The Supreme Court dealt circuitously with this conundrum of inaction via a prolonged suspension of the law. I have come up with this concept of constitutional anarchy to elucidate how and why this suspension occurred. Constitutional anarchy resolves the question of authoritative inaction and places the dynamic relationship among the three branches of the federal government as the focal point. In this regard, this book offers a distinctive view of how the Court triangulates decision making in relation to itself, in relation to the other branches, and in relation to the people. Most analysts of the Court have prioritized one relation over all others.

Whether it is seeking to situate the Court solely in relation to itself[3] or in relation to happenings outside the Court,[4] these one-dimensional approaches seek to ground constitutional law on a single foundation.[5] Another viewpoint has conjectured a more dynamic relationship. With that approach, the Court's relationship with the other branches and the people is depicted as being more complex than the one-dimensional analysis provided by more traditional analysts.[6] The analysis in this book centers on interbranch relations as they pertain to a single issue over time.

Rather than dealing with the issue head-on, the Supreme Court instead created legally bounded regions of lawlessness. These pockets of anarchy were administered indirectly by the state in that the state actively withdrew, thereby allowing other entities to do the administering. Thus, there were concurrent jurisdictional orders operating simultaneously in a hierarchical fashion, which precluded criticisms that the state was too weak to enforce its own laws and that it was too totalizing to have to accept responsibility.

With regard to the legacy of Reconstruction, Karen Orren and Stephen Skowronek, leading scholars in American political development, stated: "[C]onstitutional changes that were all but dead-on-arrival, their paper persistence a mockery of democratic pretention, became important vehicles of transformation a century later, while leaving Reconstruction's own legacy no less clear."[7] Picking up from Orren and Skowronek, this book follows through with revisiting Reconstruction in light of what occurred approximately a century later. Although this retrospective revisiting of the past is susceptible to a presentist bias, it also calls into question why previous scholarship has not addressed how and why the federal government was able to re-engage with federal rights enforcement in the manner that it did during the 1960s.

The presumption that what happened during the 1880s had no bearing whatsoever to what happened during the 1960s—and that the Supreme Court justices during the 1960s simply interpreted law as they saw fit with no recourse to precedent—raises more questions than answers. Although many presume the Constitution is a "living law" that has adapted over time, it is important to parse out exactly when it is living anew and when it is reverting back to something it did previously. Although notions that the Court changes its mind to adapt to new times can sometimes shed light on the changing nature of American jurisprudence, it can also obscure the underlying complexity of judicial decision making. With regard to lynchings, the Supreme Court did not simply enact new law as it saw fit, but reactivated old law to fit in response to changing political conditions. This course of action is aligned with one of the core values of the judiciary. According to Alexander Hamilton, one of the essential qualities of a judiciary is its steadiness. It is the quality that helps the judiciary be "an excellent barrier to the despotism of the prince" as well as "a no less excellent barrier to the encroachments and oppressions of the representative government."[8] The whole function of the doctrine of stare decisis is to maintain this core value of steadiness. To presume discontinuity without exhausting how it could and was made continuous suggests a level of anomalous reasoning that defies the historical evidence as well as the very basis of stare decisis.

The extended period between the 1880s and 1960s when the Supreme Court was for the most part not taking on cases except for a few notable exceptions, suggests the Court was primarily concerned with maintaining constitutional continuity and staying in accord with the other branches. Constitutional anarchy is, admittedly, an obscure concept; but, its obscurity is more indicative of the difficulties of addressing racial violence primarily through the language of the law. Oftentimes, studies that focuses exclusive on the American system of jurisprudence ignores the democratic nature of American lawmaking. It is important to remember the inherent tension within a liberal democracy. David Garland elaborates further on this point: "Recall that liberalism and democracy, though today usually conjoined, are not quite the same thing. Democracy's central commitment is not to equality, nor to civil liberties, nor even to limited government, but to a form of rule in which 'the people' govern themselves."[9] Oftentimes when there is a conflict between the two, the democratic forces win. As legal historian Michael Klarman noted, "Constitutional law generally has sufficient flexibility to accommodate dominant public opinion, which the justices have little inclination, and limited power, to resist. . . . Ironically, when a minority group suffering oppression is most in need of judicial protection, it is least likely to receive it."[10] Thus, the democratic pressues to enforce or not enforce a law is as important and sometimes even more important than the law itself.

In many ways, the American system of jurisprudence is ill-equipped and ill-suited to combat something like lynchings. The law itself can be a hindrance. Political scientist Stephen Halpern elaborates this point with regard to education policies and argues that "the legal process itself limits both the questions asked and the solutions considered" because "lawyers must frame their analysis in terms of contrived concepts, issues, questions, and remedies that the legal system recognizes and deems legitimate."[11] With regard to the applicability of racial inequalities in education, he goes on to state: "[T]he litigation strategy asks too much of the courts and legal process and too little of ourselves as citizens of a democratic political order. It is a strategy doomed to frustrate and fail."[12] The same can be said of lynchings. Although the law can and has been used to address racial violence, the legal concepts of racial discrimination are nevertheless inadequate analytical tools for understanding and dismantling the tacit acceptance of lynchings.

The incapacity, inability and inherent shortcomings of the judiciary all point to what legal scholar Mark Graber refers to as "constitutional evil." Graber defines constitutional evil as "the practice and theory of sharing civic space with people committed to evil practices or pledging allegiance to a constitutional text and tradition saturated with concessions to evil."[13] When it came to lynchings in the late nineteenth to mid twentieth century, the people committed to evil practices made up the majority of the American electorate. This deadly combination of illiberal majoritarianism underscores why the greatest extension of rights for blacks had occurred during exceptional ruptures – Reconstruction and the Civil Rights Era of the 1960s. It is only those rare times when the ubiquity of racial violence transcends its own banality does it become politically viable. Other than that, it hides in plain sight.

This marginalization is not exclusive to African-Americans. The selective enforcement of the law that constitutional anarchy illuminates is similar to what happens whenever a marginalized group is demarcated spatially. In describing Chinatown in New York City, Asian American Studies Professor Peter Kwong noted:

> [Chinatown] is maintained by the informal political structure in Chinatown, with the tacit agreement of outside government officials. . . . Lack of government intervention has meant de facto rule of the community by a traditional Chinatown elite.[14]

In his investigation on homelessness, political scientist Leonard Feldman uncovered how homeless people have been "consigned to a subordinate legal and political status: the outlaw–citizen."[15] This consignment is actualized spatially. Homeless people "become the constitutive outside of the consumptive public sphere, a blockage—both physical and ideological—to the free movement of goods and consumers but a blockage that simultaneously constitutes the boundaries of public space."[16] Although both instances vary widely, the fact that the law is applied differentially to certain areas and certain inhabitants within that area suggests that constitutional anarchy could help in uncovering the legal operationalization occurring in both situations. References to Guantanamo Bay as a black hole also connote a sense of a legally bounded space of lawlessness.[17] It is not anarchy, because the rule of law was suspended only for certain people in a certain area. It is not orderly either, because the rule of law stopped itself short of total jurisdiction. A black hole is in between a full-blown state of nature and a pure rule-of-law regime. It is a *framework of contrived anarchy*.

Although lynchings have receded, racial violence against blacks nevertheless persists. In what is sometimes referred to as a *legalized lynching*, capital punishment is functionally analogous to lynchings.[18] According to David Garland, "if we look beyond forms and consider the practice substantively, many of the same social forces that once prompted lynchings nowadays prompt capital punishment; many of the same social functions performed by lynchings then are performed by capital punishment now."[19] At the same time however, he goes on to say:

> Viewed alongside lynchings, today's death penalty suggests a radical inversion of form, a mirror image, a reformed present that vehemently rejects its past. This negative symmetry is so striking that we must suppose that the contemporary American death penalty has, in important respects, been designed to be an antilynching.[20]

Although both lynchings and the death penalty share the same attributes of being a highly localized and racialized affair, the death penalty is nevertheless highly medicalized, bureaucratized, and performed by state actors in the confines of a centralized location. It is as if the proponents of the death penalty went to great pains to make sure the death penalty appeared to be nothing like lynchings, although it practically served the same function. Unlike lynchings, which is administered primarily by informal actors such as lynch mobs, the death penalty is decided on mainly by local prosecutors who are elected democratically and are "overlaid with ambivalence, anxiety and embarrassment, striving hard to appear lawful and nonviolent."[21] The formal authority of the local prosecutor replaced the anarchic nature of lynch mobs.

There has also been an upsurge of racialized killings by law enforcement officials. In 2012, it was reported that a black man was killed extrajudicially once every twenty-eight hours.[22] Another report noted that a young black male was twenty-one times greater to be shot dead by police than whites.[23] Journalist Rachel Levinson-Waldman evoked Fraenkel's dual state to illuminate how the legalism surrounding the grand jury decisions not to indict police officers in the death of Michael Brown and Eric Garner enabled lawlessness.[24]

Although there are many accounts of police brutality in communities of color, it is also the case that these communities have experienced a lack of law enforcement.[25] In 1990, a popular hip-hop group named Public Enemy came out with the song "911 is a joke," which opened with the following line: "I dialed 911 a long time ago/ Don't you see how late they're reactin'?" In Detroit, which is predominantly black, the *Wall Street Journal* recently reported that the Detroit police take fifty-eight minutes on average to respond to emergency calls. The national average is eleven minutes.[26] In his account of Chicago's Southside, sociologist Sudhir Venkatesh found: "Residents routinely protest for better policing. They request greater police presence around parks and abandoned areas as well as on children's routes to schools. Such requests may result in modest or temporary increases in local police presence, but there is widespread opinion based on decades of experience that this will not last longer than a few days or weeks. So, few rest their hopes on the police for long-term guarantees of security."[27]

Although lynchings were obscured by their problematic situatedness as somehow outside the law, these new modes of racialized violence are obfuscated because they are situated squarely within the law. Naomi Murakawa argues that "carceral violence was so lethal precisely because it was not arbitrary . . . [S]o long as state-sponsored racial violence, or white violence enabled and administered by the criminal justice system, was predictable, it might be construed as legitimate."[28] Cord Jefferson elaborates on the legitimacy of the current forms of racial violence and the difficulties this creates for journalists:

> [I]n America the racist traumas are widespread. How about the next time a black person is stopped and patted down without cause? How do you write about that humiliation in a way that's different from what you wrote when Forest Whitaker received the same treatment last year, and a New York City police chief before him, and thousands of other innocent black and Latino men before them? What new column shall the writer write when an unarmed black person is killed for doing nothing but frightening an armed white person? The same thing he wrote when Trayvon Martin was killed? And that's to say nothing of when Oscar Grant was killed. Or when Ramarley Graham was killed. Or when Timothy Stansbury Jr. was killed. Or when Amadou Diallo was killed. Or when Jordan Davis was killed. Or when Ousmane Zongo was killed. Or when Jonathan Ferrell was killed. Or when Renisha McBride was killed.[29]

The murder of African-Americans has been normalized to the extent that it not only makes it difficult for journalists to chronicle it in ways that can transcend the banality and yet expose the brutality, but also it alludes to why it often takes an extraordinary act of political will to engage.

Unlike lynchings, which begged the question of what the relationship between the state and society was, contemporary iterations of racial violence are mainly about the state and its relationship to itself.[30] With regard to the death penalty and police killings, there is no other referent in that the state is both the provocateur and the mediator. Lynchings were a tragedy that was democratic in form, and the response was for more law enforcement, stronger courts, and more government involvement. Unlike with lynchings, for which the question of state action was constantly an issue of debate, there is no doubt what state action constitutes when it comes to the death penalty or police killings. With lynchings, blacks looked to the state to stop lynch mobs, but when the state is the one doing the killing, where is there to go? The understood hope and remedy for many activists during the era of lynchings was for a liberal state, with the rule of law, checks and balances, and party politics that would hopefully reign in the racist excesses of the majoritarian democracy. But, now the very machinations of liberalism have come not only to administer the killing, but also to exonerate the killer and admonish those who are angry about the killing. Critics of racial violence who propose liberal remedies as they once did during lynchings are losing any basis on which to stand.

The unfolding of time is not indicative of any teleological sense of progress, but rather a complex dynamic of inclusion and oppression. The persistence of racial violence is emblematic of what Clarissa Rile Hayward and Todd Swanstrom refer to as "thick injustice: unjust power relations that are deep and densely concentrated, as well as opaque and relatively intractable. We argue that the historical roots of metropolitan justice, its relation to the structure of local governance in the United States, and its imbrication with physical space render it difficult to see and difficult to assign responsibility for it—and hence difficult to change."[31]

That said, it is important to note the resiliency of racial violence is also predicated in part on its ability to adapt. In his famous Ballot or Bullet speech, Malcolm X stated that "You and I in America are faced not with a segregationist conspiracy, we're faced with a government conspiracy."[32] In this speech, he is trying to shift the focus from the particular instantiation and institutionalization of racism of the current moment to the overarching framework of racism that is the basis by which the particular is embedded. But unlike Malcolm X who is at times prone to analyze racism as a meta-narrative that is somehow transhistorical in nature, I have endeavored to situate racial violence within a strict historical frame that highlights the ways in which it was both instrumental and malleable. Race as a socio-political construct suggests a level of contingency that precludes any semblance of transhistorical argumentation. But this contingent understanding of racism is strained by the fact that racism has nevertheless seemingly endured the test of time. In exposing the ways in which persistence is predicated on change, I hope to show how racism is not something intrinsically preordained but rather something instrumentally reconfigured. Racism is a socio-political construct that is constantly being reconstructed. The persistence lies not in anything intrinsic about race, but rather on the instrumental value of it as a construct and the ways in which American liberal democracy and its susceptibility to illiberal majoritarianism have been able to adapt and adjust.

Although lynchings appeared to represent the outright failure of liberal democracy to live up to even its most minimalist requirement, I have hopefully demonstrated how a liberal democracy dealt internally with its seeming contradiction. Constitutional anarchy illuminates how liberalism can at times be a "fighting creed" against itself.[33] As Richard Pildes noted, "[C]onstitutional law played a role in sustaining the blatant manipulations of political institutions that kept America from fully becoming a democracy."[34] It was easy for the federal government to wash its hands of lynchings and yet extremely difficult when it wanted to reengage. Constitutional anarchy evaded sweeping gestures when it was instituted, but required sweeping gestures for it to end. The subtlety added to its enduring quality. But, this subtlety of accommodating something that was anything but subtle reveals the dark side of the constitutional flexibility Roosevelt mentioned in his 1933 inaugural address. If it is the case that "our Constitution is so simple and practical that it is possible always to meet extraordinary needs by changes in emphasis and arrangement without loss of essential form," then what exactly is the point of having a Constitution?[35]

ↄ—

CHAPTER I

1. Franklin Delano Roosevelt, "First Inaugural Address, Washington D.C., March 4, 1933," in *Great Speeches*, ed. John Grafton (Mineola: Dover Publications, 1999), 32.

2. *Lynching in America* ed. Christopher Waldrep (New York: NYU Press, 2006), 231.

3. The National Association for the Advancement of Colored People (NAACP) made a collage of newspaper headlines dramatizing advance notice of Neal's fate. See James McGovern's Anatomy *of a Lynching: The Killing of Claude Neal* (Baton Rouge: Louisiana State University Press, 1982), 104.

4. In 1970, political historian Richard Hofstadter noted, "there are, for example, descriptive and statistical books on lynching, as well as works of moral protest; but there is no great history of the subject that assesses its place in the political culture of the South." Richard Hofstadter, "Reflections on Violence in the United States," in *American Violence: A Documentary History*, ed. Richard Hofstadter and Michael Wallace (New York: Vintage Books, 1971), 4. In his research, historian Michael Pfeifer found that "southern historians have focused little on how lynching reflected a perspective on law." Michael Pfeifer, *Rough Justice: Lynching and American Society, 1874–1947* (Urbana: University of Illinois Press, 2006), 5. When people do focus on the government's role, it is usually with respect to its failure to pass antilynching legislation. Perhaps the best example of this is seen in historian Claudine L. Ferrell's book, *Nightmare and Dream: Antilynching in Congress, 1917–1922* (New York: Garland Publishing, 1986).

5. Journalist Ida B. Wells wrote *On Lynchings* (Amherst: Humanity Books, 1892. Economist James Cutler wrote *Lynch-Law: An Investigation into the History of Lynching in the United States* (New York: Negro University Press, 1905). Law Professor James Chadbourn wrote *Lynching and*

the Law (Chapel Hill: University of North Carolina, 1933). Sociologist Arthur Raper wrote *The Tragedy of Lynching* (Chapel Hill: Arno Press, 1969). Sociologists Stewart Tolnay and Elwood M. Beck wrote *A Festival of Violence: An Analysis of Southern Lynchings, 1882–1930* (Urbana: University of Illinois, 1995). Historian W. Fitzhugh Brundage wrote *Lynching in the New South: Georgia and Virginia, 1880–1930* (Urbana: University of Illinois, 1993). Historian Christopher Waldrep wrote two books, *The Many Faces of Judge Lynch: Extralegal Violence and Punishment in America* (New York: Palgrave, 2002) and *A History in Documents: Lynching in America* (New York: NYU Press, 2006).

6. Those who have proffered explanations for lynching all seem to agree that the federal government played a minor role. In *The Promise of the New South: Life after Reconstruction* (Oxford: Oxford University Press, 1992), Edward Ayers argues that lynchings were related to population densities and black migration patterns. Stewart Tolnay and Elwood M. Beck correlate the number of lynchings with cotton production in their book *A Festival of Violence*. Charles S. Sydnor provides a cultural argument for lynching in his article, "The Southerner and the Laws," *The Journal of Southern History* 6 (1940): 3–23. Arthur Raper argues that "political scientists in the grip of consensus theory tended to treat episodes of mass violence in America as insignificant or aberrational—temporary exceptions to the norm of peaceful progress. . . . the effect not only of minimizing group violence in America, but of depriving it of political content" (Raper, *The Tragedy of Lynching*, editorial note

7. William E. B. Du Bois, *The Souls of Black Folk* (New York: Dover, 1994); Valdimer O. Key, *Southern Politics in State and Nation* (Knoxville: University of Tennessee Press, 1984); Ira Katznelson, *Fear Itself* (New York: Liveright, 2013).

8. Frederick Douglass, "Why Is the Negro Lynched?" in *Life and Writings of Frederick Douglass*, vol. IV, ed. Philip Foner (New York: International Publishers, 1955), 491.

9. In my designation of the "South," I include all eleven ex-Confederate States. They consist of Alabama, Arkansas, Florida, Georgia, Louisiana, Mississippi, North Carolina, South Carolina, Tennessee, Texas, and Virginia.

10. Ernst Fraenkel, *The Dual State: A Contribution to the Theory of Dictatorship*, trans. by E.A. Shils, (Oxford, 1941).

11. Although this is not the first time the United States has been characterized as a dual state, this is the first systematic attempt to link it to Ernst Fraenkel's particular concept. Richard Young and Jeffrey Meiser described the American dual state in the following manner: "a contract state, premised on the rule of law, that promoted the growth of a prosperous liberal democratic society of Anglo-Americans, and a predatory state that financed white liberal society through its ruthless exploitation of Indian lands and African American labor." Richard Young and Jeffrey Meiser, "Race and the Dual State in the Early American Republic," in *Race and American Political Development*, ed. Joseph Lowndes, Julie Novkov, and Dorian Warren (New York, Routledge, 2008), 31–32. Their version of the dual state and the dual state that I am proposing share many similarities, including centering their analysis on the federal level, emphasizing federal complicity with southern racism, and excavating the democratic basis for racism. The crucial difference is that their conception of the dual state deals mainly with the "centrality of state action" in establishing, maintaining, and adapting a racially predatory state, whereas my conception focuses primarily on the centrality of state inaction. Young and Meiser, "Race and the Dual State in the Early American Republic," 35. Thus, there is a duality within the dual state and, as such, the dual state I propose is less of a negation of Young and Meiser's conception as it is a supplement.

12. Ashraf Rushdy states that lynchings are "confounded by a problem of definition" and that "lynching is a term more evocative than descriptive." Ashraf Rushdy, *American Lynching*, (New Haven, Yale University Press, 2012), 3–6.

13. As quoted in James Harmon Chadbourn's *Lynching and the Law* (Chapel Hill: University of North Carolina Press, 1933), 29.

14. I have to thank Professor Christopher Waldrep for pointing this out to me. There is a common misperception that lynchings were exclusively a Southern phenomenon. This misperception is a result, in part, of the political agenda of data-collecting organizations such as the NAACP and the Tuskegee Institute to focus primarily on the South, thereby undercounting other areas. For example, William D. Carrigan and Clive Webb state that "the files at Tuskegee Institute contain the most comprehensive account of lynching victims in the United States, but they only refer to the lynching of fifty Mexicans in the states of Arizona, California, New Mexico and Texas. Our own research has revealed a total of 216 victims during the same time period." William D. Carrigan and Clive Webb, "The Lynching of Persons of Mexican Origin or Descent in the United States, 1848 to 1928," *Journal of Social History* 37 (Winter 2003): 412. For more information regarding the debate on the definition and number of lynchings, see Christopher Waldrep, "War of Words: The Controversy over the Definition of Lynching, 1899–1940," *The Journal of Southern History* LXVI (2000): 75–100; Ken Gonzales-Day, *Lynching in the West: 1850–1935* (Durham: Duke University Press, 2006); Carrigan and Webb, "The Lynching of Persons of Mexican Origin or Descent in the United States, 1848 to 1928," 411–438; Jean Pfaelzer, *Driven Out: The Forgotten War against Chinese Americans* (New York: Random House, 2007); and Waldrep, *Lynching in America*.

15. With that said, steps are being made to try and cull a comprehensive account. See Lisa Cook, "Converging to a National Lynching Database," *Historical Methods* 45 (2012): 55–63.

16. Tolnay and Beck, *A Festival of Violence*, 20–21.

17. William E. B. Du Bois, *Dusk of Dawn* (New York: Oxford University Press, 2007), 34.

18. Raper, *The Tragedy of Lynching*, editorial note.

19. Amy Louise Wood, *Lynching and Spectacle* (Chapel Hill: University of North Carolina Press, 2009).

20. Ibid., 27.

21. Winthrop Sheldon, "Shall Lynching Be Suppressed, and How?" in *The Arena*, Vol. 36, No. 202(September 1906): p. 227

22. Arthur Raper divided the accusations against persons lynched into seven categories: homicide, felonious assault, rape, attempted rape, robbery and theft, insult to whites, and all other causes (Raper, *The Tragedy of Lynching*, 482–483). James Cutler divided the accusations into eight categories: murder, rape, assault, minor offenses, desperadism, theft, arson, and unknown (Cutler, *Lynch-Law*, 175). Stuart Tolnay and Elwood M. Beck concluded that "murder—not rape—was the most common rationalization for lynching African-Americans" (Tolnay and Beck, *A Festival of Violence*, 50).

23. W. Fitzhugh Brundage, *Lynching in the New South: Georgia and Virginia, 1880–1930* (Urbana: University of Illinois Press, 1993), 19.

24. The racialized nature of lynchings was not exclusive to the South. In her book documenting the atrocities that befell Chinese Americans in the West during the late nineteenth century, Jean Pfaelzer wrote that "southern traditions of lynching, racial violence, Black Codes, arson, and policies denying land ownership to racial minorities surfaced in California, Oregon and the

Washington Territory . . . in the eyes of the American legal system, the Chinese were becoming black." Jean Pfaelzer, *Driven Out: The Forgotten War against Chinese Americans* (New York: Random House, 2007), 52–59. Carrigan and Webb argue that "the danger of lynching for a Mexican resident in the United States was nearly as great, and in some instances greater, than the specter of mob violence for a black person in the American South" ("The Lynching of Persons of Mexican Origin or Descent in the United States, 1848 to 1928," 414). Although similarities might exist, further research is needed to confirm whether my concept of constitutional anarchy applies to these instances as well. One distinct difference about the racialized lynchings in the South, however, was the brief period of proactive involvement by the federal government during the period otherwise known as *Congressional Reconstruction*.

25. Brundage, *Lynching in the New South*, 3. Although my focus on the South might be construed as reinforcing the already strong Southern bias in much of the existing literature on lynching, I am not trying to suggest that lynchings were strictly a Southern black phenomena. Historian Gonzales-Day rightly argues "that lynching has long been thought of in terms of black and white racial categories and [thus] has contributed to the general absence of information on cases involving other nonwhite communities, and it has ultimately served to lock blacks and whites in a false binary of race" (Gonzales-Day, *Lynching in the West*, 13). Although lynchings were occurring nationwide, there were regional variations in how they were carried out, legitimated, and eventually phased out. For example, with regard to lynchings in the American West, there were many allusions, however valid, to the frontier, whereas in the American South, there were many allusions, however valid, to "Southern traditions." My goal in focusing on lynchings in the South is to historicize and schematize the federal government's accommodation of extralegal justice. Although extralegal justice was a nationwide phenomenon, I will argue that the particular instantiations of extralegal justice that emerged in the postbellum South were related directly to the fallout from the Civil War. Southerners justified lynchings, in part, from drawing on the national narrative of extralegal justice, but also from drawing on a regional narrative that formed after the war. It was this blending of the local and the national that made the South unique.

26. Roy Nash, "Memorandum for Mr. Philip G. Peabody on Lynch-Law and the Practicability of a Successful Attack Thereon," May 22, 1916, NAACP Papers, Reel 1 (as quoted in Waldrep, *Lynching in America*, 79).

27. Cutler, *Lynch-Law*, 276.

28. Waldrep, *Lynching in America*, 68.

29. Raper, *The Tragedy of Lynching*; William Gillette, *Retreat from Reconstruction, 1869–1879* (Baton Rouge: Louisiana State University Press, 1979); and Wang, *The Trial of Democracy*. Christopher Waldrep goes so far as to say that the "political process failed. . . . Mob law rendered [the decisions made by the Supreme Court] meaningless" (Waldrep, *Lynching in America*, xix).

30. There have been excellent accounts written by political scientists regarding racial violence that is associated with elections. See Pamela Brandwein, *Rethinking the Judicial Settlement of Reconstruction*, (Cambridge, Cambridge University Press, 2014); Xi Wang, *The Trial of Democracy: Black Suffrage and Northern Republicans, 1860–1910*, (Athens: University of Georgia Press, 1997); Everette Swinney, *Suppressing the Ku Klux Klan: The Enforcement of the Reconstruction Amendments, 1870–1877*, (New York: Garland, 1987). These accounts, however, primarily examine electoral violence and do not focus on what is otherwise known as lynchings. I elaborate on this point in further detail in Chapter 4.

31. Tolnay and Beck, *A Festival of Violence*, 213.

32. Tolnay and Beck stated, "the Great Migration and the shrinking black labor force made the white elite realize that mob violence was a luxury that southern society could no longer afford" (Tolnay and Beck, *A Festival of Violence*, 221).

33. Ibid., 28–29.

34. The term *political* was used explicitly in reference to include both state and federal governments. In a later section of this chapter, I address the need to distinguish between two. But for now, the question of the political relates to both.

35. Thomas Sugrue comments, "it is noteworthy that during the most important period of state expansion in American history—the New Deal and World War II—Congress passed no significant civil rights legislation and the executive branch created only two small, underfunded units to deal with racial inequality, arguably the nation's most pressing and intractable domestic problem." Thomas Sugrue, "All Politics Is Local: The Persistence of Localism in Twentieth-Century American," in *The Democratic Experiment*, ed. Meg Jacobs, William Novak, and Julian Zelizer (Princeton: Princeton University Press, 2003), 311.

36. Ibid.

37. Desmond King and Stephen Tuck, "De-centering the South: America's Nationwide White Supremacist Order after Reconstruction," in *Past and Present*, Number 194, February 2007, p., 214

38. Dewey Grantham, *The Life and Death of the Solid South* (Lexington: University Press of Kentucky, 1992); Hilary Abner Herbert, *Why the Solid South?* (Baltimore: R. H. Woodward, 1890).

39. C. Vann Woodward, *The Strange Career of Jim Crow* (Oxford: Oxford University Press, 2002); Kimberley Johnson, *Reforming Jim Crow* (Oxford 2010); Brandwein, *Rethinking the Judicial Settlement of Reconstruction*.

40. *Plessy v. Ferguson*, 163 U.S. 537 (1896)

41. An example of conflating segregation with all iterations of racism can be found in Desmond King and Robert Lieberman's article titled "American State Building: The Theoretical Challenge." In this article, King and Lieberman examine five aspects of the American state: (1) the administrative state, (2) the standardizing state, (3) the fragmented state, (4) the associational state, and (5) the segregated state. The segregated state is meant to refer to all "the puzzles and dilemmas inherent in studying the American state's relationship to race." Desmond King and Robert Lieberman, "American State Building: The Theoretical Challenge," in *The Unsustainable American State*, ed. Lawrence Jacobs and Desmond King (Oxford: Oxford University Press, 2009), 313.

42. *Plessy v. Ferguson*, 163 U.S. 537, 544.

43. These are the words Judge Emmons used to qualify his sympathy for blacks. *Charge to Grand Jury-Civil Rights Act*, 30 F. Cas. 1005, 1006–1007 (C.C. W.D. Tenn.) (1875) (as quoted in Brandwein, *Rethinking the Judicial Settlement of Reconstruction*, 354–355).

44. *United States v. Cruikshank*, 25 F. Cas. 707 (C.C.D. La. 1874) (No. 14,897), aff'd, 92 U.S. 542 (1876), 714.

45. As mentioned, although lynchings had and were occurring in areas other than the South, most notably in the West, non-Southern lynchings represented less of a frontal attack on American sovereignty if only because the federal government had deemed southern lynchings explicitly as something akin to "the war on race." The fact that the federal government, during Reconstruction, had commented and involved itself in combating Southern lynchings is what distinguishes

Southern lynchings of blacks from the other lynchings that had and were occurring in other regions. As William Forbath noted, "This New South and its racial apartheid won a special constitutional status, becoming a distinct society within the Union's new constitutional order." William Forbath, "Constitutional Change and the Politics of History," *Yale Law Journal* 108 (1999), 1924. *This* will be discussed further in chapters 2 and 3.

46. U.S. House Committee on the Judiciary, *Civil Rights: Hearings . . . on . . . Miscellaneous Bills Regarding the Civil Rights of Persons Within the Jurisdiction of the United States*, 84th Cong., 2d sess., 1956, 23.

47. Letter to Richard Brevard Russell, September 27, 1957, in *The Papers of Dwight David Eisenhower*, vol. XVIII, *The Presidency: Keeping the Peace, Part II: Civil Rights, June 1957 to September 1957*, ed. Alfred Chandler Jr, Stephen Ambrose, Louis Galambos, Daun van Ee, Joseph Hobbs, and Elizabeth Hughes (Baltimore: Johns Hopkins Press 2001) (Little Rock, AR), chap. 5.

48. At the municipal and state levels, this is a different story. I explain later in this chapter why the focus is at the federal level and not municipal or state levels.

49. Tolnay and Beck characterized the federal government's role in lynching as "state-sanctioned terrorism" (*A Festival of Violence*, 29); Robert Kaczorowski argues that the failure to enforce constitutional rights of blacks is "attributable, in part, to Congress's and the president's unwillingness to put the nation on a war footing to combat the racial and political insurrection with which the Klan confronted the nation." Robert Kaczorowski, *The Politics of Judicial Interpretation: The Federal Courts, Department of Justice, and Civil Rights, 1866–1876* (New York, Fordham University Press, 2005), xv.

50. Maurice S. Evans, *Black and White in the Southern States: A Study of the Race Problem in the United States from a South African Point of View* (London: Longsman, Green and Co., 1915), 4. Others who have compared the racial policies of these countries include John Cell, *The Highest Stage of White Supremacy* Cambridge, Cambridge University Press, 1982); George Fredrickson, *White Supremacy: A Comparative Study of American and South African History* (New York: Oxford University Press, 1982); and Stanley Greenberg, *Race and State in Capitalist Development: Studies on South Africa, Alabama, Northern Ireland and Israel* (New Haven: Yale University Press, 1980).

51. Anthony W. Marx, *Making Race and Nation: A Comparison of the United States, South Africa and Brazil* (Cambridge, Cambridge University Press, 1998), 7.

52. C. Vann Woodward, *The Strange Career of Jim Crow* (Oxford: Oxford University Press, 2002), 121.

53. Ibid., 107–121.

54. Marx, *Making Race and Nation*, 7–13.

55. Thomas Sugrue states that "localism often reinforced structural patterns of inequality by enshrining local prejudices into practice" (Sugrue, "All Politics Is Local," 310).

56. William Novak, *The People's Welfare: Law and Regulation in Nineteenth-Century America* (Chapel Hill: University of North Carolina Press, 1996), 10.

57. *Civil Rights Cases*, 109 U.S. 3, 11 (1883).

58. William Howard Taft, Inaugural Address, March 4, 1909, http://avalon.law.yale.edu/20th_century/taft.asp. Accessed June 1, 2015

59. Congress made several attempts at passing antilynching legislation. Perhaps the most famous instance was when Representative Leonidas C. Dyer, a republican congressman from Missouri, proposed what became known as the *Dyer antilynching bill*. Although this bill passed

the House in 1922, it—like every other antilynching bill—could not get passed through the Senate. Democratic Southerners effectively formed a filibuster that prevented any antilynching legislation to get through (I elaborate on this further in Chapter 2). For more information on Congressional attempts at passing antilynching in general and the Dyer antilynching bill in particular, please see Robert Zangrando, *The NAACP Crusade against Lynching, 1909–1950* (Philadelphia: Temple University Press, 1980) and Claudine Ferrell, *Nightmare and Dream: Antilynching in Congress, 1917–1921.*

60. *U.S. v. Guest*, 383 U.S. 745 (1966).

61. Taft, Inaugural Address.

62. Karen Orren and Stephen Skowronek, *The Search for American Political Development* (Cambridge, Cambridge University Press, 2004), 134.

63. Franz Neumann, *The Democratic and the Authoritarian State* (Glencoe: The Free Press of Glencoe, 1957), 22.

64. Cutler, *Lynch-Law*, 1–2.

65. Robert Dahl, *A Preface to Democratic Theory* Chicago: University of Chicago Press, 1956), 41.

66. Marx, *Making Race and Nation*, 7.

67. Katznelson, *Fear Itself*, 136, 168.

68. Naomi Murakawa, *The First Civil Right: How Liberals Built Prison America* (New York, Oxford University Press, 2014), 156.

69. See Cutler, *Lynch-Law*, 1905; Frank Shay, *Judge Lynch: His First Hundred Years*, (New York, Ives Washburn, 1938); McGovern, *Anatomy of a Lynching*; and Neil McMillen, *Dark Journey: Black Mississippians in the Age of Jim Crow* (Urbana: University of Illinois Press, 1989).

70. Leon Friedman, *Southern Justice* (New York: Pantheon Books, 1965), vii.

71. The definitive book regarding liberalism in America is Louis Hartz, *The Liberal Tradition in America* (San Diego: Harcourt, Brace 1991). For information regarding the reception of this book and the current status of this book with regard to American political science, see Phillip Abbott's article, "Still Louis Hartz after All These Years: A Defense of the Liberal Society Thesis," *Perspectives on Politics* 3 (2005): 93–109.

72. Rogers Smith, "Beyond Tocqueville, Myrdal and Hartz: The Multiple Traditions in America," *American Political Science Review* 87 (1993) p. 549–566. The main argument is that "American political culture is better understood as the often conflictual and contradictory product of multiple political traditions [which include liberalism, republicanism, and ascriptive forms of Americanism], than as the expression of hegemonic liberal or democratic political institutions" (549).

73. Ibid.

74. Rogers Smith and Desmond King, "Racial Orders in American Political Development," *American Political Science Review* 99 (2005): 75.

75. Ira Katznelson, "Books in Review: Civic Ideals: Conflicting Visions of Citizenship in U.S. History," *Political Theory* (August 1999): 568.

76. Rogers Smith, *Civic Ideals: Conflicting Visions of Citizenship in U.S. History* (New Haven: Yale University Press, 1997), 5.

77. http://www.theatlantic.com/national/archive/2013/07/trayvon-martin-and-the-irony-of-american-justice/277782/. Ta-Nehisi Coates, "Trayvon Martin and the Irony of American Justice," *The Atlantic*, July 15, 2013, accessed June 1, 2015.

78. Sean Wilentz, *The Rise of American Democracy: Jefferson to Lincoln* (New York: W.W. Norton and Company, 2005), xv.

79. Marie Gottschalk, "Hiding in Plain Sight: American Politics and the Carceral State," *Annual Review of Political Science* 11 (2008): 239.

80. For other works that examine how liberalism can and was qualified, see Uday S. Mehta, *Liberalism and Empire: A Study in Nineteenth-Century British Liberal Thought* (Chicago: University of Chicago Press, 1999); Aziz Rana, *The Two Faces of American Freedom* (Cambridge: Harvard University Press, 2010); and Katznelson, *Fear Itself*.

81. According to Desmond King and Robert Lieberman, "many leading works of scholarship on core institutions of the American state overlook how race and segregation shaped their content and policy effects. This deficiency is one reason for singling out the segregationist dimension of the American state" (King and Lieberman, "American State Building," 332).

82. Leonard Feldman, *Citizens without Shelter: Homelessness, Democracy and Political Exclusion* (Ithaca: Cornell University Press, 2004), 18.

83. Ibid., 16.

84. Dara Strolovitch, "Of Mancessions and Hecoveries: Race, Gender and the Political Construction of Economic Crises and Recoveries," *Perspective on Politics* 11 (2013): 169.

85. Scott Veitch, *Law and Irresponsibility: On the Legitimation of Human Suffering* (Abingdon: Routledge-Cavendish, 2007), 1–2.

86. This characterization of liberalism as a fighting creed is taken from Charles Taylor, "The Politics of Recognition," in *Multiculturalism: Examining the Politics of Recognition*, ed. Amy Gutmann (Princeton: Princeton University Press, 1994), 62.

87. Orren and Skowronek, *The Search for American Political Development*, 139.

88. Eric Foner, *Reconstruction: America's Unfinished Revolution, 1863–1877*, (New York: Perennial Classics, 1988), 531.

89. Kaczorowski, *The Politics of Judicial Interpretation*; and Brandwein, *Rethinking the Judicial Settlement of Reconstruction*.

90. As mentioned in note 52, even Orren and Skowronek seem to agree that the judiciary in particular and Reconstruction in general are still unclear.

91. Murakawa, *The First Civil Right*, 12.

92. Mark Graber, "The Nonmajoritarian Difficulty: Legislative Deference to the Judiciary," *Studies in American Political Development* 7 (1993): 40–43.

93. James Madison, Alexander Hamilton, and John Jay, "Federalist 78," in *The Federalist Papers*, ed. Robert Scigliano (New York: Modern Library, 2001). p. 496.

94. Robert A. Katzmann, "Foreword," in *Making Policy, Making Law: An Interbranch Perspective*, ed. Mark Miller and Jeb Barnes (Washington D.C.: Georgetown University Press, 2004), ix.

95. Jeb Barnes and Mark Miller, "Putting the Pieces Together: American Lawmaking from an Interbranch Perspective," in *Making Policy, Making Law: An Interbranch Perspective*, ed. Mark Miller and Jeb Barnes (Washington D.C.: Georgetown University Press, 2004), 11.

96. Orren and Skowronek, *The Search for American Political Development*, 114.

97. Carl Schurz, *Report on the Condition of the South* (USA: Hard Press, 2006), 48.

98. Letter from NAACP Secretary James Weldon Johnson to Senator Henry Cabot Lodge, June 14, 1922 (as quoted in Claudine Ferrell's *Nightmare and Dream*, 420).

99. Murakawa, *The First Civil Right*, 12.

100. Fraenkel, *The Dual State*.

101. William H. Sewell Jr., *Logics of History: Social Theory and Transformation* (Chicago: University of Chicago Press, 2005), 226.

102. Ibid., 11.

103. Ibid., 6.

104. Ibid., 98.

105. Raper, *The Tragedy of Lynching*, editorial note.

106. Charles Mills, "Ideal Theory as Ideology," *Hypatia* 20 (2005): 168.

107. Sewell, *Logics of History*, 172.

108. Mills, "Ideal Theory as Ideology," 170, 181.

109. Thomas McCarthy, "Political Philosophy and Racial Injustice: From Normative to Critical Theory," in *Pragmatism, Critique, Judgment: Essays for Richard Bernstein*, ed. Seyla Benhabib and Nancy Fraser (Cambridge: MIT Press, 2004), 165.

110. Ibid., 160.

111. Ibid., 166.

112. Billie Holiday, *Strange Fruit*, song lyrics: "Southern trees bear a strange fruit, Blood on the leaves and blood at the root."

113. Sewell, *Logics of History*, 28.

114. Earl Martz and Judith Baer, legal historians who have conflicting opinions on the Fourteenth Amendment, nonetheless agree that the Fourteenth Amendment "is so broad and general that they could be used to support almost anything." Judith A. Baer, *Equality under the Constitution: Reclaiming the Fourteenth Amendment* (Ithaca: Cornell University Press, 1983), 102–103.

115. Ronald Kahn and Ken Kersch, "Introduction," in *The Supreme Court and American Political Development*, ed. Ronald Kahn and Ken Kersch (Lawrence: University Press of Kansas, 2006), 15.

116. Charles Mangum Jr., *The Legal Status of the Negro* (Chapel Hill: University of North Carolina Press, 1940), 400.

117. See Jessie Daniel Ames, *The Changing Character of Lynching* (Atlanta: Commission on Interracial Cooperation, 1942); Herbert Shapiro, *White Violence, Black Response: From Reconstruction to Montgomery* (Amherst: University of Massachusetts Press, 1988); Wells, *On Lynchings*; and Zangrando, *The NAACP Crusade against Lynching*.

118. See Brundage, *Lynching in the New South*; J. Timothy Cole, *The Forest City Lynching of 1900: Populism, Racism, and White Supremacy in Rutherford County, North Carolina* (Jefferson: McFarland and Company, 2003); Barry A. Crouch, "A Spirit of Lawlessness: White Violence, Texas Blacks, 1865–1868," *Journal of Social History* 18 (1984): 217–232; Robert P. Ingalls, "Lynching and Establishment Violence in Tampa, 1858–1935," *The Journal of Southern History* 53 (1987): 613–644; Stacy Pratt McDermott, "An Outrageous Proceeding: A Northern Lynching and the Enforcement of Anti-Lynching Legislation in Illinois, 1905–1910," *The Journal of Negro History* 84 (1999): 61–78; McGovern, *Anatomy of a Lynching*; McMillen, *Black Mississippians in the Age of Jim Crow*; Robert Minor, *Lynching and Frame-up in Tennessee* (New York: New Century Publishers, 1946); Paul Ortiz, *Emancipation Betrayed: The Hidden Story of Black Organizing and White Violence in Florida from Reconstruction to the Bloody Election of 1920* (Berkeley: University of California Press, 2005); Charles David Phillips, "Exploring Relations among Forms of Social Control: The Lynching and Execution of Blacks in North Carolina, 1889–1918," *Law and Society Review* 21 (1987): 361–374; Jerrell H. Shofner, *Nor Is It over Yet: Florida in the Era of Reconstruction, 1863–1877* (Gainesville: The University Presses of Florida, 1974); Howard Smead, *Blood*

Justice: The Lynching of Mack Charles Parker (New York: Oxford University Press, 1986); and George C. Wright, *Racial Violence in Kentucky, 1865–1940: Lynchings, Mob Rule and "Legal Lynchings"* (Baton Rouge: Louisiana State University Press, 1990).

119. In *The Promise of the New South: Life After Reconstruction* (Oxford: Oxford University Press, 1992), o.Edward Ayers argues that lynchings were related to population densities and black migration patterns. Stewart Tolnay and Elwood M. Beck correlated the number of lynchings with cotton production in their book *A Festival of Violence: An Analysis of Southern Lynchings, 1882–1930*. Charles S. Sydnor provides a cultural argument for lynching in his article, "The Southerner and the Laws." Frank Coleman argues that U.S. foreign policy had a major impact in curbing lynchings. See "Freedom from Fear on the Home Front," *Iowa Law Review* 29 (1943–1944): 415–429.

CHAPTER 2

1. Franz Neumann, *The Democratic and the Authoritarian State* (Glencoe: The Free Press of Glencoe, 1957), 22.

2. Stephen Holmes, "Free Marketing: A Review of Naomi Klein's *Shock Doctrine*," *London Review of Books* (2008). Vol. 30, No. 9, http://www.lrb.co.uk/v30/n09/stephen-holmes/free-marketeering. Accessed June 2, 2015.

3. This is a quote from Stephen Skowronek, "Taking Stock," in *The Unsustainable American State*, ed. Lawrence Jacobs and Desmond King (Oxford: Oxford University Press, 2009), 332.

4. The most recent example of this claim being made is by Bruce Ackerman: "The federal government simply lacked the civilian bureaucracies required to enforce the amendments in hostile territory; a tiny band of federal judges, backed by a bunch of federal marshals, didn't have a chance." Bruce Ackerman, *The Civil Rights Revolution* (Cambridge: Belknap Press, 2014), 158.

5. W. Fitzhugh Brundage, *Lynching in the New South: Georgia and Virginia, 1880–1930* (Urbana: University of Illinois, 1993); James Chadbourn, *Lynching and the Law* (Chapel Hill: University of North Carolina, 1933); James Cutler, *Lynch-Law: An Investigation into the History of Lynching in the United States* (New York: Negro University Press, 1905); Philip Dray, *At the Hands of Persons Unknown* (New York: Random House, 2002); Ralph Ginzburg, *100 Years of Lynching* (New York: Black Classic Press, 1988); James McGovern, *Anatomy of a Lynching: The Killing of Claude Neal* (Baton Rouge: Louisiana State University Press, 1982); NAACP, *Thirty Years of Lynching in the United States, 1889–1918* (New York: Negro University Press, 1919); Arthur Raper, *The Tragedy of Lynching* (Chapel Hill: Arno Press, 1969); Frank Shay, *Judge Lynch: His First Hundred Years* (New York: Ives Washburn, 1938); Stewart Tolnay and Elwood M. Beck, *A Festival of Violence: An Analysis of Southern Lynchings, 1882–1930* (Urbana: University of Illinois, 1995); Christopher Waldrep, *Lynching in America* (New York: New York University Press, 2006); Christopher Waldrep, *The Many Faces of Judge Lynch: Extralegal Violence and Punishment in America* (New York: Palgrave, 2002); Ida B. Wells, *On Lynchings* (Amherst: Humanity Books, 2002).

6. For similar accounts that engage the traditional account of the United States critically as a "weak state," see Desmond King, *Separate and Unequal: Black Americans and the U.S. Federal Government* (Oxford: Clarendon Press, 1995); William Novak, "The Myth of the 'Weak' American State," *American Historical Review* Vol. 113, No. 3 (2008): 752–772; Kimberley Johnson,

Governing the American State: Congress and the New Federalism, 1877–1929 (Princeton: Princeton University Press, 2006); Desmond King and Robert Lieberman, "Ironies of State Building: A Comparative Perspective on the American State," *World Politics* 61 (2009): 547–588; and Desmond King and Stephen Tuck, "De-Centering the South: America's Nationwide White Supremacist Order after Reconstruction," *Past and Present* 194 (2007) 213–255.

7. Theda Skocpol, "Bringing the State Back In: Strategies of Analysis in Current Research," in *Bringing the State Back In*, ed. Peter Evans, Dietrich Rueschemeyer, and Theda Skocpol (Cambridge: Cambridge University Press, 1985), 3–43.

8. Joel S. Migdal, *Strong Societies and Weak States: State–Society Relations and State Capabilities in the Third World* (Princeton: Princeton University Press, 1988), xiii.

9. Ibid., 261.

10. Novak, "The Myth of the 'Weak' American State," 754.

11. Theda Skocpol, "Bringing the State Back In," 3–43; Stephen Skowronek, *Building a New American State: The Expansion of National Administrative Capacities, 1877–1920* (Cambridge: Cambridge University Press, 1982); Frank Dobbin and John Sutton, "The Strength of a Weak State: The Rights Revolution and the Rise of Human Resource Management Divisions," *American Journal of Sociology* 104 (1998) 447–476; Robert Lieberman, "Weak State, Strong Policy: Paradoxes of Race Policy in the United States, Great Britain, and France," *Studies in American Political Development* 16 (2002) 138–161; Paul Frymer, "Acting When Elected Officials Won't: Federal Courts and Civil Rights Enforcement in U.S. Labor Unions, 1935–1985," *American Political Science Review* 97 (2003) 483–499; Paul Frymer, "Race, Labor and the Twentieth-Century American State," *Politics and Society* 97 (2004) 475–509; John D. Skrentny, "Law and the American State," *Annual Review of Sociology* 32 (2006): 213–244; Novak, "The Myth of the 'Weak' American State," 752–772; Kimberley Johnson, *Governing the American State: Congress and the New Federalism, 1877–1929* (Princeton: Princeton University Press, 2007); Jacob Hacker, *The Divided Welfare State: The Battle over Public and Private Benefits in the United States* (Cambridge: Cambridge University Press, 2002); King and Lieberman, "Ironies of State Building," 547–588; Desmond King and Marc Stears, "The Missing State in Postwar American Political Thought," in *The Unsustainable American State*, ed. Lawrence Jacobs and Desmond King (Oxford: Oxford University Press, 2008), 116–134.

12. Stewart Tolnay and Elwood M. Beck, *A Festival of Violence An Analysis of Southern Lynchings, 1882–1930* (Urbana: University of Illinois Press, 1995).

13. Robert Zangrando, *The NAACP Crusade against Lynching* (Philadelphia: Temple University Press, 1980), 8.

14. Dray, *At the Hands of Persons Unknown*, ix.

15. In a speech made on July 16, 1918, President Woodrow Wilson iterated this sense of federal helplessness: "I therefore very earnestly and solemnly *beg* the governors of all the States, the law officers of every community, and, above all, the men and women of every community in the United States . . . to cooperate—not passively merely, but actively and watchfully—to make an end of this disgraceful evil" *Selected Addresses and Public Papers of Woodrow Wilson* (New York:, University Press of the Pacific, 2002), 271.

16. Raper, *The Tragedy of Lynching*; William Gillette, *Retreat from Reconstruction, 1869–1879* (Baton Rouge: Louisiana State University Press, 1979); Xi Wang, *The Trial of Democracy: Black Suffrage and Northern Republicans, 1860–1910* (Athens: University of Georgia Press, 1997).

17. Christopher Waldrep goes so far as to say that the "political process failed. . . . Mob law rendered [the decisions made by the Supreme Court] meaningless." *Lynching in America: A History in Documents*, xix (New York: New York University Press, 2006).

18. Those that have proffered explanations for lynching agree that the state played a minor role. In *The Promise of the New South: Life After Reconstruction* (Oxford: Oxford University Press, 1992), Edward Ayers argues that lynchings were related to population densities and black migration patterns. Stewart Tolnay and Elwood M. Beck correlate the number of lynchings with cotton production in their book *A Festival of Violence: An Analysis of Southern Lynchings, 1882–1930* (Urbana: University of Illinois, 1995). Charles S. Sydnor provides a cultural argument for lynching in his article "The Southerner and the Laws," *The Journal of Southern History* 6 (1940): 3–23.

19. Skowronek, *Building a New American State* (Cambridge: Cambridge University Press, 1982). Skowronek notes that "the great departure in American institutional development came between 1877 and 1920, when new administrative institutions first emerged free from the clutches of party domination, direct court supervision, and localistic orientations" (15). In later chapters, I argue that administrative institutions that were involved with stopping lynchings were completely in the clutches of party domination, direct court supervision, and localistic orientations.

20. John P. Nettl, "The State as a Conceptual Variable," *World Politics* 20 (1968): 559–592. Nettl divides stateness into four components: (1) state as sovereignty in law, (2) state as international actor, (3) state's relative autonomy to society, and (4) state as a sociocultural phenomenon. See also, Peter Baldwin, "Beyond Weak and Strong: Rethinking the State in Comparative Policy History," *Journal of Policy History* 17 (2005): 12–33.

21. Harry Scheiber, "Federalism and Legal Process: Historical and Contemporary Analysis of the American System," *Law and Society Review* 14 (1980) 679–681.

22. Ibid., 680.

23. King and Lieberman, "American State Building," 332.

24. Stephen Skowronek noted "the American state is not a coherent whole." Skowronek, "Taking Stock," 332.

25. Ira Katznelson, "Flexible Capacity: The Military and Early American Statebuilding," in *Shaped by War and Trade*, ed. Ira Katznelson and Martin Shefter (Princeton: Princeton University Press, 2002), 85.

26. There were many different white extremist groups operating in the South during this time. Groups of this nature included the Order of Pale Faces (Tennessee), the Supreme Cyclopean Council (Tennessee), the White Brotherhood (North Carolina), the Constitutional Union Guard (North Carolina), the Invisible Empire (North Carolina), the Young Men's Democratic Club (Florida), the Knights of the White Camelia (Louisiana), the Seymour Knights (Louisiana), the Knights of the Rising Sun (Texas), the Knights of the White Carnation (Alabama), the Knights of the Black Cross (Mississippi), Heggie's Scouts (Mississippi), the Washington Brothers (Mississippi), and the Ku Klux Rangers (Texas), and Democratic clubs and rifle clubs. Many of these groups lumped themselves together into the "Ku Klux movement." During the constitutional convention that redefined the Ku Klux Klan, Dr. George P. L. Reid explains that "the generic name of Ku-Klux was applied to all secret organizations in the South composed of the white natives and having for their object the execution of the first law of nature." *Constitution Adopted at a General Convention Held in the City of New Orleans, 4th of June, 1868* (copy found in New York Public Library, Walter L. Fleming Papers, 1685–1932, box 3). That said, I use the moniker *the Klan* to refer to all these extremist groups.

27. *The New York Times* reported pillaging in North Carolina (May 14, 1865, E.P. Brooks, "FROM NORTH CAROLINA.; Condition of the People Starvation Impending the Reconstructionists and the Slavery Question Railroads, &c." http://www.nytimes.com/1865/05/14/news/north-carolina-condition-people-starvation-impending-reconstructionists-slavery.html, Accessed June 2, 2015. Ed. P. Brooks, "Guerillas Still at Work—Robberies Perpetrated by Them—Discovery and Confiscation—The Career of Dr. Leach—Secesh Rejoicing Over the Assumed Non-Capture of Jeff. Davis—Union Meetings, http://www.nytimes.com/1865/05/28/news/guerrillas-still-work-robberies-perpetrated-them-discovery-confiscation-career.html, Accessed June 2, 2015; robberies in Raleigh; riots in Washington, DC (June 11, 1865, "A RIOT IN WASHINGTON; Colored Persons Beaten and Robbed by Soldiers. The Brooklyn City Directory." http://www.nytimes.com/1865/06/11/news/riot-washington-colored-persons-beaten-robbed-soldiers-brooklyn-city-directory.html, Accessed June 2, 2015; and arson in Nashville (June 13, 1865, "GREAT FIRE AT NASHVILLE.; Tremendous Destruction of Property. THE QUARTERMASTER'S DEPORT BURNED. Loss Eight to Ten Million of Dollars." June 11, 1865, http://www.nytimes.com/1865/06/11/news/great-fire-nashville-tremendous-destruction-property-quartermaster-s-depot.html, Accessed June 2, 2015. Citizens in Richmond sacked their own city as a result of the hysterical anticipation of the Union army. Defeated Confederate soldiers raided farms and their own commissaries on their way back home. Former slave owners exacted revenge on their former slaves. Victorious Union soldiers enjoyed the "spoils" of war. Roving outlaw bands such as "jayhawkers" took advantage of the lack of any strong military and/or police presence. Jay Winik, *April 1865: The Month That Saved America* (New York: Harper Perennial, 2001); Dan T. Carter, *When the War Was Over: The Failure of Self-Reconstruction in the South, 1865–1867* (Baton Rouge: Louisiana State University Press, 1985).

28. Carl Schurz, *Report on the Condition of the South* (USA: Hard Press, 2006), 20. Secretary of Treasury Hugh McCulloch reported to Congress that "lawless men, singly and in organized bands, engaged in general plunder; every species of intrigue and peculation and theft were resorted to." *House Executive Documents*, 39 Congress, 2d session, no. 97, 5.

29. Eric Foner writes: "The Proclamation represented a turning pointing in national policy as well as in the character of the war. . . . In effect, it transformed a war of armies into a conflict of societies, ensuring that Union victory would produce a social revolution within the South. In such a struggle, compromise was impossible; the war must now continue until the unconditional surrender of one side or the other." Eric Foner, *Reconstruction: America's Unfinished Revolution: 1863–1877* (New York: Harper and Row, 1988), 7. Winik argues that "not since the glory days of the Roman Empire or the subsequent sacking of the Eternal City itself by the Visigoths in the year A.D. 410, which dimmed the lights of civilization for forty generations, had war seemingly been raged by Westerners with such utter ruthlessness and with such a lack of restraint. . . . Over 620,000 lay dead, one-twelfth of the North and an astonishing one-fifth of the South; all told, it was the most battle deaths in the country's history, as great as in all of the nation's other wars combined" (Winik, *April 1865*, 354). Winik also notes: "Much of the Confederacy was an isolated wasteland: the war had not only obliterated one-quarter of the Confederacy's white men of military age and almost half of its livestock, destroyed a good 50% of the farm machinery and left tens of thousands of small farms and sizable plantations alike buried under scraps, weeds, and utter ruin, but it had also mangled thousands of miles of railroads and just as many of its telegraph wires" (287). Foner states: "The number of horses fell by 29%, swine by 35%, and farm values by half. Georgia alone reported 1 million fewer swine, 50,000 fewer horses, and 200,000 fewer

cattle, and had 3 million fewer acres under cultivation in 1870 than ten years earlier. For the South as a whole, the real value of all property, even discounting that represented by slaves, stood 30% lower than its prewar figure.... The region was all but bankrupt, for the collapse of Confederate bonds and currency wiped out the savings of countless individuals and resources.... Little money circulated and interest rates soared to exorbitant levels" (Foner, *Reconstruction*, 125).

30. Foner points out the North's "amazing leniency. No mass arrests followed the collapse of the Confederacy; only Henry Wirz, commandant of Andersonville prison camp, paid the ultimate penalty for treason. Jefferson Davis spent two years in federal prison but was never put on trial" (Foner, *Reconstruction*, 69). As George Tucker, a practicing lawyer in Virginia stated in his testimony in front of the Joint Congressional Committee on Reconstruction, "they should have been treated as rebels, and should have been made to feel that to be a rebel was dishonorable; that they have lost their caste among men, and the leaders ought to have been made to feel that they were, and ought to be, outcasts" (*Report of the Joint Committee on Reconstruction*, 39th Congress, 1st Session, 24). Although all the peace treaties signed by Confederate leaders stipulated that Confederate soldiers were supposed to turn in their arms, there was no clear enforcement mechanism to ensure such actions were being carried forth and no clear estimates of how many arms were actually returned. Whitelaw Reid reports that the soldiers under General Kirby's command simply "gone off, arms in their hands, half expecting a renewal of the war." Whitelaw Reid, *After the War, A Tour of the Southern States, 1865–1866*, (New York, Harper Torchbooks, 1965) 229. When Southerners, particularly former soldiers of the Confederate army, found Northern policies in any way inimical to their interests, they predictably just picked up the fighting again. Although leniency might have helped end the war, it encouraged hostilities to continue.

31. Historian Eric McKitrick observed that, although "we still tend to suppose that this period must have been one of busy preparations within the Republican party for what was to come, with the Democrats standing more or less passively by, during the six months from the end of May to December, 1865, there was not much purposeful organized political activity." Eric McKitrick, *Andrew Johnson and Reconstruction* (Chicago: University of Chicago Press, 1960), 52. A very similar situation occurred with regard to reconstruction in Iraq. Thomas Ricks writes: "The U.S. invasion of Iraq, Army Lt. Col. James Scudieri wrote later, 'may be the most planned operation since D-Day on 6 June 1944 and Desert Storm in 1991.' The irony is that in eighteen months of planning, the key question was left substantially unaddressed: What to do after getting to Baghdad. Franks, Rumsfeld, Wolfowitz, Feith and other top officials spent well over a year preparing to attack Iraq, but treated almost casually what would come after that.... It wasn't that there was no planning. To the contrary, there was a lot, with at least three groups inside the military and one at the State Department working on postwar issues and producing thousands of pages of documents. But much of the planning was shoddy, there was no one really in charge of it, and there was little coordination between the various groups.... The result would be that while there was much discussion, and endless PowerPoint briefings, there wouldn't be a real plan for postwar Iraq that could be implemented by commanders and soldiers on the ground." Thomas Ricks, *Fiasco: The American Military Adventure in Iraq*, (New York, Penguin Press, 2006), 78–79.

32. James Sefton, *The United States Army and Reconstruction, 1865–1877* (Baton Rouge: Louisiana State University Press, 1967), 30.

33. George Bentley, *A History of the Freedmen's Bureau* (Philadelphia: University of Pennsylvania Press, 1955), 154.

34. Sefton, *The United States Army and Reconstruction, 1865–1877*, 30.

35. Bentley, *A History of the Freedmen's Bureau*, 154.

36. Sefton, *The United States Army and Reconstruction, 1865–1877*, 48.

37. *Senate Executive Documents*, 39 Cong., 1 sess., no. 2, Letter by General Grant concerning Affairs at the South, December 18, 1865, 108.

38. Ex parte *Milligan* 71 U.S. 2 (1866).

39. Foner states that ex parte *Milligan* "threw into question the legality of martial law and Freedmen's Bureau courts" (Foner, *Reconstruction*, 272).

40. *Congressional Globe*, 39 Cong., 2 sess., 250. An example occurred in fall 1865 when six South Carolinians killed three Union soldiers on guard duty. There was a military trial during which four were found guilty. After the trial, the president had them transferred to Fort Delaware, whereupon their arrival the commander was served with a writ of habeas corpus from a federal district judge of Delaware. There was a subsequent hearing in November during which the judge ordered the prisoners released on the grounds that the civil courts of South Carolina had been open at the same time the crime was committed. The murderers were never tried again (McKitrick, *Andrew Johnson and Reconstruction*, 458).

41. See Stanley Horn, *Invisible Empire: The Story of the Ku Klux Klan 1866–1871* (Montclair, Patterson Smith, 1969).

42. Bentley argues that attempts "to bring more unity and system into the [Freedmen] Bureau's work had failed because the President would not endorse them" (Bentley, *A History of the Freedmen's Bureau*, 163).

43. Ketchum to all assistant commissioners, September 19, 1866, Bureau Records, Letters Sent, II, 333 (as quoted in Bentley, *A History of the Freedmen's Bureau*, 163).

44. Republican Congressmen John Bingham presented a bill that would have "provided that no civil courts could have jurisdiction of, or reverse any proceedings resulting from, such proclamations [regarding the military commissions]." *Congressional Globe*, 39 Cong., 2 sess., 47.

45. Petition filed under May 1, 1865, in Johnson Papers, Library of Congress (Reel 14), (as quoted in Sefton, *The United States Army and Reconstruction, 1865–1877*, 12).

46. *House Report*, 39 Cong., 2 sess., no. 16, "Report of the Select Committee on the New Orleans Riots," 443.

47. It also did not help that the occupied forces seemed intent on maintaining a weak presence in the South. U.S. Army presence in the South was reduced dramatically after the war. Trelease reports that "only 20,000 troops remained on duty in the South by the fall of 1867, and this number gradually fell to 6,000 by the fall of 1876; moreover, one-quarter to half of these men were stationed in Texas, chiefly on frontier duty." Allen Trelease, *White Terror: The Ku Klux Klan Conspiracy and Southern Reconstruction* Baton Rouge: Louisiana State University Press, 1971), xxxvi. During its first year of existence, the Freedmen's Bureau was allotted no budget. Bentley notes that "Congress did not appropriate any money for the Freedmen's Bureau until July 1866.... Its chief source of income was rent from abandoned lands, but this source dried up rapidly as President Johnson pardoned the plantation owners and restored property to them" (Bentley, *A History of the Freedmen's Bureau*, 74).

48. Sefton, *The United States Army and Reconstruction, 1865–1877*, 8.

49. Ibid., 11.

50. *Senate Executive Documents*, 39 Cong. 2 sess., no. 6, serial no. 1276, 145.

51. James Sefton notes that the only previous time the Army was involved in military occupation was in Mexico in 1847 and that was of a completely different nature than Southern

reconstruction, not to mention the fact that "of the thirty-five most important men who during the period 1865–77 held commands in the South appropriate to the rank of a general officer, seventeen either had not been in the Mexican War or had had service which did not bring them into direct contact with the problems of occupation" (Sefton, *The United States Army and Reconstruction, 1865–1877*, 5).

52. James Sefton notes that "of the high-ranking commanders, only Alfred H. Terry had studied law extensively." Ibid., 9.

53. Although Kenneth Stampp cautions against levying a blanket critique against the Freedmen's Bureau, he does admit that there were some flaws: Although "a balanced evaluation of the Freedmen's Bureau must stress its constructive achievements . . . there is some truth to the charges that some of the agents were incompetent, some were corrupt, and some used the bureau's power to win Negro votes for the Republicans." Stampp, 132–134.

54. Bentley, *A History of the Freedmen's Bureau*, 161.

55. *Daily Columbus Enquirer*, May 20, 1866, and *Augusta Weekly Constitutionalist*, April 15, 1866 (as quoted in Ellis Coulter, *The South During Reconstruction* (Baton Rouge: Louisiana University Press, 1947), 90)

56. In a report dated August 14, 1869, General Terry indicated in Georgia, "the worst of crimes are committed and no attempt is made to punish those who commit them." Report made by General A.H. Terry, August 14, 1869 (as quoted in Horn, *Invisible Empire*, 176). In a letter to Commissioner Howard that is included in a report to Congress, Assistant Commissioner Wager Swayne complained about the "non-execution [of law] in behalf of freedmen." *Senate Executive Documents*, 39th Cong. 2 sess., no. 6, serial no. 1276, 3.

57. An example is the case that involved Dr. Watson. In November 1866, Dr. Watson confessed to pursuing, shooting, and killing a local Negro for having accidentally inflicting 50¢ worth of damage on his carriage while passing it on a narrow road. In pursuance of the Congressional Act of July 16, 1866, extending military jurisdiction over a variety of cases involving freedmen, General Schofield, the local commander, ordered Watson tried by military commission, whereupon he was found guilty of murder. President Johnson, on December 21, ordered the commission dissolved and the prisoner released (McKitrick, *Andrew Johnson and Reconstruction*, 459).

58. Harold Hyman and William Wiecek noted that "Army officials, in turn, were increasingly timid by reason of the damage suits filed against them in increasing number in unfriendly state courts for alleged offenses." Harold Hyman and William Wiecek, *Equal Justice under Law: Constitutional Development 1835–1875* (New York, Harper and Row, 1982), 444

59. *Report of the Joint Committee on Reconstruction*, 39th Congress, 1st Session, Tennessee, 111.

60. Ibid., 31.

61. *Report of the Joint Select Committee to Inquire into the Conditions of Affairs in the Late Insurrectionary States*, 42d Congress, 2d session (cited hereafter as *KKK Report*), South Carolina, Vol. 3, 1483

62. For example, historian George Rable wrote that "southerners stood ready to resist any fundamental restructuring of their society." George Rable, *But There was No Peace: The Role of Violence in the Politics of Reconstruction* Athens: University of Georgia Press, 1984), 15.

63. Woodward's key contribution is distinguishing between the constancy of racism and the inevitability of Southern extremism. Southern extremism is but one form of racism and by no means is meant to refute the claim that racism has been prevalent throughout American history. C. Vann Woodward, *The Strange Career of Jim Crow* (Oxford: Oxford University Press, 2002).

For examples of the ubiquity of racism, see Mary Frances Berry, *Black Resistance/White Law* (New York: Appleton-Century-Crofts, 1971); Derrick Bell, *Race, Racism and American Law* (New York: Aspen Publishers, 2004); Valdimer O. Key, *Southern Politics in State and Nation* (Knoxville: University of Tennessee Press, 1984); and Rogers Smith, "Beyond Tocqueville, Myrdal and Hartz: The Multiple Traditions in America," *American Political Science Review* 87 (1993): 549–566.

64. In an article titled "The Central Theme of Southern History," eminent historian Ulrich B. Phillips asks what is the essence of the South: "Not state rights—Calhoun himself was for years a nationalist . . . not free trade—sugar and hemp growers have ever been protectionists . . . not slavery—in the eighteenth century this was of continental legality; and in the twentieth it is legal nowhere . . . not democracy—there were many Federalists in Washington's day and many Whigs in Clay's. . . . Yet it is a land with a unity despite its diversity, with a people having common joys and common sorrows, and, above all, as to the white folk a people with a common resolve indomitably maintained—that it shall be and remain a white man's country" (31). Ulrich B. Phillips, "The Central Theme of Southern History," *The American Historical Review* 34 (1928): 30–43

65. Captain Jos W. Gelray is reported to have stated that "a few Union soldiers eulogized and advocated [the Klan's] usefulness." Petition filed May 1, 1865, in *The War of the Rebellion: A Compilation of the Official Records of the Union and Confederate Armies (Washington, 1880–1901)*, Ser. I, Vol. XLVII, Pt. 3. Brig. Gen. Fred C. Ainsworkth and Mr. Joseph W. Kirkley, (Washington, Government Printing Office, Published under the Direction of The Honorouable Elihu Root, Secretary of War, 1902), 595–596.

66. *Southern Cultivator* XXIV (1866); 144 (as quoted in Coulter, *The South during Reconstruction*, 11).

67. Francis Fisher Browne, *The Every-Day Life of Abraham Lincoln: A Narrative and Descriptive Biography with Pen-Pictures* (Chicago: Browne & Howell Company, 1913), 577. There is reason to believe Lincoln never said this to Welles. Browne states that Gideon Welles wrote this in his diary. I have searched *The Diary of Gideon Welles* thoroughly (Boston: Houghton Mifflin Company, 1911) and was unable to find this quote.

68. Bentley, *A History of the Freedmen's Bureau*, 156.

69. Cutler, *Lynch-Law*, 205.

70. Christopher Waldrep, *Lynching in America*, 49.

71. *KKK Report*, North Carolina, 3.

72. Carl Schurz, Document 27, Letter from Samuel Thomas, *Report on the Condition of the South*, (USA, Hard Press, 2006), 121

73. *Congressional Globe*, 39th Cong., 2d sess., p. 161.

74. The prescript is printed in Stanley Horn, *Invisible Empire: The Story of the Ku Klux Klan 1866–1871* (Montclair, Patterson Smith, 1969), 381–393; in *KKK Report*, Vol XIII, Miscellaneous Testimony, 35–41, and in John Lester and DanielWilson, *Ku Klux Klan: Its Origin, Growth and Disbandment*, ed. by Walter Fleming (AMS Press, 1971), 135–150

75. Although it might seem ludicrous to consider the Klan as some sort of quasi-legitimate, jurisprudential entity, a similar kind of logic was popularly used to describe the passage of the Reconstruction Amendments. In his book *We the People 2: Transformations*, Bruce Ackerman argues that "lawlessness can be in conformity with the rule of law" (14). "The entire point of this book is to reject the dichotomy between legalistic perfection and lawless force" (116) and to show that "by breaking the law we will find higher law" (p. 14). Bruce Ackerman, *We the People 2: Transformations* (Cambridge: Belknap Press, 1998).

76. General Orders No. 1 is printed in *Historic Pulaski: Birthplace of the Ku Klux Klan, Scene of Execution of Davis* (Nashville: W.T. Richardson, 1913), 56–57. Brunson started the Klan in South Carolina. Historian James Cutler makes a more sweeping overgeneralization: "the people have committed the administration of justice to a certain machinery; so long as that machinery works without flagrant injustice, it will be left to do the work; but when it utterly breaks down, or goes in the teeth of what is right according to the rough-and-ready ideas of the Americans, the people will resume the function of dealing out punishment direct" (Cutler, 271).

77. Raper, *The Tragedy of Lynching*, 1.

78. Waldrep, *The Many Faces of Judge Lynch*, 87.

79. Hubert Howe Bancroft *Popular Tribunals* (San Francisco: History Company, 1887), 10–12 (as quoted in Waldrep, *The Many Faces of Judge Lynch*, 162).

80. Horn notes what caught the eye of many white Southerners was "the effectiveness of the Ku Klux as a medium for the pacification of the lawless element" (Horn, *Invisible Empire*, 20).

81. For examples of the bias in Southern newspapers, see Susan Jean's article, "Warranted Lynchings: Narratives of Mob Violence in White Southern Newspapers, 1880–1940," *American Nineteenth-Century History* 6 (2005): 351–372.

82. Eqbal Ahmad, "Revolutionary Warfare and Counterinsurgency," in *Guerrilla Strategies: An Historical Anthology from the Long March to Afghanistan*, ed. Gerard Chaliand Berkeley: University of California Press, 1982), 245.

83. William McFeely, "Amos T. Akerman: The Lawyer and Racial Justice," in *Region, Race and Reconstruction: Essays in Honor C. Vann Woodward*, ed. J. Morgan Kousser and James M. McPherson (New York: Oxford University Press, 1982), 412.

84. Trelease, *White Terror*, xi.

85. *KKK Report*, 66. Vol 1.

86. *Senate Executive Documents*, 39th Congress, 1st sess., No. 2, Documents Accompanying the Report of Major General Carl Schurz, No. 12, General Orders No. 22; Schurz, 88. Du Bois makes a similar point: "[A]ll the hatred that the whites had for each other [during the war] gradually concentrated on [Negroes]." William Du Bois, *Black Reconstruction in America, 1860–1880* (New York: Free Press, 1962), 125.

87. Oliver C. Cox, *Caste Class and Race: A Study in Social Dynamics* (New York: Modern Reader Paperbacks, 1948), 549.

88. Ibid., 554.

89. *KKK Report*, South Carolina, Vol. 3, 1603. Trelease notes that "the civil authorities, like the general white public, were either in sympathy with the order or intimidated by [the Klan]" (Trelease, *White Terror*, 32).

90. *KKK Report*, 39. Arkansas

91. *House Executive Documents*, 40 Cong., 2d sess., no.1, Letter from the Secretary of War, 46.

92. Gunnar Myrdal, *An American Dilemma: The Negro Problem and Modern Democracy* (New York: Harper and Brothers, 1962), 564.

93. This is the wording used by the Supreme Court in *Plessy v. Ferguson*: "In determining the question of reasonableness it is at liberty to act with reference to the established usages, customs, and traditions of the people, and with a view to the promotion of their comfort, and the preservation of the public peace and good order." *Plessy v. Ferguson*, 163 U.S. 537, 544 (1896).

94. For a survey of the violence befalling blacks following the aftermath of the Civil War, see Eric Foner, *Reconstruction*; Nicholas Lemann, *Redemption: The Last Battle of the Civil War* (New

York: Farrar, Straus and Girous, 2007); and Kwando Mbiassi Kinshasa, *Black Resistance to the Ku Klux Klan in the Wake of Civil War* (Jefferson: McFarland and Company, 2006).

95. Foner, *Reconstruction*, 457; Robert Kaczorowski, *The Politics of Judicial Interpretation: The Federal Courts, Department of Justice, and Civil Rights, 1866–1876* (New York: Fordham University Press, 2005), 65; Everette Swinney, *Suppressing the Ku Klux Klan: The Enforcement of the Reconstruction Amendments, 1870–1877* (New York: Garland Publishing, 1987), 182; Trelease, *White Terror*, 402.

96. Akerman's desire to prosecute the atrocities associated with the Ku Klux Klan went beyond simply restoring electoral order. Historian William McFeely argues that "perhaps no attorney general since his tenure—and the list of those who followed him is a long one that includes Ramsey Clark in the 1960s—has been more vigorous in the prosecution of cases designed to protect the lives and rights of black Americans" (McFeely, "Amos T. Akerman," 395).

97. "Circular Relative to the Enforcement of the Fourteenth Amendment," July 6, 1871, Circulars of the Attorneys General, Record Group 60, National Archives.

98. Stephen Cresswell notes that "the courts ran out of money with alarming regularity." Stephen Cresswell, *Mormons Cowboys, Moonshiners and Klansmen: Federal Law Enforcement in the South and West, 1870–1893* (Tuscaloosa: University of Alabama Press, 1991), 5.

99. Foner, *Reconstruction*, 457.

100. Cresswell notes that, during this period, the Department of Justice had no Bureau of Investigations: "[V]iolations of federal law were discovered only by citizen's complaint, or perhaps when a marshal read of an apparent violation in the local newspaper" (Cresswell, *Mormons Cowboys, Moonshiners and Klansmen*, 15).

101. Kaczorowski notes that "legal officers were reluctant to involve themselves in such situations, particularly when the very existence of the Klan and its crimes was so vehemently denied by the Southern press and politicians" (Kaczorowski, *The Politics of Judicial Interpretation*, 65).

102. Kaczorowski notes that "victims frequently were unwilling to bring charges or to testify against their assailants." Ibid.

103. Cresswell notes that the second head of the justice department, George Williams, "borrowed Justice Department funds to meet household expenses" (Cresswell, *Mormons Cowboys, Moonshiners and Klansmen*, 8).

104. For example, in *United States v. Blyew*, 80 U.S. (13 Wall.) 581 (1872), Blyew was defended by Jeremiah Black, former attorney general to President Buchanan and former Chief Justice of the Pennsylvania Supreme Court.

105. Kaczorowski notes that, in 1870, only 43 cases were prosecuted under the 1870 Enforcement Act. In 1871, 271 cases were prosecuted. This equates to a 630% increase. Kaczorowski, *The Politics of Judicial Interpretation*, 70.

106. Annual message, November 28, 1871, 31, in Legislative System, Messages, South Carolina Archives (as quoted in Trelease, *White Terror*, 406).

107. As quoted in Kaczorowski, *The Politics of Judicial Interpretation*, 72.

108. William Watson Davis, "The Federal Enforcement Acts," in *Studies in Southern History and Politics, Inscribed to William Archibald Dunning, Ph.D, LL.D, Lieber Professor of History and Political Philosophy in Columbia University, By His Former Pupils the Authors* (New York: Columbia University Press, 1914), 219; *KKK Report*, Mississippi, ii, 1149.

109. *House Executive Documents*, 42nd Congress, 2nd Session, No. 268, 34–41; Davis, "The Federal Enforcement Acts," 219.

110. *KKK Report*, North Carolina, 415.

111. Kaczorowski, *The Politics of Judicial Interpretation*, 213.

112. As quoted in Trelease, *White Terror*, 410.

113. The number 190 is very conservative. This is the number Gillette reports (*Retreat from Reconstruction, 1869–1879*, 44). Xi Wang reports 206 cases (*The Trial of Democracy*, 300). But, for some reason, neither Gillette nor Wang include Tennessee as part of the South. This is highly suspicious considering not only that the Ku Klux Klan started in Tennessee, but that Tennessee had 171 prosecutions in 1870 alone.

114. Again, this number does not include Tennessee.

115. See Gillette, *Retreat from Reconstruction, 1869–1879*; Wang, *Trial of Democracy*; and Richard Bensel, *Yankee Leviathan: The Origins of Central State Authority in America, 1859–1877* (New York: Cambridge University Press, 1990).

116. It is important to note, however, that many cases were carried over into 1872.

117. Kaczorowski, *The Politics of Judicial Interpretation*, 71–72.

118. Ibid., 74.

119. Alfred Terry to Adjutant General, June 11, 1871, M666, roll 17, Letters Received, Record Group 94, National Archives.

120. Kaczorowski, *The Politics of Judicial Interpretation*, 76.

121. James Sefton, *The United States Army and Reconstruction, 1865–1877*, 228.

122. Kaczorowski, *The Politics of Judicial Interpretation*, 77.

123. John Minnis to Williams, June 25 and April 1, 1872, Middle District of Alabama, Source Chronological File, in Record Group 60, "Records of the Department of Justice," National Archives (as quoted in Kaczorowski, p. 77).

124. Daniel Corbin to Williams, November 2, 1872, Northern and Middle District of Alabama, Source Chronological File, in Record Group 60, "Records of the Department of Justice," National Archives (as quoted in Kaczorowski, p. 77).

125. Hugh Lennox Bond to Anna Bond, September 21, 1871, Hugh L. Bond Papers, Maryland Historical Society.

126. Trelease, *White Terror*, 410.

127. Ibid.

128. Merrill to Adjutant General, Department of the South, January 17, 1872, 615 AGO 1872 (as quoted in Swinney, *Suppressing the Ku Klux Klan*, 235).

129. Swinney, *Suppressing the Ku Klux Klan*, 286.

130. Ibid., 318.

131. Edwin C. Woolley, "Grant's Southern Policy," in *Studies in Southern History and Politics, Inscribed to William Archibald Dunning, Ph.D, LL.D, Lieber Professor of History and Political Philosophy in Columbia University, By His Former Pupils the Authors* (New York: Columbia University Press, 1914), 184.

132. Gillette, *Retreat from Reconstruction, 1869–1879*, 246.

133. As quoted in Foner, *Reconstruction*, 523.

134. "Busted. The Radical Machine Gone to Smash," *Courier-Journal*, November 4–5, 1874 (as quoted in Gillette, p. 248).

135. Blanche Butler Ames, *Chronicles from the Nineteenth Century; Family Letters of Blanche Butler and Adelbert Ames, Married July 21st, 1870*, Vol. 2 Clinton, Privately Published 1957), 216.

136. In his May 22, 1873, Proclamation, President Grant states that "it is provided in the laws of the United States that in all cases of insurrection in any State, or of obstruction to the laws thereof, it shall be lawful for the President of the United States, on application of the legislature of such State, or of the executive when the legislature can not be convened, to call forth the militia of any other State or States . . . he shall forthwith by proclamation command such insurgents to disperse and retire." Ulysses S. Grant, *The Papers of Ulysses S. Grant*, Vol. 24, ed. John Y. Simon (Carbondale: Southern Illinois University Press, 1995), 122. Grant subsequently sent two companies of federal troops into Grant Parish. The military findings are located in "The Use of the Army in Certain of the Southern States," *Congressional Globe*, 44th Cong., 2d Sess., Ex. Doc. No. 30 (1875), 436. In a recent book chronicling the Colfax Massacre, Charles Lane writes: "In Boston, a crowd at Faneuil Hall repudiated the army's actions in Louisiana. The Ohio and Pennsylvania legislatures condemned the alleged invasion of their Louisiana counterpart. Senator Carl Schurz of Missouri, who had joined the Liberal Republicans in 1872, gave a speech suggesting that Congress itself might be the next legislature invaded." Charles Lane, *The Day Freedom Died: The Colfax Massacre, The Supreme Court, and the Betrayal of Reconstruction* (New York: Henry Holt and Company, 2008), 227.

137. *New York Herald*, January 18, 1874. "General Grant's New Departure – Notice to the Republican Party and its Monstrosities," p. 6.

138. Although no explicit reason was given, there is evidence to suggest that a scandal involving the railroad industry forced Akerman to resign.

139. C. Vann Woodward, *Reunion and Reaction: The Compromise of 1877 and the End of Reconstruction* (Boston: Little, Brown and Company, 1966), 8.

140. Some, most notably Pamela Brandwein, have contended that 1891 marked the end of Reconstruction with the failure of Congress to pass the Lodge-Hoar elections bill. She argues that the Lodge bill was the last attempt to reconstruct the South, "the failure of which marked the Republican party's abdication of rights enforcement." Pamela Brandwein, *Rethinking the Judicial Settlement of Reconstruction* (Cambridge: Cambridge University Press, 2011), 183. I address this claim directly in Chapter 4 but, for now, it is important to note that the Republican Party chose to abandon its broad enforcement efforts.

141. *The Slaughter-house Cases*, 83 U.S. (16 Wall.) 36 (1873); *U.S. v. Cruikshank*, 92 U.S. 542 (1875); *United States v. Harris*, 106 U.S. 629 (1883); *The Civil Rights Cases of 1883*, 109 U.S. 3 (1883). Quote from Foner, *Reconstruction*, 531.

142. This view—that, during Reconstruction, the Supreme Court did not abandon federal rights enforcement for blacks completely—is supported by the following works: Michael Les Benedict, "Preserving Federalism: Reconstruction and the Waite Court," in *The Supreme Court Review* (1978), 39–79; Ronald Labbe and Jonathan Lurie, *The Slaughterhouse Cases: Regulation, Reconstruction, and the Fourteenth Amendment* (Lawrence: University Press of Kansas, 2003); Michael Ross, *Justice of Shattered Dreams: Samuel Freeman Miller and the Supreme Court during the Civil War Era* (Baton Rouge: Louisiana State University Press, 2003); Brandwein, *Rethinking the Judicial Settlement of Reconstruction*; Pamela Brandwein, "A Judicial Abandonment of Blacks? Rethinking the 'State Action' Cases of the Waite Court," *Law and Society Review* 41 (2007): 343–386; Leslie Friedman Goldstein, "The Specter of the Second Amendment: Rereading Slaughterhouse and Cruikshank," *Studies in American Political Development* 21 (2007): 131–148.

143. Pamela Brandwein illustrates how "innovations in legal education, practiced by well-respected experts, helped hide the older legal context of the 1870s and 1880s—a context that gave greater support to black civil and political rights" (Brandwein, *Rethinking the Judicial Settlement of Reconstruction*, 213).

144. Arthur Kinoy, "The Constitutional Right of Negro Freedom," *Rutgers Law Review* 21 (1966–1967): 438.

145. In many respects, this account of political calculus is meant to supplement Richard Valelly's work on the political conditions necessary for biracial coalition-making. Although Valelly emphasizes the significant role that political leaders and the federal judiciary played in maintaining and altering biracial coalition making, he does not explore sufficiently the relationship among the branches. This lack is somewhat understandable considering the discrepancy among the numerous accounts of the nuanced differences and challenges facing the Reconstruction Congress and the rather one-dimensional accounts of the Court at that time, although recent research, such as that provided in Pamela Brandwein's *Rethinking the Judicial Settlement of Reconstruction*, has begun to rectify the discrepancy. Richard Valelly, *The Two Reconstructions: The Struggle for Black Enfranchisement* (Chicago: University of Chicago Press, 2004).

146. Zangrando, *The NAACP Crusade against Lynching*, 146.

147. Claudine Ferrell, *Nightmare and Dream: Antilynching in Congress, 1917–1922* (New York: Garland Publishing, 1986), 207.

148. Ibid., 382.

149. William Ford, "Constitutionality of Proposed Federal Anti-Lynching Legislation," *Virginia Law Review* 34 (1948): 944–953.

150. Ibid., 947.

151. *U.S. v. Cruikshank*, 92 U.S. 542, 556–557.

152. Ferrell, *Nightmare and Dream*, 481.

153. *Congressional Record*, 67 cong., 2 Sess., 860, 405–406.

154. John W. H. Crim to W. D. Johnson, June 8, 1922, Record Group 60, No. 158260–202 (as quoted in Ferrell, *Nightmare and Dream*, 221).

155. Assistant Attorney General R. R. Stewart to Arthur A. Schomburg, September 20, 1919, Record Group 60, No. 158260-2-11 (as quoted in Ferrell, *Nightmare and Dream*, 221).

156. Lawrence Baum and Lori Hausegger, "The Supreme Court and Congress: Reconsidering the Relationship," in *Making Policy, Making Law: An Interbranch Perspective*, ed. Mark Miller and Jeb Barnes (Washington D.C: Georgetown University Press, 2004), 107–108.

157. Mark Miller, "The View of the Courts from the Hill: A Neoinstitutional Perspective," in *Making Policy, Making Law: An Interbranch Perspective*, ed. Mark Miller and Jeb Barnes (Washington D.C.: Georgetown University Press, 2004), 65–66.

158. As quoted in Miller, "The View of the Courts from the Hill," 59.

159. *Congressional Record*, 67 Cong., 3 Sess., 332.

160. As quoted in Ferrell, *Nightmare and Dream*, 475.

161. "Senate Democrats Start Filibuster, Stop All Business," *New York Times*, November 29, 1922, 1.

162. "The Senate's Surrender," *New York Times*, December 4, 1922, 16

163. As quoted in Ferrell, *Nightmare and Dream*, 477.

164. Robert Zangrando, *The NAACP Crusade against Lynching*, 69.

165. Ibid., 63, 71, 67

166. As quoted in John T. Elliff, *The United States Department of Justice and Individual Rights, 1937–1962* (New York: Garland Publishing Inc., 1987), 68.

167. Ira Katznelson, Kim Geiger, and Daniel Kryder, "Limiting Liberalism: The Southern Veto in Congress, 1933–1950," *Political Science Quarterly* 108 (1993): 283–306; Robert Lieberman, *Shifting the Color Line: Race and the American Welfare State* (Cambridge: Harvard University Press, 2001).

168. *U.S. v. Price*, 383 U.S. 787 (1966); *U.S. v. Guest*, 383 U.S. 745 (1966).

169. *U.S. v. Price*, 383 U.S. 787 (1966).

170. Ibid., 794.

171. Ibid., 806.

172. Ibid., 803.

173. Derrick Bell, *Race, Racism, and American Law*, 5th ed. (New York: Aspen Publishers, 2004), 380.

174. *United States v. Williams*, 341 U.S. 70 (1951).

175. *U.S. v. Guest*, 383 U.S. 745 (1966).

176. Michael Klarman, *From Jim Crow to Civil Rights* (Oxford: Oxford University Press, 2004), 294.

177. Jackson draft concurrence, School Segregation Cases, March 15, 1954, 1–2; case file: Segregation Cases, Box 184, Jackson Papers; Klarman, *From Jim Crow to Civil Rights*, 305.

178. Klarman, *From Jim Crow to Civil Rights*, 303.

179. Ibid., 306.

180. Douglas memorandum, January 25, 1960, in *The Douglas Letters: Selections from the Private Papers of Justice William O. Douglas*, ed. Philip Urofsky Bethesda: Adler and Adler, 1987), 169; Klarman, *From Jim Crow to Civil Rights*, 310.

181. E. Barrett Prettyman to Jackson, n.d., 1,3, Box 184, Jackson Papers; Burton conference notes, School Segregation Cases, December 12, 1953; Klarman, *From Jim Crow to Civil Rights*, 306.

182. Klarman, *From Jim Crow to Civil Rights*, 302.

183. *U.S. v. Guest*, 383 U.S. 745, 783.

184. Michal R. Belknap, *Federal Law and Southern Order: Racial Violence and Constitutional Conflict in the Post-Brown South* (Athens: University of Georgia Press, 1987), 180.

185. Ibid., 176.

186. *U.S. v. Guest*, 383 U.S. 745, 755.

187. Ibid.

188. Ibid.

189. Ibid.

190. Ibid.

191. Alfred Avins, "The Ku Klux Klan Act of 1871: Some Reflected Light on State Action and the Fourteenth Amendment," *St. Louis University Law Journal* 11 (1966–1967): 381.

192. *U.S. v. Guest*, 383 U.S. 745, 755.

193. Ibid., 761.

194. Ibid., 782.

195. Ibid., 755.

196. These are the words Judge Emmons used to qualify his sympathy for blacks. *Charge to Grand Jury-Civil Rights Act*, 30 F. Cas. 1005, 1006–1007 (C.C. W.D. Tenn.) (1875) (as quoted in Pamela Brandwein, "A Judicial Abandonment of Blacks? Rethinking the 'State Action' Cases of the Waite Court," *Law and Society Review*, 41, 2, 2007, 354–355).

197. William Trotter, editor of the *Boston Guardian*, found it "incomprehensible that the federal government, while lecturing Europe on the responsibilities of democracy and equality, could do nothing about a crime against which states took no action" (as quoted in Ferrell, *Nightmare and Dream*, 236–237).

198. Letter to Richard Brevard Russell, September 27, 1957, *The Papers of Dwight David Eisenhower*, Volume XVIII—The Presidency: Keeping the Peace, Part II: Civil Rights, June 1957 to September 1957 (Little Rock, AR), chap 5. Ed. Louis Galambos and Daun Ee Van, (Baltimore: Johns Hopkins Press, 2001).

199. Eugene Gressman stated that, starting with *Slaughterhouse*, the Supreme Court enacted a "judicial coup d'état against Reconstruction." Eugene Gressman, "The Unhappy History of Civil Rights Legislation," *Michigan Law Review* 50 (1952): 1337. Political scientist Richard Valelly notes how "the entire arc of jurisprudence-building was influenced by the *Slaughterhouse Cases*" (Valelly, *The Two Reconstructions*, 112). Legal historian Robert Kaczorowski wrote, "The Supreme Court selected the *Slaughter-House Cases* as the instrument for its interpretation of national civil rights enforcement authority. . . . Justice Miller's opinion overturned the growing body of judicial interpretations of the impact of the Thirteenth and Fourteenth Amendments upon American constitutionalism as fixing sovereignty in the nation and as establishing the primacy of national citizenship and the concomitant national authority to secure the civil rights of American citizens. . . .[The significance of Miller's decision] lays in the Court's reversal of the constitutional developments in the nation's courts" (Kaczorowski, *The Politics of Judicial Interpretation*, 116–123).

200. Anthony W. Marx, *Making Race and Nation: A Comparison of the United States, South Africa and Brazil* (Cambridge: Cambridge University Press, 1998), 7–13

201. King and Tuck, "De-Centering the South, 240, 244.

202. Perveen Ali, "I Am Iraq: Law, Life and Violence in the Formation of the Iraqi State," *Utrecht Law Review* 7 (2011): 5.

203. Robert Dahl, *A Preface to Democratic Theory* (Chicago: University of Chicago Press, 1956), 41.

204. Timothy Stanley and Alexander Lee, "It's Still Not the End of History," *The Atlantic*, September 1, 2014, http://www.theatlantic.com/politics/archive/2014/09/its-still-not-the-end-of-history-francis-fukuyama/379394/. Accessed June 2, 2015.

205. Michal Belknap reiterated this point: "The department [of Justice] and the White House commonly insisted that limitations on federal jurisdiction kept the national government from doing more to combat anti-civil rights violence." Michal Belknap, *Federal Law and Southern Order: Racial Violence and Constitutional Conflict in the Post-Brown South* Athens: University of Georgia Press, 1987), 39.

206. In juxtaposing the political against that of the legal, by no means am I trying to suggest that garnering the political will for federal rights enforcement was easy. Rather, it is that the political difficulties surrounding federal rights enforcement be seen as primarily political issues to be resolved, rather than legal issues that needed to be overcome. For an in-depth analysis of the political difficulties surrounding federal rights enforcement, see Richard Valelly, *The Two Reconstructions*

207. Amos T. Akerman to B. Silliman, November 9, 1871, Amos T. Akerman Papers, University of Virginia.

208. Carl Schmitt, *Political Theology: Four Chapters on the Concept of Sovereignty*, trans. George Schwab (Chicago: University of Chicago Press, 1995), 5.

209. U.S. Constitution, Article II, Section 3.

210. Desmond King and Stephen Tuck make a similar argument in stating that characterizing the United States as weak pays "insufficient attention to the racial dimensions of government policy from the 1880s which contributed to the spread of segregation across the nation" (King and Tuck, "De-Centering the South," 236).

211. Neumann, *The Democratic and the Authoritarian State*, 22.

212. King and Tuck, "De-Centering the South," 214.

CHAPTER 3

1. Frederick Douglass, "What the Black Man Wants" [original publication date 1865], in *The Life and Writings of Frederick Douglass*, Vol. IV, *Reconstruction and After*, ed. Philip Foner (New York: International Publishers, 1955), 163.

2. Walter Benjamin, "Theses on the Philosophy of History," in *Illuminations: Essays and Reflections*, ed. Hannah Arendt (New York: Shocken, 1969), 257.

3. This is the (in)famous statement made by Chief Justice Roger Taney in the Dred Scott Case: *Dred Scott v. Sanford*, 60 U.S. 393, 408 (1856).

4. Robert Kaczorowski, *The Politics of Judicial Interpretation: The Federal Courts, Department of Justice, and Civil Rights, 1866–1876* (New York: Fordham University Press, 2005).

5. *Slaughter-House Cases*, 83 U.S. 36 (1873). My analysis of *Slaughter-House* is very similar to that of Pamela Brandwein. However, unlike Brandwein, who predicated her analysis on state action, my analysis is predicated on this concept of an emergency. Pamela Brandwein, *Rethinking the Judicial Settlement of Reconstruction* (Cambridge: Cambridge University Press, 2011).

6. *The Slaughterhouse Cases.*

7. *U.S. v. Cruikshank*, 92 U.S. 542 (1875).

8. *U.S. v. Harris*, 106 U.S. 629 (1883).

9. *The Civil Rights Cases*, 109 U.S. 3 (1883).

10. Eric Posner and Adrian Vermeule, *Terror in the Balance: Security, Liberty and the Courts* (Oxford: Oxford University Press, 2007), 5.

11. For more information on the traditional concept of emergencies, see Clinton Rossiter, *Constitutional Dictatorship: Crisis Government in the Modern Democracies* (New Brunswick: Transaction Publishers, 2002); Oren Gross and Fionnuala Ni Aolian, *Law in Times of Crisis: Emergency Powers in Theory and Practice* (Cambridge: Cambridge University Press, 2006); and Ian Zuckerman, "One Law for War and Peace? Judicial Review and Emergency Powers between the Norm and the Exception," *Constellations* 13 (2006): 522–545.

12. Hoong Phun Lee, *Emergency Powers* (Sydney: Law Book Co., 1984), 4.

13. Jane Perry Clark, "Emergencies and the Law," *Political Science Quarterly* 49 (1934): 269.

14. Ibid., 281.

15. In the National Recovery Act, it states: "A national emergency productive of widespread unemployment and disorganization of industry, which burdens interstate and foreign commerce, affects the public welfare, and undermines the standard of living of the American people, is hereby declared to exist." The National Recovery Act of 1933, Section 1.

16. Gross and Ni Aolian, *Law in Times of Crisis*, 1036.

17. Gross and Ni Aolian state: "Recognizing a separate reality of extralegal activity in the face of emergency may help in maintaining the integrity of the ordinary legal system.... Keeping the ordinary legal system clean and distinct from the dirty and messy reality of emergency prevents the perversion of that system in order to give answers to the hard, exceptional cases. Ordinary rules need not be modified or adapted so as to facilitate governmental crisis measures. Insofar as exceptional measures are required to deal with the crisis, these measures are viewed precisely as such, 'exceptional.' They are not allowed to penetrate the ordinary legal system and 'contaminate' it. Once an emergency has terminated, a return to normalcy may be possible without the ordinary legal system being marred by scars of emergency legislation or by interpretive stretch marks" (Ibid., 1132–1133).

18. Dara Strolovitch, "Of Mancessions and Hecoveries: Race, Gender and the Political Construction of Economic Crises and Recoveries," *Perspective on Politics* 11 (2013); 169.

19. Ibid., 171.

20. Ibid., 168.

21. Charles Beard and Mary Beard, *The Rise of American Civilization* (New York: Macmillan Company, 1946), 53, 121.

22. Morton Keller, "Powers and Rights: Two Centuries of American Constitutionalism," *The Journal of American History* 74 (1987): 681.

23. Bruce Ackerman, *We the People, Vol. 2: Transformations* (Cambridge: Belknap Press, 1998), 199.

24. *Congressional Globe*, 39th Congress, 1st session, 1292.

25. Michael Les Benedict, *A Compromise of Principle: Congressional Republicans and Reconstruction, 1863–1869*, (New York, Norton, 1974), 123.

26. The major exception was the Fugitive Slave Acts of 1793 and 1850. These acts secured the property right of slaveholders in their slaves.

27. Ironically, the Fugitive Slave Act would be the basis for the Civil Rights Act of 1866. See Robert Kaczorowski's article, "The Enforcement Provisions of the Civil Rights Act of 1866: A Legislative History in Light of *Runyon v. McCrary*," *Yale Law Journal* 98 (1989): 565–595.

28. Harold Hyman and William Wiecek, *Equal Justice under Law: Constitutional Development 1833–1875* (New York: Harper and Row, 1982), 299.

29. *Congressional Globe*, 40th Congress, 2nd session, 2603.

30. Benedict, *A Compromise of Principle*, 103.

31. "Reconstruction in South Carolina," *New York Times*, June 26, 1865, p. 5

32. Eric Foner, *Reconstruction: America's Unfinished Revolution, 1863–1877* (New York: Perennial Classics, 1988), 246.

33. Foner, *Reconstruction*, 199

34. Benjamin F. Flanders to Henry C. Warmoth, November 23, 1865, Warmoth Papers (as quoted in Foner, *Reconstruction*, 199).

35. William W. Davis, *The Civil War and Reconstruction in Florida* (New York: Columbia University, 1913), 425.

36. Hyman and Wiecek note that "the southern delegates [to Congress] of December, 1865, included the Confederacy's former vice-president and two C.S.A. generals" (Hyman and Wiecek, *Equal Justice under Law*, 311). They go on to say that President Johnson "left virtually all determination of state residents' political and civil status in the hands of southern whites, most of whom were recent rebels he had amnestied or pardoned.... Johnson encouraged pardoned ex-rebels to

dominate both federal and state offices in the South, the former in defiance of the oath law" (Hyman and Wiecek, *Equal Justice under Law*, 314).

37. In addition to the violence mentioned in Chapter 2, there were two riots in particular that discredited President Johnson's policies in the eyes of many congressmen who had hitherto supported him. One was the Memphis Riots of 1866. On May 1, 1866, a full-scale battle that lasted forty hours occurred in the downtown area of Memphis, Tennessee, resulting in the death of forty-six blacks and two whites. A congressional committee reported that blacks in Memphis enjoyed "no protection from the law whatever." Majority Report, *Memphis Riots and Massacres: The Reports of the Committees of the House of Representatives Made during the First Session, Thirty-Ninth Congress, 1865–1866* (Washington: Arno Press, 1969), 30. Also see James G. Ryan, "The Memphis Riots of 1866: Terror in a Black Community During Reconstruction," *The Journal of Negro History* 62 (1977): 243–257. The second riot was the New Orleans Riot of 1866. On July 30, 1866, what General Philip H. Sheridan described as an "absolute massacre" occurred in which thirty-four blacks and three whites were killed, along with over a hundred people injured in Louisiana.

38. Eric McKitrick asked: "How is one to explain their almost brazen willingness to put forward so many of their most forthright secessionists in public office? What of their incredible black codes? Why should these men have disregarded so completely President Johnson's suggestion, made to all intents and purposes in good faith, that they grant the suffrage to a small and very highly qualified class of their colored freedmen? That step alone, so relatively easy compared with all they would have to undergo in later years, could beyond doubt have effected a revolution in Northern sentiment." Eric McKitrick, *Andrew Johnson and Reconstruction* (Chicago: University of Chicago Press, 1960), 153.

39. *Congressional Globe*, 39th Congress, 1st session, 474.

40. As quoted in Foner, *Reconstruction*, 263.

41. Foner, *Reconstruction*, 262.

42. Joseph Holt to Henry C. Warmoth, August 1, 1866, Henry C. Warmoth Papers, UNC (as quoted in Foner, *Reconstruction*, 263).

43. Foner, *Reconstruction*, 263.

44. Benedict, *A Compromise of Principle*, 206

45. The use of the term *radical* has been one way of delineating those who wanted a qualitative change from the past. But, as Michael Les Benedict points out, "Johnson and renegade Republican allies deliberately lumped all Republicans together as radicals, insisting that the entire congressional party had come under the domination of the 'fanatics,' Thaddeus Stevens and Charles Sumner. From this time forward all anti-Johnson Republicans were called—and called themselves—Radical Republicans and it was this journalistic and political convention which for so long submerged the incontestable fact that many 'Radicals' were radical with a capital R only" (Benedict, *A Compromise of Principle*, 23).

46. Ibid., 27.

47. Ibid., 35.

48. Ibid., 38.

49. *Congressional Globe*, 39th Congress, 1st session, 2764.

50. I have omitted the 1866 bill to extend the Freedmen's Bureau for two reasons. First, unlike the Civil Rights Bill, Congress did not override the President's veto. Second, unlike the Civil Rights Bill, Congress justified it under the war powers (see *Congressional Globe*, 39 Congress, 1st session, 364–366).

51. *Congressional Globe*, 39th Congress, 1st session, 211.

52. Ibid.

53. Ibid., 813.

54. Some have pointed erroneously to the actions of the Freedmen's Bureau as a gauge of how the Civil Rights Act was and should be interpreted. After ratification of the Civil Rights Act, the Freedmen's Bureau was ordered to enforce the Civil Rights Act, but under military authority. Agents were instructed to arrest persons who were charged with offenses against citizens "in cases where the civil authorities have failed, neglected, or are unable to arrest and bring such parties to trial" (Kaczorowski, *The Politics of Judicial Interpretation*, 24). Although such wording would appear to entail broad powers, the Freedmen's Bureau, under the command of General Howard, decided that "nothing could be done under the Civil Rights Act until the local Courts shall have been tested" (27). Kaczorowski concludes that Howard's declaration had more to do with political considerations and practical difficulties than it had to do with a particular legal interpretation of the law (30). Kaczorowski's argument is buffeted by the fact that the Freedmen's Bureau did, in fact, prosecute people without first testing the local courts (28), arrest and prosecute judges and state officers who refused or neglected "to perform any official act required by law" (31), assumed primary jurisdiction and law enforcement functions, and prosecuted private individuals (32). But, too much should not be read into the actions of the Freedmen's Bureau with regard to their interpretation of the Civil Rights Act because their actions were conducted under war powers.

55. Eric McKitrick argues that "it is important in any diagnosis of Johnson's subsequent downfall not to belittle the fact that virtually every Republican paper in the country, including those later to be designated as 'radical,' was initially on the President's side. Even the most extreme of these journals would remain with him for a number of months, and the majority would not fully sever connections until early in 1866" (McKitrick, *Andrew Johnson and Reconstruction*, 21).

56. On February 19, 1866, President Johnson vetoed the bill to extend the Freedmen's Bureau. On March 29, 1866, President Johnson vetoed the bill to extend the Civil Rights Bill of 1866.

57. Kaczorowski, *The Politics of Judicial Interpretation*, 41.

58. Ibid., 38–39.

59. McKitrick, *Andrew Johnson and Reconstruction*, 421.

60. Ackerman, *We the People*, 182.

61. McKitrick, *Andrew Johnson and Reconstruction*, 366.

62. Foner, *Reconstruction*, 264.

63. Ibid., 265.

64. As quoted in McKitrick, *Andrew Johnson and Reconstruction*, 428.

65. Ibid., 448.

66. The four states were readmitted in 1870.

67. Grant carried twenty-six states, collecting 214 electoral votes and amassing 3,013,650 popular votes. Seymour carried eight states, collecting eighty electoral votes and amassing 2,708,744 popular votes. Texas, Mississippi, and Virginia were not yet readmitted to the Union and therefore their population could not vote.

68. Act of May 31, 1870 (Enforcement Act), 16Statutes at Large, 140–146

69. Ibid.

70. Ibid.

71. Act of April 20, 1871 (Ku Klux Act), 22Statutes at Large, 13–15.

72. Ibid., 13–15.

73. Ibid., 13–15.

74. "The Problem at the South," *The Nation*, March 23, 1871, p. 192.

75. Benjamin Butler stated that "if the Federal Government cannot pass laws to protect the rights, liberty, and lives of citizens of the United States in the States, why were guarantees of those fundamental rights put in the Constitution at all?" (*Congressional Globe*, 42d Congress, 1st Session, Appendix, 299).

76. For example, the House vote on the Civil Rights Act of 1866 was 122 to 41 whereas the House vote on the Ku Klux Act of 1871 was 118 to 91.

77. *Congressional Globe*, 42d Congress, 1st session, 364.

78. Ibid., 577.

79. Ibid., 576.

80. Carl Schurz to E. L. Godkin, March 31, 1871, E. L. Godkin Papers, Houghton Library, Harvard University (as quoted in Foner, *Reconstruction*, 456).

81. Foner, *Reconstruction*, 456.

82. Kaczorowski, *The Politics of Judicial Interpretation*, 45. In this same vein, he also states that "it is curious that Northern Republicans did not perceive Klan terrorism as a revival of the South's rebellion against the United States" (45). Kaczorowski seems to imply that because the Klan was "a paramilitary operating fighting a rear-guard action in continuation of the Civil War," the best means of fighting the Klan would have been through extralegal means (44).

83. In 1868, Grant garnered 3,013,650 popular votes and 214 electoral college votes. In 1872, Grant garnered 3,598,235 popular votes and 286 electoral college votes.

84. In 1870, only Virginia, Tennessee, North Carolina, and Georgia shifted to Democratic control.

85. *Columbia Daily Union*, November 22, 1872 (as quoted in Michael Perman, *The Road to Redemption: Southern Politics, 1869–1879* Chapel Hill University of North Carolina Press, 1984), 136.

86. Kerr to Marble, June 13, 1872, in Marble Papers (as quoted in William Gillette, *Retreat from Reconstruction, 1869–1879* [Baton Rouge: Louisiana State University Press, 1979], 63).

87. John Mosby to Captain A. G. Babcock, Warrenton, Virginia, May 13, 1872, *Columbia Daily Union*, May 23, 1872 (as quoted in Perman, *The Road to Redemption*, 109).

88. Greeley was, in fact, the nominee of the Liberal Republican Party. In terms of electoral college votes, Grant received 286 electoral college votes, Greeley received sixty-six electoral college votes, and four other candidates collected sixty-three electoral college votes.

89. Perman, *The Road to Redemption*, 106.

90. Ibid., 88.

91. Ibid., 88.

92. Ibid., 103.

93. Foner, *Reconstruction*, 439.

94. Gillette, *Retreat from Reconstruction, 1869–1879*, 51.

95. Andrew Slap, *The Doom of Reconstruction: The Liberal Republicans in the Civil War Era* (New York: Fordham University Press, 2006); Matthew Downey, "Horace Greeley and the Politicians: The Liberal Republican Convention in 1872" *The Journal of American History* 53 (1967): 727–750.

96. Perman, *The Road to Redemption*, 108.

97. Gillette, *Retreat from Reconstruction, 1869–1879*, 70.

98. Raleigh *Sentinel*, November 16, 1872 (as quoted in Perman, *The Road to Redemption*, 123).

99. Perman, *The Road to Redemption*, 150.

100. Samuel B. Maxey to his wife, Washington, DC, June 26, 1876, Samuel Bell Maxey Papers (as quoted in Perman, *The Road to Redemption*, 130).

101. James W. Throckmorton to Ashbel Smith, Mckinney, Texas, November 11, 1872, Ashbel Smith Papers (as quoted in Perman, *The Road to Redemption*, 124).

102. Perman, *The Road to Redemption*, 79.

103. An apt analogy would be the 2006 midterm elections. The Democratic victories in 2006 were seen by many as a call for change regarding America's occupation in Iraq. Although the electoral results clearly signaled public desire for change, it was not clear in 2006 whether that change meant full withdrawal, a definite exit strategy, and/or troop reduction.

104. William M. Wiecek, "The Reconstruction of Federal Judicial Power, 1863–1875," *The American Journal of Legal History* 13 (1969): 333.

105. Ibid., 334.

106. Homer Cummings and Carl McFarland, *Federal Justice: Chapters in the History of Justice and the Federal Executive* (New York: Macmillan Company, 1937).

107. *Congressional Globe*, 41st Congress, 2d session, 3034–3039, 3065–3067.

108. Kaczorowski, *The Politics of Judicial Interpretation*, 63.

109. Foner, *Reconstruction*, 258.

110. Kutler argues that "as the stalemated political system made a political settlement of the issue almost impossible, leading party spokesmen expressed a desire for an authoritative judicial decree on the constitutional issues." Stanley Kutler, *Judicial Power and Reconstruction Politics* (Chicago: University of Chicago Press, 1968), 33.

111. The prevailing thought among many Republicans was that when the ex-Confederate states were back in, they would nullify whatever Republicans had in plan for them. In a letter to Thaddeus Stevens dated January 1866, Republican A. Noble exclaimed that "now is the time to take our guarantees. If we don't do it now, we never will have them." A. Noble to Thaddeus Stevens, January 13, 1866, in Stevens Papers (as quoted in William Nelson, *The Fourteenth Amendment: From Political Principle to Judicial Doctrine*, (Cambridge, Harvard University Press, 1988), 44) Many congressional Republicans thought that by extending and broadening the Court's power, Reconstruction would be able to continue unabated if and when the Democrats regained control of the political branches. Because the federal judiciary was the least susceptible to dramatic shifts in opinion, congressional Republicans believed they could stack the judiciary with justices sympathetic to their cause, and the judiciary could subsequently act as a bulwark against the anticipated Democratic counteroffensive. In other words, the Reconstruction Congress had placed its hopes on the most conservative branch to preserve its radical program.

112. A whole host of factors, including electoral fatigue, economic downturns, westward expansion, and racism, led to the rapid diminution of electoral support for extending rights to blacks (Foner, *Reconstruction*; Perman, *The Road to Redemption*; William Gillette, *Retreat from Reconstruction, 1869–1879*). Congressional Republicans were, in many ways, more progressive than their respective constituencies. In 1867, one year after the Republicans won a resounding electoral victory for congressional Reconstruction in general and the Fourteenth Amendment in particular, voters in Ohio, Pennsylvania, New York, and New Jersey voted to reject Negro suffrage. Thus, there was not only a fear of backlash from their own constituency, but also a fear that whatever compassion Northerners might have had for blacks in the South would turn quickly into compassion fatigue. In other ways, congressional Republicans were more conservative than

their respective constituencies. The emergence of labor movements in the North and their concomitant demands for equality, freedom, and protection under the law made many Republican legislators fearful that the same arguments they were making for racial equality for blacks in the South would be used against them by their own constituents. William Du Bois, *Black Reconstruction in America, 1860–1880*, (New York, Free Press, 1962), 356, 359; Richard Bensel, *Yankee Leviathan: The Origins of Central State Authority in America, 1859–1877* (New York: Cambridge University Press, 1990), 421.

113. McKitrick, *Andrew Johnson and Reconstruction*, 96.

114. See William Dunning, "The Constitution of the United States in Reconstruction," *Political Science Quarterly* 2 (1987): 558–602; and McKitrick, *Andrew Johnson and Reconstruction*, 96–119.

115. McKitrick, *Andrew Johnson and Reconstruction*, 102.

116. Ibid., 113.

117. *Luther v. Borden*, 48, U.S. 1, 42 (as quoted in McKitrick, *Andrew Johnson and Reconstruction*, 114).

118. Cases deemed nonjusticiable means they are not capable of being settled by law or by the action of a court.

119. *U.S. v. Rhodes*, 27 F. Cas. 785 (No 16151) (C.C. Ky. 1867).

120. *re Turner*, 24 Fed. Cas. 339, Abb. U.S. 89, #14, 247 (C.C.C. Md., 1867).

121. *Live Stock Dealers and Butchers Association v. Crescent City Livestock Landing and Slaughterhouse Co.*, 1 Woods 21, 15 Fed. Cas. 649 at 652, #8408 (C.C.D. La., 1870).

122. *U.S. v. Hall*, 26 Fed. Cas. 79 at 81–82, #15, 282 (C.C.S.D. Ala., 1871); *U.S. v. Hall*, 26 Fed. Cas. 1147, #15, 712 (C.C.S.D. Ala., 1871).

123. *U.S. v. Rhodes*.

124. *The American Law Register (1852–1891)* 16 (1868): 249.

125. Ibid., 246.

126. *re Turner*.

127. *Live Stock Dealers and Butchers Association v. Crescent City Livestock Landing and Slaughterhouse Co.*

128. *U.S. v. Hall* and *U.S. v. Hall*.

129. The Court's apprehension to lead during times of crises is in line with the general behavior of the judiciary during crises. During emergencies, Samuel Issacharoff and Richard Pildes concluded that often the Courts seek "to shift the responsibility for difficult decisions away from themselves and toward the joint action of the most democratic branches of the government." Samuel Issacharoff and Richard Pildes, "Emergency Contexts without Emergency Powers: The United States' Constitutional Approach to Rights during Wartime," *International Constitutionalism* 2 (2004): 297.

130. *Georgia v. Stanton*, 73 U.S. 50 (1867).

131. *Mississippi v. Johnson*, 71 U.S. 475 (1867).

132. Ex parte *McCardle*, 74 U.S. 506 (1868).

133. Kutler, *Judicial Power and Reconstruction Politics*, 113.

134. *Texas v. White*, 74 U.S. 700 (1869).

135. Kutler, *Judicial Power and Reconstruction Politics*, 6.

136. Hyman and Wiecek, *Equal Justice under Law*, 383.

137. Ibid.

138. *Congressional Globe*, 39 Cong., 2 sess., 250. An example is seen in fall 1865 when six South Carolinians killed three Union soldiers on guard duty. There was a military trial in which four were found guilty. After the trial, the president had them transferred to Fort Delaware, whereupon their arrival the commander was served with a writ of habeas corpus from a federal district judge of Delaware. There was a subsequent hearing in November during which the judge ordered the prisoners released on the grounds that the civil courts of South Carolina had been open at the same time the crime was committed. The murderers were never tried again. McKitrick, *Andrew Johnson and Reconstruction* 458.

139. Charles Warren, *The Supreme Court in United States History, 1865–1918*, vol. 3 (Boston: Beard Books, 1999), 164–165.

140. In 1871, *Milligan was* the basis for the defense in the South Carolina Klan trials. See Kermit Hall, "Political Power and Constitutional Legitimacy: The South Carolina Ku Klux Klan Trials, 1871–1872," *Emory Law Journal* 33 (1984): 921–952.

141. Ex parte *Milligan*, 71, U.S. 2, 140–141.

142. Samuel Freeman Miller to William Pitt Ballinger, February 6, 1867, box 1, folder 4, Samuel Freeman Miller Papers, Library of Congress.

143. Historian Eric Foner wrote, "a series of Supreme Court decisions during Grant's second term undercut the legal rationale for an [interventionist Southern policy.]... The first pivotal decision, in the *Slaughterhouse Cases*, was announced in 1873" (Foner, *Reconstruction*, 529–531).

144. For an excellent history of the entire case, see Ronald Labbe and Jonathan Lurie, *The Slaughterhouse Cases: Regulation, Reconstruction, and the Fourteenth Amendment* (Lawrence: University Press of Kansas, 2003).

145. Ibid.; William E. Nelson, *The Fourteenth Amendment: From Political Principle to Judicial Doctrine* (Cambridge: Harvard University Press, 1988); Kaczorowski, *The Politics of Judicial Interpretation*; Hyman and Wiecek, *Equal Justice under Law*; Michael A. Ross, *Justice of Shattered Dreams: Samuel Freeman Miller and the Supreme Court during the Civil War Era* (Baton Rouge: Louisiana State University Press, 2003); Michael Les Benedict, "Preserving Federalism: Reconstruction and the Waite Court," *Supreme Court Review* (1978): 39–62; Pamela Brandwein, *Rethinking the Judicial Settlement of Reconstruction*; Leslie Friedman Goldstein, "The Spectre of the Second Amendment: Rereading *Slaughterhouse* and *Cruikshank*," *Studies in American Political Development* 21 (2007): 131–148.

146. Ronald Labbe and Jonathan Lurie argue that "race is one of the less important features of the *Slaughterhouse* story" (Labbe and Lurie, *The Slaughterhouse Cases*, 9).

147. Historian Eric Foner wrote, "a series of Supreme Court decisions during Grant's second term undercut the legal rationale for an [interventionist Southern policy.]. . . The first pivotal decision, in the *Slaughterhouse Cases*, was announced in 1873. . . . Attributes of national citizenship had been defined so narrowly in *Slaughterhouse* as to render them all but meaningless to blacks" (Foner, *Reconstruction*, 529–531). Legal historian Robert Kaczorowski wrote, "The Supreme Court selected the *Slaughter-House Cases* as the instrument for its interpretation of national civil rights enforcement authority. . . . Justice Miller's opinion overturned the growing body of judicial interpretations of the impact of the Thirteenth and Fourteenth Amendments upon American constitutionalism as fixing sovereignty in the nation and as establishing the primacy of national citizenship and the concomitant national authority to secure the civil rights of American citizens. . . . [The significance of Miller's decision] lays in the Court's reversal of the constitutional

developments in the nation's courts" (Kaczorowski, *The Politics of Judicial Interpretation*, 116–123). Lewis LaRue, "The Continuing Presence of *Dred Scott*," *Washington and Lee Law Review* 42 (1985): 57–63.

148. Michael Les Benedict, "Preserving Federalism"; Labbe and Lurie, *The Slaughterhouse Cases*; Michael Ross, *Justice of Shattered Dreams*; Brandwein, *Rethinking the Judicial Settlement of Reconstruction*; Goldstein, "The Specter of the Second Amendment."

149. According to Labbe and Lurie, "there is no evidence of any reluctance on Miller's part to enforce the new amendment on behalf of the ex-slave" (Labbe and Lurie, *The Slaughterhouse Cases*, 16).

150. Slaughterhouse, 71–72.

151. Ibid., 77–78.

152. Ibid., 78.

153. Ibid., 79.

154. Ibid., 82.

155. Ibid., 124.

156. Ibid.

157. Ibid., 130.

158. Ibid., 91.

159. Ibid.

160. Ibid., 93.

161. This is analogous to the arguments made in the *Bakke* decision regarding reverse discrimination. *Regents of the University of California v. Bakke,* 438 U.S. 265 (1978).

162. Samuel Freeman Miller to William Pitt Ballinger, February 6, 1867, box 1, folder 4, Samuel Freeman Miller Papers, Library of Congress.

163. Letter from Francis Cope to Laura Towne, November 19, 1877. Reprinted in Willie Lee Rose, *Rehearsal for Reconstruction: The Port Royal Experiment*, (New York, Oxford University Press, 1976), 403–404 (1964).

164. Slaughterhouse.

165. Ibid., 75.

166. Lewis LaRue writes, "*Slaughterhouse Cases* begin to look like the deep mirror image of Dred Scott. . . . With the adoption of the fourteenth amendment, blacks become citizens, but Miller gutted the meaning of that by stripping citizenship of any important legal consequences. So long as blacks cannot be citizens, enormous importance is attached to the concept; as soon as blacks can become citizens, the concept is drained of all meaning. (It is this sort of thing that gives paranoia a good name)." Lewis LaRue, "The Continuing Presence of *Dred Scott*," *Washington and Lee Law Review* 42 (1985): 60. Kaczorowski, *The Politics of Judicial Interpretation* 122; Foner, *Reconstruction*, 531.

167. Alexander Bickel, *The Morality of Consent* (New Haven: Yale University Press, 1975), 45–46; Jonathan Lurie, *The Chase Court: Justices, Rulings and Legacy* (Santa Barbara: ABC-CLIO, 2004), 83.

168. For example, in his denunciation of Miller's decision, Rogers Smith simply quotes Miller's use of "distinct" to make his point. Rogers Smith, *Civic Ideals: Conflicting Visions of Citizenship in U.S. History* (New Haven: Yale University Press, 1997), 331.

169. For other accounts that treat race as an emergency, see Mahmood Mamdani, *Citizen and Subject: Contemporary Africa and the Legacy of Late Colonialism* (Princeton: Princeton

University Press, 1996); and Partha Chatterjee, "Civil Liberties, Terrorism and Difference," presented at Columbia University, February 4, 2006.

170. *Evil* is a term used by Miller in *Slaughter-House* to explain the intent of the Fourteenth Amendment: "No one can fail to be impressed with the one pervading purpose found in them all, lying at the foundation at each, and without which none of the would have been even suggested; we mean the freedom of the slave race, the security and firm establishment of that freedom, and the protection of the newly-made freeman and citizen from the oppressions of those who had formerly exercised unlimited dominion over him . . . in any fair and just construction of any section or phrase of these amendments, it is necessary to look to the purpose which we have said was the pervading spirit of them all, the evil which they were designed to remedy" (*Slaughter-House*, 71–72).

171. *Mitchell v. Harmony*, 54, US. 115 (1851).

172. Ibid., 135.

173. *U.S. v. Cruikshank*, 92 U.S. 542 (1875).

174. As quoted in James Hogue, *Uncivil War: Five New Orleans Street Battles and the Rise and Fall of Radical Reconstruction* (Baton Rouge, Louisiana University Press, 2006), 150.

175. *United States v. Cruikshank*, 714.

176. "Ordinary felonies" and "the war of race" were the terms used by Justice Bradley in his circuit court decision of *U.S. v. Cruikshank* (Ibid.).

177. Amos T. Akerman to B. Silliman, November 9, 1871, Amos T. Akerman Papers, University of Virginia.

178. Amos T. Akerman to Charles Sumner, April, 2, 1869, Sumner Papers, Harvard University.

179. *U.S. v. Cruikshank*, 92 U.S. 542, 554

180. *U.S. v. Cruikshank*, 556.

181. Ibid.

182. Ibid., 557.

183. Ibid.

184. Pamela Brandwein, "A Judicial Abandonment of Blacks? Rethinking the 'State Action' Cases of the Waite Court," *Law and Society Review* 41 (2007): 362.

185. *Dred Scott v. Sanford*, 60 U.S. (19 How.) 393 (1857).

186. Waite to Bond, April 4, 1876, Letterbooks (as quoted in Peter Magrath, *Morrison R. Waite: The Triumph of Character*, (New York, Macmillan, 1963), 129).

187. *U.S. v. Harris*, 106 U.S. 629 (1883).

188. Ibid., 640.

189. *U.S. v. Hall*, 26 Fed. Cas. 79 at 81–82, #15, 282 (C.C.S.D. Ala., 1871).

190. *U.S. v. Harris*, 640.

191. *Civil Rights Cases*, 109 U.S. 3, 25 (1883).

192. *U.S. v. Cruikshank*, 25 F. Cas. 707 (C.C.D. La. 1874) (No. 14897), aff'd, 92 U.S. 542 (1876), 714.

193. In the Compromise of 1877, Rutherford B. Hayes agreed to withdraw all federal troops in the South to resolve the disputed electoral results of 1876 made by Samuel Tilden. For further details, see C. Vann Woodward, *Reunion and Reaction: The Compromise of 1877 and the End of Reconstruction* (Boston: Little, Brown and Company, 1966). Others, including Pamela Brandwein, have disputed this claim that Reconstruction ended in 1877, and contend that 1891 marked the end of Reconstruction with the failure of Congress to pass the Lodge–Hoar elections bill,

and point to Miller's decision in ex parte *Yarbrough* as evidence of the Supreme Court's continued efforts at curtailing racial violence. Although it is understandable to interpret the Supreme Court in *Yarbrough* as indicative of the Court's proactive stance in quelling racial violence, it is important to note the limited scope of Miller's decision in this case. In *Yarbrough*, the Supreme Court restricted its focus on the application for a writ of habeas corpus. Miller stated explicitly, "the court has no general authority to review on error or appeal the judgments of the circuit courts" or "to convert the writ of habeas corpus into a writ of error" (*Ex parte Yarbrough*, 110, U.S. 651, 654 (1884)). The Supreme Court was focused only on whether the circuit court had the jurisdiction to make the ruling it did. In other words, Miller made clear that the Supreme Court was neither endorsing nor refuting the circuit court decision to prosecute *Yarbrough*; rather, it was simply deciding whether the circuit court had the authority to make such a decision. To suggest, then, as Brandwein does that the Supreme Court in *Yarbrough* was proceeding proactively with Reconstruction, is a mistake that Miller tried explicitly to avoid. (Pamela Brandwein, *Rethinking the Judicial Settlement of Reconstruction*, (New York, Cambridge University Press, 2011), 148–151.

194. *Giles v. Harris*, 189 U.S. 475, 486–488 (1903).

195. Brandwein, "A Judicial Abandonment of Blacks?" 352.

196. Ibid., 355.

197. Ibid.

198. These are the words Judge Emmons used to qualify his sympathy for blacks. *Charge to Grand Jury-Civil Rights Act*, 30 F. Cas. 1005, 1006–1007 (C.C. W.D. Tenn.) (1875) (as quoted in Brandwein, "A Judicial Abandonment of Blacks?," 354–355).

199. "The State Rights Issue Settled," *Nation*, July 21, 1887, 46.

200. For more information on the solidity of Southerners to vote against anything that might extend to blacks, see Valdimer O. Key, *Southern Politics in State and Nation* (Knoxville: University of Tennessee Press, 1984); and Ira Katznelson, Kim Geiger, and Daniel Kryder, "Limiting Liberalism: The Southern Veto in Congress, 1933–1950," *Political Science Quarterly* 108 (1993): 283–306.

201. U.S. Commission on Civil Rights, Law Enforcement 13 (1965).

CHAPTER 4

1. Frederick Douglass, "Southern Barbarism: Speech on the Occasion of the Twenty-Fourth Anniversary of Emancipation in the District of Columbia, Washington, DC, 1886," in *Life and Writings of Frederick Douglass*, Vol. IV, ed. Philip Foner (NewYork: International Publishers, 1955), 431.

2. Corey Robin, *Fear: The History of A Political Idea* (Oxford: Oxford University Press, 2006), 70.

3. Letter from NAACP Secretary James Weldon Johnson to Senator Henry Cabot Lodge, June 14, 1922. As quoted in Claudine Ferrell's *Nightmare and Dream: Anti-Lynching in Congress, 1917–1922* (NewYork: Garland Publishing, 1896), 420.

4. Oliver C. Cox, *Caste Class and Race: A Study in Social Dynamics* (New York: Modern Reader Paperbacks, 1948), 549.

5. Ibid., 554.

6. Robert Dahl, *A Preface to Democratic Theory*, (Chicago: University of Chicago Press, 1956), 41.

7. Ernst Fraenkel, *The Dual State: A Contribution to the Theory of Dictatorship*, trans. E. A. Shils (New York: Oxford: 1941); Gerald Neuman, "Surveying Law and Borders: Anomalous Zones," *Stanford Law Review* 48 (1996): 1197–1234.

8. *Moore v. Dempsey*, 261 U.S. 86 (1923).

9. *Logan v. U.S.*, 144 U.S. 263 (1892).

10. James Madison, Alexander Hamilton, and John Jay, "Federalist 78," in *The Federalist Papers*, ed. Robert Scigliano (New York: Modern Library, 2001) 496.

11. Christopher Waldrep, *The Many Faces of Judge Lynch: Extralegal Violence and Punishment in America* (New York: Palgrave, 2002), 67.

12. Ibid., 78.

13. Ibid., 67.

14. *Report of the Joint Committee on Reconstruction*, 39th Congress, 1st Session, Tennessee, 111.

15. *Report of the Joint Committee on Reconstruction*, 39th Congress, 1st Session, 31.

16. *Report of the Joint Select Committee to Inquire into the Conditions of Affairs in the Late Insurrectionary States*, 42d Congress, 2d session (cited hereafter as *KKK Report*), South Carolina, Vol. 3, 1483.

17. Eric Foner, *Reconstruction: America's Unfinished Revolution, 1863–1877*, (New York: Perennial Classics, 2002), 425.

18. Allen Trelease, *White Terror: The Ku Klux Klan Conspiracy and Southern Reconstruction*, (Baton Rouge, Louisiana State University Press, 1971), xi.

19. Richard Zuczek, *State of Rebellion: Reconstruction in South Carolina* (Columbia: University of South Carolina Press, 1996). His characterization of the Klan as insurgency is taken from the work of Robert Tomes and Eqbal Ahmad. In "Relearning Counterinsurgency Warfare," they outline four elements that characterize an insurgency, "cell-networks that maintain secrecy, terror used to foster insecurity among the population and drive them to the movement for protection, multifaceted attempts to cultivate support in the general population, often by undermining the new regime, and attacks against the government." Robert Tomes and Eqbal Ahmad, "Relearning Counterinsurgency Warfare," *Parameters* Vol. 34, Spring (2004): 18. The use of the term *guerrilla warfare* comes from the work of Eqbal Ahmad, "Revolutionary Warfare and Counterinsurgency," in *Guerrilla Strategies: An Historical Anthology from the Long March to Afghanistan*, ed. Gerard Chaliand (Berkeley: University of California Press, 1992), 245–260. In this article, Chaliand outlines several characteristics of guerrilla warfare that are an apt characterization of what the Klan did, including the importance of popular support, local autonomy, self-management, rapid social mobility, accountability of the leaders and cadres to the populace, and the need to depict the guerrilla's actions as "extragovernmental efforts to dispense justice long overdue" (250–252).

20. *Congressional Globe*, 39th Cong., 1st session, 1118–1119. As quoted in Pamela Brandwein, *Rethinking the Judicial Settlement of Reconstruction* (New York: Cambridge University Press, 2011), 36.

21. Brandwein, *Rethinking the Judicial Settlement of Reconstruction*, 29.

22. Eric Foner, *Forever Free: The Story of Emancipation and Reconstruction* (New York: Alfred A. Knopf, 2005), 196.

23. Waldrep, *The Many Faces of Judge Lynch*, 83.

24. Waldrep, *The Many Faces of Judge Lynch*, 84.

25. Gunnar Myrdal, *An American Dilemma: The Negro Problem and Modern Democracy* (New York: Harper and Brothers, 1962), 564. Herbert Shapiro has a more critical stance: "Polite

southern society was likely to pronounce lynching distasteful and to see lynching as the work of poor whites, but the leaders of society did nothing to put a stop to the practice and in actuality tended to see lynching as most regrettable but justifiable." Herbert Shapiro, *White Violence and Black Response* (Amherst: University of Massachusetts Press, 1988), 31. James Silver, a history professor at Ole Miss, remarked that Mississippi "had erected a totalitarian society which has eliminated the ordinary processes through which change can come about." James Silver, *Mississippi: The Closed Society* (New York: Harcourt, Brace and World, 1963), 155.

26. Howard Odum, "Lynchings, Fears and Folkways," *Nation*, December 30, 1931, 719–720.

27. Waldrep, *The Many Faces of Judge Lynch*, 83.

28. Albert Bandura, *Aggression: A Social Learning Analysis* (Englewood Cliffs, Prentice Hall, 1973); David Gilmore, *Aggression and Community: Paradoxes of Andalusian Culture* (New Haven: Yale University Press, 1987).Edward Ayers, *Vengeance and Justice* (New York: Oxford University Press, 1985); Jacquelyn Hall, *Revolt against Chivalry* (New York: Columbia University Press, 1979).

29. Ulrich B. Philips, "The Central Theme of Southern History," *The American Historical Review* 34 (1928): 30–43.

30. Stewart Tolnay and Elwood M. Beck, *A Festival of Violence: An Analysis of Southern Lynchings, 1882–1930* (Urbana: University of Illinois, 1995); Carl Iver Hovland and Robert Sears, "Minor Studies of Aggression: VI. Correlation of Lynchings with Economic Indices," *Journal of Psychology* 9 (1940), 301–310.

31. James Cutler, *Lynch-Law: An Investigation into the History of Lynching in the United States* (New York: Negro Universities Press, 1969), 276.

32. Ibid., 269.

33. "Federal Intervention in the States for the Suppression of Domestic Violence: Constitutionality, Statutory Power, and Policy," *Duke Law Journal* 1996 (1966): 440.

34. Douglass, "Southern Barbarism," 501–503.

35. This point is similar to the one made by Ashraf Rushdy to resituate lynchings as political acts. But whereas Rushdy wants to focuses on the continuities of racial violence before, during and after Reconstruction, I want to provide a more nuanced defense of discontinuity by outlining how lynchings were politically de-politicized. Ashraf Rushdy, *American Lynching*, (New Haven, Yale University Press, 2012).

36. See Chapter 2.

37. James McGovern, *Anatomy of a Lynching: The Killing of Claude Neal*, (Baton Rouge, Louisiana State University Press, 1982), 10–11.

38. James McGovern's *Anatomy of a Lynching: The Killing of Claude Neal* (Baton Rouge: Louisiana State University Press, 1982), 11.

39. Brandwein, *Rethinking the Judicial Settlement of Reconstruction*, 152–153.

40. Ibid., 153.

41. Ibid., 61.

42. Ashraf Rushdy, *American Lynching*, (New Haven, Yale University Press, 2012), 14.

43. For excellent accounts of electoral violence, see Everette Swinney, *Suppressing the Ku Klux Klan: The Enforcement of the Reconstruction Amendments, 1870–1877* (New York: Garland, 1987); Xi Wang, *The Trial of Democracy: Black Suffrage and Northern Republicans, 1860–1910* (Athens: University of Georgia Press, 1997); and Brandwein, *Rethinking the Judicial Settlement of Reconstruction.*

44. Tolnay and Beck, *A Festival of Violence*, 47–48.

45. In her book, *Rethinking the Judicial Settlement of Reconstruction,* Pamela Brandwein rightfully points out the "efforts to protect black voting rights between 1877 and the early 1890s" (7) to refute the claim that Reconstruction did not end with the Compromise of 1877. But in so doing, she empties the Compromise of 1877 of any political content and even goes so far as to describe the Compromise as a "myth" (228), thereby making her susceptible to the very critique she was trying to make initially, which is that Reconstruction was not this monolithic entity. Reconstruction was dismantled incrementally and, although the Compromise of 1877 did not mark the end of Reconstruction, it did mark the end to one component of Reconstruction, which was federal rights enforcement against the general category of racial violence. After 1877, Republicans narrowed their focus to that of electoral violence. Nonelectoral violence was effectively off the table.

46. According to Tolnay and Beck, 92% of lynchings that occurred after Reconstruction were the result of allegations of sexual norm violations, rape and murder, theft and robbery, arson, incendiarism, and racial prejudice. Violence related to voting was so uncommon that it fell under the rubric of "miscellaneous" (Tolnay and Beck, *A Festival of Violence,* 48).

47. Although the timing is different, the schema is somewhat similar in that both categories of violence were never completely outside the purview of the federal government. Rather, the government chose an active policy of nonintervention that was predicated primarily on the choice not to act, as opposed to any inherent relinquishing of authority. *U.S. v. Reese* (92 U.S. 214 [1876]), which declared the Fifteenth Amendment did not allow Congress to redress interferences with a citizen's qualifying to vote unless there is explicit showing of the state's racial animus, is akin to *Cruikshank* (*United States v. Cruikshank,* 25 F. Cas. 707 [C.C.D. La. 1874] [No. 14897], aff'd, 92 U.S. 542 [1876]), in that it seemed to quell all efforts of federal rights enforcement for blacks. But, as was the case with lynchings, a comprehensive dismantling was not the case. Ex parte *Yarbrough* (110 U.S. 651 [1884]) upheld the application of the Fifteenth Amendment to private interference. Although *James v. Bowman* (190 U.S. 127 [1903]) held that state action was required by the Fifteenth as well as the Fourteenth Amendment, in *Terry v. Adams* (345 U.S. 461 [1953]), the Supreme Court, according to the *Yale Law Journal,* "discarded state action requirement altogether and returned to the more liberal doctrine of the nineteenth century." "The Strange Career of 'State Action' under the Fifteenth Amendment," *Yale Law Journal* 74 (1965): 1455.

48. Ferrell, *Nightmare and Dream,* 481.

49. Ibid., 477.

50. Christopher Waldrep goes so far to even say, "Mob law rendered [the decisions made by the Supreme Court] meaningless." *A History in Documents: Lynching in America,* (New York: Palgrave, 2002), xix.

51. Ashraf Rushdy makes a similar point: "we must also search through the rhetorical apologia for lynching in order to detect the ways that these statements hid their politics within more popularly accepted justifications. . . . these attacks are justified through subterfuge." Ashraf Rushdy, *American Lynching,* 14.

52. Ernst Fraenkel, *The Dual State.*

53. Ibid., xiv.

54. Ibid., xiii.

55. Ibid., 46.

56. When Fraenkel states that "martial law as such does not necessarily clash with the rule of civil law" (Ibid., 91), he is arguing against the claim of mutual exclusivity.

57. Ibid., 71, 62.

58. Ibid., 58–59.

59. Ibid., 70.

60. For a comparison between Nazi Germany and the American South, see Johnpeter Horst Grill and Robert L. Jenkins, "The Nazis and the American South in the 1930s: A Mirror Image?" *The Journal of Southern History* 58 (1992): 667–694.

61. Fraenkel, *The Dual State*, xiii.

62. Foner, *Reconstruction*, 425.

63. Trelease, *White Terror*, xlvi.

64. This quote was taken from the testimony of Alabama Provisional Governor Lewis Parsons in the *KKK Report*,, 42d Congress, 2d session (cited hereafter as the *KKK Report*), Vol. 1, 66.

65. Fraenkel, *The Dual State*, 206.

66. Ibid., 71.

67. See Paul R. Viotti and Mark V. Kauppi, *International Relations Theory: Realism, Pluralism, Globalism and Beyond*, 3rd ed. (Boston: Allyn and Bacon, 1999), 68.

68. Jack Hirshleifer, "Anarchy and its Breakdown," *Journal of Political Economics*, Vol. 103, no.1, Feb. 1995, 26

69. Foner, *Reconstruction*, 425.

70. *Atlanta Constitution*, May 19, 1863. Quoted in Susan Jean and W. Fitzhugh Brundage, "Legitimizing 'Justice': Lynching and the Boundaries of Informal Justice in the American South," in *Informal Criminal Justice*, ed. Dermot Feenan (Aldershot: Ashgate, 2002), 159.

71. Neuman, "Surveying Law and Borders," 1201.

72. Ibid., 1224.

73. Ibid.

74. Ibid., 1208.

75. Partha Chatterjee, "Civil Liberties, Terrorism and Difference." Presented at Columbia University, February 4, 2006.

76. Ibid., 4–8.

77. Ibid., 9–10.

78. Mahmood Mamdani, *Citizen and Subject: Contemporary Africa and the Legacy of Late Colonialism* (Princeton: Princeton University Press, 1996), 18.

79. Ibid., 17.

80. Ibid., 22.

81. Ibid., 51.

82. Ibid.

83. Ibid., 61.

84. Ibid., 51.

85. Ibid., 110.

86. United States v. Cruikshank, 714.

87. Ibid.

88. *New York Herald*, January 18, 1874. "General Grant's New Departure – Notice to the Republican Party and its Monstrosities," p. 6.

89. Foner, *Reconstruction* 531.

90. Ibid.

91. Eugene Gressman, "The Unhappy History of Civil Rights Legislation," *Michigan Law Review* 50 (1952): 1337; *Slaughter-House Cases*, 83 U.S. 36 (1873).

92. Leonard Levy and Kenneth Karst, eds., *Encyclopedia of the American Constitution*, Vol. 2 (New York: Macmillan Reference, 2000); *U.S. v. Cruikshank*.

93. *Civil Rights Cases*, 109 U.S. 3, 11 (1883).

94. Robert Kaczorowski, *The Politics of Judicial Interpretation: The Federal Courts, Department of Justice, and Civil Rights, 1866–1876* (New York: Fordham University Press, 2005).

95. Brandwein, *Rethinking the Judicial Settlement of Reconstruction*.

96. Michal R. Belknap, *Federal Law and Southern Order: Racial Violence and Constitutional conflict in the Post-Brown South* (Athens: University of Georgia Press, 1987), xi.

97. In *Price*, Justice Abe Fortas wrote in the majority decision that "to act under color of law does not require that the accused be an officer of the State. It was enough that he was a willful participant in joint activity with the State or its agents" (*United States v. Price*, 383 U.S. 787, 794 (1966)). In *Guest*, Justice Stewart writes in the majority decision that "no determination of the threshold level that state action must attain . . . allegation of state involvement is sufficient" (*United States v. Guest*, 383 U.S. 745, 755 (1966).

98. Arthur Kinoy, "The Constitutional Right of Negro Freedom," *Rutgers Law Review* 21 (1966–1967): 438.

99. Michal Belknap reiterated this point: "The department [of Justice] and the White House commonly insisted that limitations on federal jurisdiction kept the national government from doing more to combat anti-civil rights violence"(Michal R. Belknap, *Federal Law and Southern Order*, 39).

100. Charles Mangum Jr., *The Legal Status of the Negro* (Chapel Hill: University of North Carolina Press, 1940), 400.

101. *U.S. v. Harris*, 106 U.S. 629 (1883).

102. *Plessy v. Ferguson*, 163 U.S., 537 (1896).

103. Ibid.

104. *Plessy v. Ferguson*, 163 U.S., 537, 544 (1896).

105. Michael Klarman, *From Jim Crow to Civil Rights* (Oxford: Oxford University Press, 2004), 23.

106. Jeremy Waldron, "Torture and Positive Law: Jurisprudence for the White House," *Columbia Law Review* Vol. 105, (2005): 1681–1750.

107. Ibid., 1724.

108. Ibid., 1725. *Brown v. Board of Education*, 347 U.S. 483 (1954)

109. "Federal Intervention in the States for the Suppression of Domestic Violence: Constitutionality, Statutory Power, and Policy," *Duke Law Journal* 1996 (1966): 440.

110. *Plessy v. Ferguson*, 544.

111. These are the words Judge Emmons used to qualify his sympathy for blacks. *Charge to Grand Jury-Civil Rights Act*, 30 F. Cas. 1005, 1006–1007 (C.C. W.D. Tenn.) (1875) (as quoted in Brandwein, *Rethinking the Judicial Settlement of Reconstruction*, 354–355).

112. See Christopher Waldrep, *The Many Faces of Judge Lynch*, 68. See also Richard Maxwell Brown, *Strain of Violence: Historical Studies of American Violence and Vigilantism* (New York: Oxford University Press, 1975) and Michael J. Pfeifer, *Rough Justice: Lynching and American Society, 1874–1947* (Urbana: University of Illinois Press, 2004).

113. *U.S. v. Harris*.

114. Neuman, "Surveying Law and Borders," 1205.

115. James Cutler, *Lynch-Law*; Philip Dray, *At the Hands of Persons Unknown* (New York: Random House, 2002); NAACP, *Thirty Years of Lynching in the United States, 1889–1918* (New York: Negro University Press, 1919); Arthur Raper, *The Tragedy of Lynching* (Chapel Hill: Arno

Press, 1969); Frank Shay, *Judge Lynch: His First Hundred Years* (New York: Ives Washburn, 1938); Christopher Waldrep, *Lynching in America* (New York: New York University Press, 2006); Ida B. Wells, *On Lynchings* (Amherst: Humanity Books, 1892).

116. Ashraf Rushdy has argued against this line of reasoning. Rushdy argues against the idea of spontaneity: "Lynching in these terms is not a spontaneous event, but a strategic ritual publicly affirming white supremacy and enforcing black terror" and that lynch mobs should be seen "as an institution of civil society equal to the CIC, ASWPL and NAACP." Rushdy, *American Lynching*, (New Haven, Yale University Press, 2012), 82–85.

117. *Moore v. Dempsey*, 261 U.S. 86, (1923), 90–91.

118. Ibid., 90.

119. *Logan v. U.S.*, 144 U.S. 263 (1892).

120. Ibid., 275.

121. Ibid., 295.

122. Ibid., 265.

123. Belknap, *Federal Law and Southern Order*, xi.

124. The 2005 Senate Resolution Apologizing for Lynching states "that 99 percent of all perpetrators of lynching escaped from punishment." http://landrieu.senate.gov/priorities/Resolution-Apologizing-for-Lynching.cfm

125. Philip Dray, *At the Hands of Persons Unknown* (New York: Random House, 2002).

126. *U.S. v. Shipp*, 214 U.S. 386 (1909).

127. Ibid., 414.

128. Ibid., 425.

129. *Corpus Juris*, 328; as quoted in James Harmon Chadbourn, *Lynching and the Law* (Chapel Hill: University of North Carolina Press, 1933), 29.

130. In *The Promise of the New South: Life After Reconstruction* ed. by Christopher Waldrep and Donald Nieman (Oxford: Oxford University Press, 1992), Edward Ayers argues that lynchings were related to population densities and black migration patterns. Stewart Tolnay and Elwood M. Beck correlated the number of lynchings with cotton production in their book *A Festival of Violence*.

131. Cutler, *Lynch-Law*, 194.

132. For information regarding the local variations of lynch law, please see Christopher Waldrep and Donald Nieman, eds., *Local Matters: Race, Crime, and Justice in the Nineteenth Century South* (Athens: University of Georgia Press, 2001); W. Fitzhugh Brundage, ed., *Under Sentence of Death: Lynching in the South* (Chapel Hill: University of North Carolina Press, 1997); and James Cutler, *Lynch-Law*.

133. Neuman, "Surveying Law and Borders," 1197.

134. Ibid., 1224.

135. Ibid., 1201.

136. Ibid., 1202.

137. Ibid., 1207.

138. Letter from NAACP Secretary James Weldon Johnson to Senator Henry Cabot Lodge, as quoted in Ferrell's *Nightmare and Dream*, 420.

139. Trelease, *White Terror*, 205.

140. U.S. Congress, Senate, Subcommittee on Constitutional Rights of the Committee on the Judiciary, *Civil Rights Hearings on S 3296 . . . and S 3170*, 89th Cong., 2d sess., 1966, 1:497 (as quoted in Belknap, *Federal Law and Southern Order*, 189).

141. *Giles v. Harris*, 189 U.S. 475, 486–488 (1903).

142. John A. Marin to "Dear Senator," February 22, 1877, Hayes Papers (as quoted in Foner, *Reconstruction*, 581).

143. Historian Eric Foner has argued the Supreme Court decision in *Cruikshank* has "rendered national prosecution of crimes committed against blacks virtually impossible, and gave a green light to acts of terror where local officials either could not or would not enforce the law" (Foner, *Reconstruction*, 531).

CHAPTER 5

1. *Elmore v. Rice*, 72 F. Supp. 516, 528 (E.D.S.C.), aff'd, 165 F. 2 387 (4th Cir. 1947), cert. denied, 333 U.S. 875 (1948); as quoted in Michael Klarman, *From Jim Crow to Civil Rights: The Supreme Court and the Struggle for Racial Equality* (Oxford: Oxford University Press, 2004), 244.

2. Michal R. Belknap, *Federal Law and Southern Order: Racial Violence and Constitutional Conflict in the Post-Brown South* (Athens: University of Georgia Press, 1987), xi.

3. Michael Klarman, *From Jim Crow to Civil Rights*, 82.

4. Ida B. Wells, *On Lynchings* (Amherst: Humanity Books, 2002); Alfreda Duster, ed., *Crusade for Justice: The Autobiography of Ida B. Wells* (Chicago: University of Chicago Press, 1970); Angela Davis, *Women, Race and Class* (New York: Random House, 1981); Mildred I. Thompson, *Ida B. Wells-Barnett: An Exploratory Study of an American Black Woman, 1893–1930* (Brooklyn: Carlson Publishing, 1990).

5. Jessie Daniel Ames, *The Changing Character of Lynching: Review of Lynching, 1931–1941, with a Discussion of Recent Developments in this Field* (New York: AMS Press, 1973); Jacquelyn Dowd Hall, *Revolt against Chivalry: Jessie Daniel Ames and the Women's Campaign against Lynching* (New York: Columbia University Press, 1993); John Shelton Reed, "An Evaluation of an Anti-Lynching Organization," *Social Problems* 16 (1968): 172–182.

6. J. Edgar Hoover, Cabinet Briefing on the morning of March 9, 1956; as quoted in John T. Elliff, *The United States Department of Justice and Individual Rights, 1937–1962* (New York: Garland Publishing, 1987), 796.

7. In 1920, blacks in Jacksonville, Florida, canceled their policies with a white life insurance company after some of its agents led a lynch mob. *Chicago Defender*, January 24, 1920; as quoted in W. Fitzhugh Brundage, "The Roar on the Other Side of Silence: Black Resistance and White Violence in the American South, 1880–1940," in *Under Sentence of Death: Lynching in the South*, ed. W. Fitzhugh Brundage (Chapel Hill: University of North Carolina Press, 1997), 278.

8. Ibid., 275; Stewart Tolnay and Elwood M. Beck, "Black Flight: Lethal Violence and the Great Migration, 1900 to 1930," *Social Science History* 14 (1990): 347–370.

9. Brundage points to an instance when black farmhands appealed to their employer, Mitchell Price, a rich white planter who subsequently proclaimed that further mob violence would be suppressed, and even threatened prosecution of members of the mob (Brundage, The Roar on the Other Side of Silence," 276).

10. In 1899, a crowd of blacks gathered around a jail to prevent Henry Denegal from getting lynched (Ibid., 278).

11. Paul Ortiz chronicles a group of black Floridians who took up arms to prevent a lynching. Paul Ortiz, *Emancipation Betrayed* (Berkeley: University of California Press, 2005).

12. Brundage, "The Roar on the Other Side of Silence."

13. Klarman, *From Jim Crow to Civil Rights*, 173.

14. "Negroes, Nazis, and Jews," *The Crisis*, December 1938, 393, editorial 1.

15. Alexander Keyssar, *The Right to Vote: The Contested History of Democracy in the United States* (New York: Basic Books, 2000). Other books that point out the civil rights impact of World War II include Daniel Kryder, *Divided Arsenal* (Cambridge: Cambridge University Press, 2000); Ronald Krebs, *Fighting for Rights: Military Service and the Politics of Citizenship* (Ithaca: Cornell University Press, 2006); David Mayhew, "Events and Causes: The Case of American Politics," in *Political Contingency: Studying the Unexpected, the Accidental, and the Unforeseen*, ed. Ian Shapiro and Sonu Bedi (New York: New York University Press, 2007); Reeve Huston, "Battling over the Boundaries of the American Electorate," *Reviews in American History* 29 (2001): 628–634.

16. Harvard Sitkoff, "Harry Truman and the Election of 1947: The Coming of Age of Civil Rights in American Politics," *Journal of Southern History* 37 (1971): 613.

17. Robert Zangrando, *The NAACP Crusade against Lynching*, (Philadelphia, Temple University Press, 1980), 15.

18. Ibid., 28.

19. Christopher Waldrep, *Lynching in America: A History in Documents* (New York: New York University Press, 2006), 207.

20. Ibid., 222.

21. Elliff, *The United States Department of Justice and Individual Rights, 1937–1962*, 68.

22. Ibid., 70.

23. Robert K. Carr, *Federal Protection of Civil Rights: Quest for a Sword* (Ithaca: Cornell University Press, 1947), 164.

24. Elliff, *The United States Department of Justice and Individual Rights, 1937–1962*, 68.

25. Klarman, *From Jim Crow to Civil Rights*, 181.

26. Harvard Sitkoff, "Harry Truman and the Election of 1948," 602–603, 610.

27. Ibid., 611.

28. Night letter to Russell, September 27, 1957, box 261, Administration Series, Ann Whitman File (as quoted in Belknap, *Federal Law and Southern Order*, 49).

29. Belknap, *Federal Law and Southern Order*, 68–69.

30. Burke Marshall, *Federalism and Civil Rights* (New York: Columbia University Press, 1964), 69–70; Ibid., 89.

31. Belknap, *Federal Law and Southern Order*, 70.

32. "Federal Criminal Jurisdiction Over Violations of Civil Liberties," Memo accompanying Circular No. 3356 (Supplement 1), O. John Rogge, Assistant Attorney General, To All United States Attorneys, May 21, 1940.

33. Here is a brief list of books and articles that have engaged in this debate: Robert Kaczorowski, *The Politics of Judicial Interpretation, The Federal Courts, Department of Justice, and Civil Rights, 1866–1876* (New York: Fordham University Press, 2005); Pamela Brandwein, "A Judicial Abandonment of Blacks? Rethinking the 'State Action' Cases of the Waite Court," *Law and Society Review* 41 (2007): 343–386; "Federal Power to Prosecute Violence against Minority Groups," *Yale Law Journal* 57 (1948); <pg>855–873; Belknap, *Federal Law and Southern Order*; John T. Elliff, *The United States Department of Justice and Individual Rights, 1937–1962*; Horace E. Flack, *The Adoption of the Fourteenth Amendment* (Baltimore: Johns Hopkins University

Press, 1908); Jacobus TenBroek, *The Antislavery Origins of the Fourteenth Amendment* (Berkeley: University of California Press, 1951); William M. Wiecek, *The Sources of Antislavery Constitutionalism in America, 1760–1848* (Ithaca: Cornell University Press, 1977); Howard Jay Graham, *Everyman's Constitution: Historical Essays on the Fourteenth Amendment, the Conspiracy Theory, and American Constitutionalism* (Madison: State Historical Society of Wisconsin, 1968); Chester J. Antieau, *The Original Understanding of the Fourteenth Amendment* (Tucson: Mid-America Press, 1981); Judith A. Baer, *Equality under the Constitution: Reclaiming the Fourteenth Amendment* (Ithaca: Cornell University Press, 1983); Michael Kent Curtis, *No State Shall Abridge: The Fourteenth Amendment and the Bill of Rights* (Durham: Duke University Press, 1986); Raoul Berger, *Government by Judiciary: The Transformation of the Fourteenth Amendment* (Cambridge: Harvard University Press, 1977), 18. See also Alexander M. Bickel, "The Original Understanding and the Segregation Decision," *Harvard Law Review* 69 (1955): 1–65; Charles Fairman, "Does the Fourteenth Amendment Incorporate the Bill of Rights? The Original Understanding," *Stanford Law Review* 2 (1949): 5–139; Earl M. Maltz, "The Fourteenth Amendment as Political Compromise: Section One in the Joint Committee on Reconstruction," *Ohio State Law Journal* 45 (1984): 933–980.

34. Elliff, *The United States Department of Justice and Individual Rights, 1937–1962*, 126.

35. *United States v. Sutherland*, 37 F. Supp. 344 (N.D. Ga. 1940)

36. Ibid., 109–110.

37. Ibid., 156. *United States v. Sutherland*, Case No. 144–41-8 (1943)

38. *United States v. Classic*, 313 U.S. 299 (1941).

39. Ibid., 327.

40. Elliff, *The United States Department of Justice and Individual Rights, 1937–1962*, 123.

41. *United States v. Trierweiler*, Department of Justice, Division of Communications and Records, Case No. 144–24-5, 52 F. Supp. 4 (1943); as quoted in Carr, *Federal Protection of Civil Rights*, 172.

42. *Screws v. United States*, 325 U.S. 91 (1945).

43. Robert K. Carr, "*Screws v. United States*: The Georgia Police Brutality Case," in *Cornell Law Quarterly* 31 (1945–1946): 48.

44. *Screws v. United States*, 103–104.

45. Eugene Gressman, "The Unhappy History of Civil Rights Legislation," *Michigan Law Review* 50 (1952): 1353.

46. *U.S. v. Price*, 383 U.S. 787 (1966); *U.S. v. Guest*, 383 U.S. 745 (1966).

47. For more information, please see Dominic J. Capeci, Jr., "The Lynching of Cleo Wright: Federal Protection of Constitutional Rights during World War II," *The Journal of American History* 72 (1986): 859–887.

48. Elliff, *The United States Department of Justice and Individual Rights, 1937–1962*, 153.

49. Ibid., 526.

50. Ibid., 525.

51. Clayborne Carson, *In Struggle: SNCC and the Black Awakening of the 1960s* (Cambridge: Harvard University Press, 1981), 37.

52. Ibid., 86.

53. Belknap, *Federal Law and Southern Order*, 136.

54. As quoted in Klarman, *From Jim Crow to Civil Rights*, 434.

55. As quoted in Mark Stern, *Calculating Visions: Kennedy, Johnson, and Civil Rights* (New Brunswick: Rutgers University Press, 1992), 80.

56. Klarman, *From Jim Crow to Civil Rights,* 436; Ibid.

57. Stern, *Calculating Visions*, 120.

58. Carter Wesley, *Houston Informer*, February 6, 1954; as quoted in Ibid., 124.

59. Stern, *Calculating Visions*, 124.

60. Arthur Schlesinger, *A Thousand Days: John F. Kennedy in the White House* (New York: Fawcett Crest, 1965), 361–362.

61. Lyndon B. Johnson, *Congressional Record*, 81st Cong., 1st sess., 2041–2049.

62. Transcript, Vice-President Lyndon Johnson to Ted Sorensen, 6/3/1963. http://digital. lbjlibrary.org/record/DOC-1963-06-03_Sorensen-LBJ_tele2a Accessed June 9, 2015

63. Public Papers of the President: Lyndon B. Johnson, 1963–1964, (Washington D.C., Government Printing Office, 1965), Vol. I, entry 11, 9.

64. Lyndon B. Johnson, *The Vantage Point: Perspectives on the Presidency, 1963–1969*, (New York, Holt, Rinehart and Winston, 1971), 162–3. In a meeting with civil rights advocates, LBJ reiterated his determination: "We are not going to have anything else hit the Senate floor until this bill is passed." Joseph L. Rauh, Jr., "Notes on Meeting: President Johnson, Clarence Mitchell, and Joe Rauh," January 21, 1964, Rauh Papers, Box 26, Library of Congress.

65. Lyndon B. Johnson, *The Vantage Point: Perspectives of the Presidency, 1963–1969* (New York: Holt, Rinehart, and Winston, 1971), 163; Stern, *Calculating Visions*, 225.

66. Congressional Quarterly, *Congress and the Nation* (Washington, DC: Congressional Quarterly, 1969), 357; Stern, *Calculating Visions*, 226.

67. This view of the Court is in line with the work done by Robert Dahl, Gerald Rosenberg, and Michael Klarman, who generally regard the Supreme Court as operating mostly in accordance with democratic pressures. Robert Dahl, "Decision-Making in a Democracy: The Supreme Court as a National Policy-Maker," *Journal of Public Law* 6 (1957): 279–295; Michael Klarman, *From Jim Crow to Civil Rights*; Gerald Rosenberg, *The Hollow Hope: Can Courts Bring about Social Change?* (Chicago: University of Chicago Press, 1993).

68. Belknap, *Federal Law and Southern Order*, xi.

69. Ibid.

70. Amos T. Akerman to B. Silliman, November 9, 1871, Amos T. Akerman Papers, University of Virginia.

71. Amos T. Akerman to Charles Sumner, April, 2, 1869, Sumner Papers, Harvard University.

72. Clayborne Carson, *In Struggle*, 37.

73. Klarman, *From Jim Crow to Civil Rights*, 429.

74. Burt Neuborne, "The Gravitational Pull of Race on the Warren Court," *The Supreme Court Review* 2010 (2011): 82.

75. *U.S. v. Guest.*

76. Clark Conference notes, *Brown v. Board of Education*, Box A27, Tom C. Clark Papers, Tarleton Law Library, University of Texas.

77. Michael Klarman, *From Jim Crow to Civil Rights*, 310. Michal Belknap also states that "Southerners, concerned about the breakdown of law and order in their communities, had accepted, and became willing to act upon, the responsibility for protecting Blacks" (Belknap, "The Legal Legacy of Lemuel Penn," 521).

78. Lee White to Anthony Town, February 5, 1965, Gen. HU2/ST 24, White House Central Files, Lyndon Baines Johnson Presidential Library, Austin, TX.

79. Burt Neuborne, "The Gravitational Pull of Race on the Warren Court," 69, 95.

80. Memorandum from William J. Brennan, Jr., to the Conference, re: No. 65 *United States v. Guest*, February 4, 1966, Clark Case File 65.

81. Michal, "The Legal Legacy of Lemuel Penn," 468.

82. Jacob Hacker, *The Divided Welfare State* (Cambridge: Cambridge University Press, 2002), 291.

83. After signing the 1964 Civil Rights Act, Lyndon Johnson said, "I think we just delivered the South to the Republican Party for a long time to come." Bill Moyers, *Moyers on America: A Journalist and His Times* (New York: Anchor, 2005), 167.

84. The 1964 presidential election marked the last time a majority of whites voted for a Democratic presidential candidate.

85. *Youngstown Sheet & Tube Co. v. Sawyer*, 343 U.S. 579 (1952).

86. Ibid., 637.

CONCLUSION

1. Derrick Bell, *And We are Not Saved: The Elusive Quest for Racial Justice* (New York: Basic Books, 1989), 175–176.

2. Senate Resolution 39–109, Congress: Lynching Victims Senate Apology Resolution, 2005. Available at http://www.govtrack.us/congress/bills/109/sres39 (accessed November 8, 2013).

3. This approach is perhaps best epitomized by the legal formalism expounded by Hans Kelsen. His rubric includes originalism, formalism, intratextualism, and moralism. Hans Kelsen, *General Theory of Law and State*, (New York: Russell and Russell, 1961).

4. Critical Legal Studies is an example of this line of reasoning. It deduces law as simply an outgrowth of politics.

5. Legal analysts Daniel Farber and Suzanna Sherry labeled all these approaches as "foundationalism." Daniel Farber and Suzanna Sherry, *Desperately Seeking Certainty: The Misguided Quest for Constitutional Foundations* (Chicago: University of Chicago Press, 2002), 1.

6. Mark Miller and Jeb Barnes, *Making Policy, Making Law: An Interbranch Perspective* (Washington D.C.: Georgetown University Press, 2004); Mark Graber, "The Nonmajoritarian Difficulty: Legislative Deference to the Judiciary," *Studies in American Political Development* 7 (1993): 35–73.

7. Karen Orren and Stephen Skowronek, *The Search for American Political Development* (Cambridge: Cambridge University Press, 2004), 134.

8. James Madison, Alexander Hamilton, and John Jay, "Federalist 78," in *The Federalist Papers*, ed. Robert Scigliano (New York: Modern Library, 2001), 496).

9. David Garland, *Peculiar Institution: America's Death Penalty in an Age of Abolition*, (Cambridge, Belknap Press, 2010), 142.

10. Michael Klarman, *From Jim Crow to Civil Rights*, (Oxford: (Oxford University Press, 2004), p. 449–450.

11. Stephen Halpern, *On the Limits of the Law: The Ironic Legacy of Title VI of the 1964 Civil Rights Act*, (Baltimore: Johns Hopkins University Press, 1995), p. ix.

12. Ibid., Halpern, p. 3.

13. Mark Graber, *Dred Scott and the Problem of Constitutional Evil* (New York: Cambridge University Press, 2006), 1.

14. Peter Kwong, *The New Chinatown*, rev. ed. (New York: Hill and Wang, 1996), 80–81.

15. Leonard Feldman, *Citizens without Shelter: Homelessness, Democracy and Political Exclusion* (Ithaca: Cornell University Press, 2004), 50.

16. Ibid., 44.

17. Gerald Neuman, "Anomalous Zones," *Stanford Law Review* 48 (1996): 1197–1234.

18. Charles Ogletree and Austin Sarat, eds. *From Lynch Mobs to the Killing State: Race and the Death Penalty in America* (New York: New York University Press, 2006).

19. David Garland, *Peculiar Institution: America's Death Penalty in an Age of Abolition* (Cambridge: Belknap Press, 2010), 35.

20. Ibid., 34.

21. Ibid.

22. Malcolm X Grassroots Movement, "Operation Ghetto Storm." Available at http://mxgm.org/wp-content/uploads/2013/04/Operation-Ghetto-Storm.pdf. Accessed June 9, 2015.

23. Available at http://www.propublica.org/article/deadly-force-in-black-and-white. Ryan Gabrielson, Ryann Grochowski Jones and Eric Sagara, "Deadly Force, in Black and White," October 10, 2014. Accessed June 9, 2015.

24. Rachel Levinson-Waldman, "When Legalism Enables Lawlessness," *The Atlantic*, December 24, 2014. Available at http://www.theatlantic.com/politics/archive/2014/12/when-legalism-enables-lawlessness/383965/. Accessed June 9, 2015.

25. Jill Leovy, *Ghettoside: A True Story of Murder in America* (New York: Spiegel & Grau, 2015).

26. Carl Biali, "Detroit Police Response Times No Guide to Effectiveness," August 2, 2013. Accessed June 9, 2015. Available at http://online.wsj.com/news/articles/SB10001424127887323997004578642250518125898.

27. Sudhir Alladi Venkatesh, *Off the Books: The Underground Economy of the Urban Poor* (Cambridge: Harvard University Press, 2006), 79.

28. Naomi Murakawa, *The First Civil Right: How Liberals Built Prison America* (Oxford: Oxford University Press, 2014), 44.

29. Cord Jefferson, "The Racism Beat: What It's Like to Write about Hate Over and Over." June 9, 2014. Available at https://medium.com/matter/the-racism-beat-6ff47f76cbb6. Accessed June 9, 2015.

30. Murakawa even argues that the liberal response to lynchings actually created the conditions for the carceral state: "[L]iberal law-and-order depoliticized white violence by dividing 'private' white lawlessness from prejudiced administration, correcting the former through criminalization and the latter through rationalization" (Murakawa, *The First Civil Right*, 29).

31. Clarissa Rile Hayward and Todd Swanstrom, "Introduction: Thick Injustice," in *Justice and the American Metropolis*, ed. Clarissa Rile Hayward and Todd Swanstrom (Minneapolis: University of Minnesota Press, 2011), 4.

32. Malcolm X, "The Ballot or the Bullet," in *Malcolm X Speaks*, ed. By George Breitman, (New York, Grove Weidenfeld, 1990), 30.

33. This characterization of liberalism as a fighting creed is taken from Charles Taylor, "The Politics of Recognition," in *Multiculturalism: Examining the Politics of Recognition*, ed. Amy Gutmann (Princeton: Princeton University Press, 1994), 62.

34. Richard Pildes, "Democracy, Anti-Democracy and the Canon," *Constitutional Commentary* 17 (2000): 296.

35. Franklin Delano Roosevelt, "First Inaugural Address, Washington, DC, March 4, 1933," in *Great Speeches*, ed. John Grafton (USA: Dover Publications, 1999), 32.

INDEX